an
introduction to
moral
philosophy

Jonathan Wolff

Blavatnik School of Government, University of Oxford

W. W. NORTON & COMPANY

NEW YORK · LONDON

To my nephews, Dan and Tom

W. W. Norton & Company has been independent since its founding in 1923, when William Warder Norton and Mary D. Herter Norton first published lectures delivered at the People's Institute, the adult education division of New York City's Cooper Union. The firm soon expanded its program beyond the Institute, publishing books by celebrated academics from America and abroad. By midcentury, the two major pillars of Norton's publishing program—trade books and college texts—were firmly established. In the 1950s, the Norton family transferred control of the company to its employees, and today—with a staff of four hundred and a comparable number of trade, college, and professional titles published each year—W. W. Norton & Company stands as the largest and oldest publishing house owned wholly by its employees.

Editors: Ken Barton, Peter Simon
Assistant Editors: Shannon Jilek, Quynh Do
Project Editor: Diane Cipollone
Editorial Assistant: Gerra Goff
Manuscript Editor: Christianne Thillen
Managing Editor, College: Marian Johnson
Managing Editor, College Digital Media: Kim Yi
Production Managers: Ashley Horna, Benjamin Reynolds
Media Editor: Erica Wnek
Media Assistant Editor: Ava Bramson
Media Project Editor: Cooper Wilhelm
Digital Production: Lizz Thabet, Mateus Teixeira
Marketing Manager, Philosophy: Michael Moss
Design Director: Lissi Sigillo
Composition: Jouve International
Manufacturing: Quad Graphics—Taunton

ISBN: 978-0-393-92359-9 (pbk.)

W. W. Norton & Company, Inc., 500 Fifth Avenue, New York, NY 10110
wwnorton.com
W. W. Norton & Company Ltd., 15 Carlisle Street, London W1D 3BS

1 2 3 4 5 6 7 8 9 0

brief contents

contents

CHAPTER 10 Deontology: Kant   163

CHAPTER 11 Challenges for Kantian Ethics   182

preface

One of the key ideas when reflecting on a moral problem is to consider how things look from the other person's point of view. This, in my opinion, is just as important in writing about morality as it is for morality itself. In all my writing, including this book, I have aimed to write what I would have wanted to read myself at the relevant stage of my life; in this case, at the start of my study of moral philosophy. I have been led by the dictum of the great moral philosopher Immanuel Kant in his text "What is Enlightenment?" To be enlightened is to *think for yourself,* rather than taking on other people's ideas without reflecting for yourself how they might be justified.

This book is aimed at helping those new to the subject to think for themselves about moral philosophy. I want to help you come to a better understanding of how you should think, feel, and act, if you are to do so with moral confidence. I have not attempted to tell you *what* to think, but rather to help you think independently about moral questions—not only about the issues in this book, but also about other questions that may occur in your life and in your thought. In other words, although saying this could give rise to false expectations, the point of this book is to help set you out on the path toward moral enlightenment (at least in Kant's sense of the term *enlightenment*). It is not, however, a matter of knowing the answers, but rather of having the equipment to think hard about the questions.

The main focus of this book is theoretical or conceptual. It is aimed at introducing the reader to the main debates, theories, and concepts that currently structure moral philosophy both as a subject studied in the university and applied to real life. In doing so I often use examples, but there is not enough space in just one book to examine practical questions in full depth. Accordingly, this book is accompanied by another one, called *Readings in Moral Philosophy*, that provides selections from many of the texts discussed here, as well as readings on many critical debates in applied ethics. Together these books provide a comprehensive introduction to moral philosophy, although each one can also be used independently of the other.

One goal of this book is to reflect moral philosophy in its growing diversity of approaches and subject matter. Thus it includes illustrations from a wide array of other disciplines that students might be studying, such as psychology, anthropology, literature, biological sciences, and so on. In addition, students will find an expansive and contemporary discussion of gender and race included across much of the text. In particular, I have tried to avoid the common trap of restricting feminist ethics to the ethics of care.

Each chapter ends with a summary, from three to five discussion questions, separate lists of key terms and thinkers, and a further reading section. At the end of this book is a glossary of key terms and a list of key thinkers found in the book. The book is also supported by a full test bank and a coursepack of assignable quizzes and discussion prompts that loads into most learning management systems. Access these resources at digital.wwnorton.com/intromoral.

ACKNOWLEDGMENTS

In writing this book I have acquired many debts. I think the first person to suggest that I write this book for W. W. Norton was Roby Harrington. Ken Barton broke down my resistance, and then Peter Simon was the first Norton editor I worked with until Ken returned to take over that role. I have worked with Ken most on this book, but Michael Moss has also played an important role, as have Diane Cipollone, Shannon Jilek, Christianne Thillen, Marian Johnson, Quynh Do, Gerra Goff, Benjamin Reynolds, Ashley Horna, Erica Wnek, Lissi Sigillo, and other colleagues in bringing it safely to print and beyond. I am exceptionally grateful to all of these people for their encouragement and firm advice at many points.

I have received an abundance of comments at many stages. The response that led to the most significant rethinking was from my former PhD student, the moral and political philosopher Rajeev Sehgal, who generously wrote up comments on two successive drafts of the book, each time expressing a rich variety of forms of dissatisfaction with what I had written. I learned from all these suggestions, and adopted many of them, though I fear not enough to dispel all of Raj's doubts. But even if it is far from perfect, the book is greatly improved as a result. I've also benefited enormously from feedback from a good number of others. Michael Klenk, Doug Reeve, Dan Guillery, Showkat Ali, Khatiji Haneef, and Don Berry all provided comments on all or part of the first draft.

I also greatly appreciate the excellent feedback on later drafts provided by the following people: Paul Abela, Acadia University; Caroline T. Arruda, University of Texas at El Paso; Luisa Benton, Richland College; Andrew D. Chapman, University of Colorado, Boulder; Laura T. Di Summa-Knoop, Fairfield University; Eric Gampel, California State University–Chico; Don Hatcher, Baker University; Carol Hay, University of Massachusetts, Lowell; Debby Hutchins, South Texas College; Rodger Jackson, Stockton University; Alex King, University at Buffalo, SUNY; Julie Kirsch, D'Youville College; Alice MacLachlan, York University; Michael McKeon, Barry University; Timothy J. Nulty, University of Massachusetts, Dartmouth; Andrew Pavelich, University of Houston; Arina Pismenny, Montclair State University; Aleksandar Pjevalica, University of Texas at El Paso; Weaver Santaniello, Penn State University; Susanne Sreedhar, Boston University; Daniel Star, Boston University; Glenn Tiller, Texas A&M University Corpus Christi; Lori Watson, University of San Diego; and Bryan Weaver, Ohio State University.

I would particularly like to thank Derek Bowman, Providence College; Rory Kraft, York College of Pennsylvania; and Joanna Smolenski, CUNY, for their work in preparing the test bank and coursepack.

about the author

Jonathan Wolff is the Blavatnik Chair in Public Policy at the Blavatnik School of Government, University of Oxford. Previously he was Professor of Philosophy, and Dean of Arts and Humanities, at University College London. His books include *Robert Nozick: Property, Justice and the Minimal State* (1991), *An Introduction to Political Philosophy* (1996, 3rd ed. 2016), *Why Read Marx Today?* (2002), *Disadvantage* (with Avner de-Shalit) (2007), *Ethics and Public Policy* (2011), and *The Human Right to Health* (2012). He has been a member of the Nuffield Council of Bioethics, and has worked on questions of the ethics of risk and the valuation of life and health with regard to the railway and pharmaceutical industries in the UK, as well as the government. He writes a regular column for *The Guardian* newspaper.

CHAPTER 1

Moral Philosophy and Moral Reasoning

Let no one be slow to seek wisdom when he is young nor weary in the search of it when he has grown old. For no age is too early or too late for the health of the soul. And to say that the season for studying philosophy has not yet come, or that it is past and gone, is like saying that the season for happiness is not yet or that it is now no more. Therefore, both old and young alike ought to seek wisdom, the former in order that, as age comes over him, he may be young in good things because of the grace of what has been, and the latter in order that, while he is young, he may at the same time be old, because he has no fear of the things which are to come.

EPICURUS, LETTER TO MENOECEUS

THE POINT OF MORAL PHILOSOPHY

In one sense of the word *introduction*, no one reading this book needs an introduction to morality. Even before we can speak, we receive training in morality; we are taught to share and to take turns. We are told not to bite, pinch, or scratch or to take toys that belong to others. Once we can speak, we are instructed not to lie, and not to make promises we don't intend to keep. We are shown how to be considerate of others' feelings, and we find it easy to detect when we have been unfairly treated. Some children take to these rules easily; others have to be reminded again and again. Some never learn. But morality, and moral questions, are all around us from the start.

If morality comes early, moral philosophy, which is the name for thinking and reflecting about morality, comes later if it comes at all. Although the Ancient Greek philosopher Epicurus (341–270 BCE) in the opening quote invites everyone to take an early interest in philosophy, another view from the earliest recorded days of philosophy was that moral philosophy is not for the young. Aristotle (384–322 BCE), whom we will look at in detail later in this book, wrote:

> Hence a young man is not a proper hearer of lectures on [moral philosophy], for he is inexperienced in the actions that occur in life, but its discussions start from these and are about these; and further, since he tends to follow his

passions, his study will be vain and unprofitable, because the end aimed at is not knowledge but action. (Aristotle, *Ethics*, Book 1, iii)

Aristotle suggests that the young man is not ready to study moral philosophy for he lacks experience of life, as well as self-control. For the young woman, Aristotle appears to assume that the question simply does not arise, which reflects common Ancient Greek views about women's place in society (again, something we will look at later). Yet, Aristotle went on to add, youthfulness is not to be measured in years: You could be old but immature and the value of moral philosophy pass you by (Book 1, iii). For the purposes of this book I will assume that even if Aristotle is right that moral philosophy needs life experience, then you, female or male, have reached a level of maturity in outlook and behavior that will allow you to benefit from thinking hard about the nature of morality—from doing moral philosophy.

Developing a Moral Outlook

But what, more exactly, is moral philosophy, and why study it? From time to time people turn to moral philosophy because they face a serious moral difficulty in their own life that they hope will be resolved, or at least eased, by understanding the works of the great philosophers. Those with such hopes treat philosophers rather like some people approach religious leaders: as a source of moral wisdom and comfort. But as things are, it is the rare moral philosopher who is trained or equipped to help in this very direct fashion.

Nevertheless moral philosophy is a *practical* subject, albeit with many significant and important theoretical elements. What moral philosophy can do, at its best, is to help you develop your moral outlook on life. By this I mean that it can help you come to a keener sense of what does and does not matter from a moral point of view. It can help you form a view of what considerations do, and do not, need to be taken seriously, and how we should develop our reasoning, attention, and emotions. Most importantly, it can help you think through the nature of your relationships with other people, and with other things of value, such as the animal world and the natural environment. It can help you think about how best to use your talents and energy, and what your goals in life should be. It can also have implications for how you should try to influence and, where appropriate, educate those around you. Although, as we will see, many moral philosophers have offered guidance to help in particular situations, often what the best moral philosophers do is inspire you to come to a way of seeing the world and the individuals within it.

To give examples of some of the major philosophers discussed here, from the Ancient Greek philosopher Plato (429?–347 BCE) we can learn how hard it is to reject the idea that, deep down, there are objective truths of morality. From Aristotle, whom I have just been discussing, we can learn that morality is as much about human character as it is about action. From the German philosopher Immanuel Kant (1724–1804), we can appreciate how important it is to treat other people with respect. From the British philosophers Jeremy Bentham (1748–1832) and John Stuart Mill (1806–73), we can consider whether we agree that primarily what matters is the happiness of human beings and other sentient creatures. And from the German philosopher Friedrich Nietzsche (1844–1900), we can comprehend that genuine morality should not be confused with what we happen to approve or disapprove of at this time in history. All of these thinkers developed their insights in much more depth and very often held detailed moral positions that emphasize their own concerns to the exclusion of others. But they all have something to teach us, not just intellectually, but practically. Their insights can help inform and inspire your moral outlook on life, whether or not you endorse the details of their views.

I said that these great thinkers have something to teach us not just intellectually, but practically. Nevertheless many readers will want to reject some of the ideas that I have just outlined, just as many of these philosophers rejected the ideas of other philosophers. To take just one example, Bentham and Mill insisted that human (or animal) happiness is the foundation of all morality. Kant thought this was a fundamental error, arguing that respecting the will of other rational creatures, rather than a concern for their happiness, is the basis of morality. Nietzsche was even more dismissive, memorably asserting that only the Englishman cares about happiness. Yet many will side with Bentham and Mill against Kant and Nietzsche. In this book I do not try to argue that one particular way of thinking about moral questions is the right one, although it may become obvious where my sympathies lie. My aim, rather, is to introduce some of the best philosophical writing about morality, providing a sense of the options available to guide our reflections.

Traditions of Moral Philosophy

Even for those who want to reject some, or perhaps all, of the ideas mentioned above as part of their practical approach to morality, the ideas of these thinkers are vitally important and should be studied by anyone who wishes to think seriously about morality. First of all, it is important to gain an understanding of a view in its subtlety and complexity before trying to evaluate it, rather than dismissing it without proper understanding. But equally, these views are a major part of our intellectual inheritance in the

Western world, and the spread of Western ideas, for good or ill, has meant that their influence is worldwide. We must therefore be aware of the major traditions of Western moral philosophy if we are to understand world history, literature, or culture or even to participate in debates about war and peace, about life and death, and much else besides.

Nevertheless, I certainly do not want anyone to get the impression that I believe that Western theories of morality are the only ideas worth examining: Chinese, Indian, Arabic, African, and other traditions of ethics are full of wisdom and insight and are worthy of deep study. Some of these, especially Indian traditions, have influenced some of the thinkers discussed here. (I have included references to introductory texts in these traditions in "Further Reading" at the end of this chapter.) But a single book cannot possibly cover everything in detail, and I have chosen to concentrate on Western traditions of ethical thought rather than produce a more superficial sample with wider scope. Although I do sometimes mention other traditions (especially in Chapter 2, "Cultural Relativism"), they play a minor role here.

THE NATURE OF MORAL INQUIRY

Morality is a puzzle. It's not like science, where we make observations and conduct experiments to gain and improve knowledge. It is not like literary fiction, which, if we have the skill, we can conjure up out of our imaginations. There seem to be moral rules, or at least moral standards. What are they? What do they require of us? Where do they come from? How do we know what they are? Are moral rules like the truths of basic arithmetic, true for all times, all places, and most importantly, all people? If so, then they would seem to have a high degree of **objectivity**. Or are they more like rules of fashion, coming and going, varying in time and place, at the whim of a few leaders in the field—in the case of fashion, by designers and journalists; in the case of morality, by priests, prophets, and perhaps philosophers? If morality is so variable, then the objectivity of morality would seem to be threatened. Or are both comparisons misleading, and is morality nothing like either mathematics or fashion?

Looking more carefully, we can see that it is possible to group these questions into different types. Some of them seem more deeply philosophical in nature, by which I mean that they ask about the fundamental nature of reality and how we can know about it: Where do moral standards come from, and how do we know what they are? Others look more practical: What are the rules, and what do they require of us? In fact, philosophers have made a three-way distinction among areas of moral philosophy: meta-ethics;

normative ethics; and applied ethics. We will now explore the meaning and significance of these terms.

Meta-Ethics

The term *meta* may be relatively familiar now, from information technology and website design. We use the term *meta-data* as a way of picking up the most important content on a website, which in turn will be indexed by a search engine. This gives the sense of *meta* as meaning "of a higher order." Many philosophical questions are "meta-questions" in this sense. For example, while scientists want to find out the laws of nature, philosophers want to understand what it means to say that something *is* a law of nature. Like philosophers of science, many moral philosophers are interested in meta-questions. For moral philosophers, questions concerning the nature of value, where the rules of ethics come from, and how we can learn about them are questions of **meta-ethics**.

In fact, for many people their first meta-ethical discussion might occur very early in life and run along the following lines:

"Be nice to your sister."
"Who says I have to?"

Of course a tired and frustrated parent may be unlikely to have the patience to engage in philosophical ruminations, but this snippet of dialogue raises some fundamental meta-ethical questions. A child is questioning the authority of a moral rule, yet at the same time is making what might be a mistaken assumption: that the only source of authority would be an authoritative human being (by asking "Who says?" rather than "Why should I?"). And, of course, the child is implicitly—and impudently—questioning the authority of whomever she is speaking to. The child's possible mistake is to assume that moral rules can have authority only if some person with the right to lay down rules has done so. But could it be that moral rules can come to be binding on us in some other way? These are the types of questions explored in the early chapters of this book, where we will look at questions of cultural relativism, skepticism, and subjectivism.

Normative Ethics

The sassy child could have asked another question when told to be nice to her sister: "Do I really have to?" And this could have been the result of genuine puzzlement. Suppose that her sister has been horrible to her. Does she still really have to be nice back? If so, why? Are there moral rules that tell you how to behave in these and other much more serious circumstances?

The study of these more practical questions of what, morally, we ought to do is often called **normative ethics**, in contrast with meta-ethics. The source of the term *normative* is the word *norm*, which means "standard." But the notion of a standard is ambiguous, for in ordinary life we use the term in two ways that are completely opposed to each other. One way that we understand the idea of *norm* or *standard* is "average," in the sense of what is normal (think of the phrase "well within the norm"). But we can think of standards in another way: not statistically, but ideally. For example, a health professional might tell us that in some parts of the world 90 percent of all adults are overweight. In making this judgment they are not comparing individual weight to an average derived from a statistical survey. Rather, they have a theory about the ideal weight for people, relative to their height and other factors, and are using that as a norm or standard in the sense of an ideal model. They are presenting a normative view, for it says that many people are heavier than they ought to be, rather than heavier than is statistically normal. This presupposition of a benchmark or standard is the sense of *norm* that is implied by the phrase "normative ethics." Normative ethics, then, is the branch of ethics that asks: What moral rules, principles, or doctrines should we accept? What benchmarks or standards should we live by (whether or not we actually do)?

One problem we have already touched on is that if a normative view presupposes an ideal standard, where does that ideal come from? In the case of human weight, physiologists have a view about the healthy functioning of a human body and what is needed to maintain it. We may decide, eventually, that they are wrong; but they do have a theory to back up their judgments. But what about morality? Where do the ideal standards come from? These questions return us to meta-ethics. Clearly, then, questions of normative ethics and meta-ethics can have strong connections, although meta-ethics is seemingly the "deeper" subject for it raises the most fundamental issues of truth and justification. In this book, we start at the deep end by considering questions of meta-ethics first.

Applied Ethics

Many people become interested in moral philosophy because of a concern, whether practically or theoretically, with a particular moral problem. Under what circumstances, if any, is abortion permitted? How do you draw the line between consensual sex and rape, especially when alcohol is involved? Or, on a different level, was it right for the United States to drop an atomic bomb on Japan in the Second World War? Can terrorism ever be justified? These issues of real life cry out for moral analysis, and **applied ethics** is the name for how it is done.

Applied ethics differs from normative ethics primarily in focus and emphasis. In normative ethics we try to form a general approach to morality that, we hope, will have wide application. In contrast, applied ethics tends to begin with a specific problem and then looks for values, principles, or other normative standards that can be applied to the problem to resolve it. Some problems, it seems, can be resolved easily by applying a particular moral theory. For example, a theory that prohibits all violence would, it would seem, rule out dropping an atomic bomb or carrying out acts of terrorism. But in fact that just pushes the problem one stage back, into normative ethics: Why do you think that this is the right theory? Therefore, in applied ethics it is common to look at a problem from various points of view to see which arguments appear the strongest and most compelling. In this book, although I will use many examples as illustrations and discussion points, we will not look at any applied ethics questions in full detail. Rather, in studying this book you will gain the necessary background to examine in-depth questions of applied ethics, further study of which is possible by consulting the selections in *Readings in Moral Philosophy* (Wolff, 2018).

Before moving on, one quick point about terminology. To this point I have used the terms *morality* and *ethics* interchangeably. In ordinary life it is not unusual to hear or read someone, often a politician or a journalist, argue that "there is no valid moral or ethical objection to" whatever it is that he or she proposes. It's not clear what distinction such people intend between the moral and the ethical, and I'm not sure they have anything in mind other than to make their point more emphatically by using two words when they could have used one—a bad habit that afflicts most of us. Most philosophers use the two terms with the same meaning. Some do make a distinction, but when they do, they explain it carefully, and different philosophers make different distinctions between the two. Generally, unless explicitly stated otherwise, I will use the terms *ethical* and *moral* as synonyms.

MORAL REASONING

How, though, is moral philosophy to be done? What are its methods? Frustratingly, there is no definitive answer to this very good question. How you do moral philosophy is itself a question in moral philosophy, and as such the correct answer is highly disputed. In fact, the same applies to many disciplines of thought. As we go through the questions raised in this book I will occasionally highlight some methodological issues and explain them in context, but before moving on it is worth exploring some of the more common methodologies used in moral philosophy. This should help you develop the ability to apply some of the techniques discussed here to other moral questions. Nevertheless, it is important not to treat any proposed methodology as if it is a rule book. Moral philosophy, like so many other areas of inquiry, is still developing, and that means some new methods could be invented tomorrow, or those used for centuries might fall into disuse. And the reverse can happen: Methodologies previously rejected are sometimes resurrected. Remember that moral philosophy is a tradition of thought, rather than a set of doctrines to be learned. Any of us can add to it at any time. I will split this discussion into four areas: logical principles of reasoning that apply to all subject matters; less formal techniques of argument that also apply to all subject areas; thought experiments and moral intuitions; and specific methodological devices used in moral philosophy.

Formal Logic: Validity, Soundness, Equivocation, Circularity

Starting with some general logical techniques that should apply to any rigorous form of inquiry, whether in philosophy, science, or elsewhere, the most basic notion to introduce is that of an **argument**. In ordinary language we typically use the term *argument* to refer to a dispute between two or more people that may, in fact, have little to do with calm rationality. And we sometimes use the term *logical* to mean "sensible." But in philosophy, both terms mean something much more specific. An argument is a way of lending support for a particular conclusion by reasoning from other claims that function as some form of support for it. Logic is a formal method of argument.

I will start with some basic principles of logic and then move on to other types of argument. One common and simple form of argument moves from two initial statements, known as premises, to a conclusion. Consider, for example:

Argument 1

Premise 1: Socrates is a human being.

Premise 2: All human beings are mortal.

Therefore

Conclusion: Socrates is mortal.

An argument is said to be **logically valid** when the conclusion logically follows from the premises. This is so whenever it is impossible for the conclusion to be false when the premises are true. In other words, an argument is valid when, if the premises are true, the conclusion must be true too. Consequently, a good way of testing the validity of an argument is to try to imagine a world in which the conclusion is false and the premises are true. We can tell that this first argument is valid because it is impossible to imagine a world in which Socrates is a man, and all men are mortal, but it isn't true that Socrates is mortal. That would be a **contradiction**, and hence impossible.

Consider now a second argument:

Argument 2

Premise 1: Socrates is mortal.

Premise 2: All human beings are mortal.

Therefore

Conclusion: Socrates is a human being.

At first sight, this may appear to be a minor reordering of the first argument. The premises are true and so is the conclusion. But in fact, by means of this reordering we have now produced an invalid argument. From the facts that Socrates is mortal, and all human beings are mortal, it does not at all follow that Socrates is a human being: For all we know from the premises, he could be any mortal creature, such as a cat. If Socrates were a cat, the two premises could still be true. Therefore the conclusion that he is a human being does not follow. There is no contradiction in saying that Socrates is mortal, all human beings are mortal, but Socrates is not a human being.

Validity is obviously important. But to see that more is needed from an argument, consider this:

Argument 3

Premise 1: Socrates is a cat.

Premise 2: All cats have ten legs.

Therefore

Conclusion: Socrates has ten legs.

This is a logically valid argument (to test, once again try to imagine the premises being true but the conclusion false). But it is hardly a compelling basis for concluding that Socrates has ten legs. The problem, of course, is that the premises are false, and it is impossible to establish the truth of a conclusion based on reasoning from false premises. What we are looking for are valid arguments from true premises: Such arguments are said to be **sound** as well as valid. A sound argument is powerful, and it can act as a type of proof. But it has to be based on true premises. Argument 1, above, is an example of a sound argument.

We have, so far, looked at simple forms of argument. Often arguments will be much more complicated, with multiple premises and sub-conclusions along the way. But still, we can see the value of trying to work out what philosophers call the **logical form** of an argument, rigorously formulating it into a series of premises and a conclusion. We will do this at several points in the book, for it allows a complex issue to be broken down into a series of steps, each of which can be investigated separately. We can look at the premises one by one and also at the logical validity of the steps in the argument. Having said that, it is not always straightforward to see how to formulate an argument, and there are various traps and fallacies that we need to avoid.

For example, one fallacy is known as **equivocation**, in which the same word has different meanings in different premises. Here is an example typical of those used by philosophers:

Argument 4

Premise 1: Every river has two banks.

Premise 2: A bank is a financial institution.

Therefore

Conclusion: Every river has two financial institutions.

The fallacy of equivocation here is particularly easy to spot. *Bank* can mean "side of a river" or "financial institution" or, indeed, other things too. In this case it means different things in the different premises, and the apparently valid logical deduction is no such thing. But equivocation can be much harder to see when a word has close, though different, meanings. For example, the term *man* is sometimes used to mean "human being" and sometimes "male human being." Arguments using the term *man* are probably much more liable to equivocation than those using the term *bank*.

A different fallacy is that often called a **circular argument** (also known as **begging the question**). A circular argument is one in which, although the conclusion validly follows from the premises, the premises already assume the truth of the conclusion. This can be hard to spot, especially in a long and complex argument, and it is often a matter of dispute; but there are clear cases. To take an example from outside ethics, suppose a friend is trying to convince you that God exists, and offers the argument that it says that God exists in the Bible. You ask why the Bible can be trusted, and your friend replies that it can be trusted because it is the word of God. Now whatever the merits of your friend's scholarship or faith, it is easy to see that this is a bad argument. To say that the Bible is the word of God already assumes that God must exist, but that is what the argument was setting out to prove.

Hence, in assuming what it aims to demonstrate, the argument is circular and proves nothing. As I said, this was an easy case. But in a more complex argument it can be much harder to tell whether an argument is circular, as we will see when we look at an example later in this book.

We will also, in the coming chapters, look at other logical techniques, such as arguments by dilemma and arguments by elimination, but these are much more easily introduced in the context of real examples, and so we will hold off from exploring them for the moment.

Analogy, Induction, Argument to the Best Explanation

Logically sound arguments, in providing a form of proof, can be satisfying. But there are other ways in which it is possible to find support for a conclusion through patterns of reasoning that fall short of strict proof. For example, one type of argument that I have already briefly used is that of **analogy**. Earlier, I asked whether we should think of morality as being like mathematics or fashion. If we think that it is like mathematics, then it seems there should be moral truths that hold for all times and all places and are capable of rigorous demonstration. If we think it is like fashion, then moral truths would vary over time and place. The power of an argument from analogy is that if we can make a convincing comparison between two fields of enquiries, we can use knowledge gained in one field to illuminate another, and this can be fruitful. For example, in teaching students about electrical circuits, it can be helpful to make a comparison with pumping water around a heating system. On the other hand, the disadvantages are clear too. If the analogy is inappropriate, it can be misleading. In any case, as the folk wisdom has it, analogies always break down somewhere, because any two areas are unlikely to be exactly comparable at all levels of detail. A broken electrical circuit behaves very differently from a broken water circuit. Looking for analogies can, nevertheless, be a useful strategy in reasoning, provided it is done with care.

We should also ask whether scientific reasoning provides further valuable models for moral reasoning. Of course scientists will use logical reasoning as well as arguments from analogy, but there is also thought to be a distinctive scientific method of accumulating evidence to arrive at general principles. A simple view of science is that it is a process of accumulating data to a point where it becomes possible to develop a general principle or law: I see one white swan, then another, then another, and because all the swans I see are white, I formulate the law that "all swans are white." This procedure is known as **induction**. It can be a helpful way of generating evidence to support hypotheses (although you need to formulate a hypothesis before you can even know what evidence to look for) but the problem is obvious. However many times you see white swans, or however many times you see the sun rise in the morning, you have no guarantee that the next swan you see won't be a different color, or that tomorrow morning the sun simply doesn't rise. Induction is never proof—but at its best it can provide strong evidence.

But how precisely can scientific reasoning be a helpful model for moral reasoning? As we noted, morality is a normative discipline, looking for an understanding of how things *ought to be* rather than evidence of how things are. For example, only a generation or two ago it was common for parents to discipline their children by hitting them with a belt or cane. There was plenty of evidence that this practice happened. But that, on its own, is hardly enough to convince us it is right. Induction, then, does not look directly applicable to moral philosophy in its pure form; but in an extended form, induction has much greater use.

This extended form is another methodology commonly used in science and elsewhere, known as **inference to the best explanation**, sometimes called **abduction** (no connection with the practice of abduction as a crime involving the taking of another person). Consider the important medical and scientific example of the relation between smoking and lung cancer. Although not all smokers developed lung cancer, and although some people suffered from lung cancer without smoking, nevertheless it became clear, by the use of induction (the accumulation of evidence) that there is a strong association between lung cancer and smoking. It would be easy to jump straight to the conclusion that smoking tends to cause lung cancer. But even though the conclusion is correct, it would not be right to adopt it just on the basis of the inductive evidence linking smoking and lung cancer. Induction on its own says nothing about the causal relation, for it is consistent with the evidence that what comes first is some sort of underlying condition that causes you both to develop lung cancer and to smoke. In other words, the evidence is consistent with the hypothesis that being the sort of person liable to develop lung cancer makes you smoke. And indeed this conclusion was suggested as a possibility by those who wanted to defend the tobacco industry. Although false, it isn't completely crazy. It could have been, for example, that some people had a form of extreme anxiety disorder that led them not only to want to smoke but also to develop lung cancer.

So there are at least two competing hypotheses consistent with the data: First, that smoking tends to cause lung cancer; and, second, there is an underlying factor that causes both the tendency to develop lung cancer and smoking. Today we are likely to regard the second possible hypothesis as ridiculous, lacking any evidence, and to argue that the first, more familiar claim is a much better explanation of the data. What makes it a better explanation is related to knowledge about human physiology. Therefore, in deciding on a theory we are asking: "What theory best explains the data?" rather than "What theory is consistent with the data?" In practice, then, we are much more comfortable with the idea of appealing to inference to the best explanation, looking for an underlying causal mechanism, reason, or theory rather than pure induction alone. And we will see this technique used widely in moral philosophy, as I will now illustrate.

Thought Experiments and Moral Intuitions

Consider the following example, from the philosopher William Godwin (1756–1836):

> In a loose and general view I and my neighbor are both of us men; and of consequence entitled to equal attention. But in reality it is probable that one of us is a being of more worth and importance than the other. A man is of more worth than a beast; because, being possessed of higher faculties, he is capable of a more refined and genuine happiness. In the same manner the illustrious archbishop of Cambray [Fénelon (1651–1715)] was of more worth than his chambermaid, and there are few of us that would hesitate to pronounce, if his palace were in flames, and the life of only one of them could be preserved, which of the two ought to be preferred.
>
> Supposing the chambermaid had been my wife, my mother or my benefactor. This would not alter the truth of the proposition. The life of Fénelon would still be more valuable than that of the chambermaid; and justice, pure, unadulterated justice, would still have preferred that which was most valuable. Justice would have taught me to save the life of Fénelon at the expense of the other. What magic is there in the pronoun "my," to overturn the decisions of everlasting truth? My wife or my mother may be a fool or a prostitute, malicious, lying or dishonest. If they be, of what consequence is it that they are mine? (Godwin, 1798/2013, pp. 53–54)

From the fire, should you rescue the illustrious Archbishop Fénelon, or your mother, the chambermaid? In a later edition of the book, Godwin changed the example from a (female) chambermaid to a (male) valet, perhaps to avoid the apparent sexism of the example. But chambermaid or valet, what would you do? Godwin was clearly impressed with Archbishop Fénelon, writing:

> In saving the life of Fénelon, suppose at the moment when he was conceiving the project of his immortal *Telemachus*, I should be promoting the benefit of thousands, who have been cured by the perusal of it of some error, vice and

consequent unhappiness. Nay, my benefit would extend farther than this, for every individual thus cured has become a better member of society, and has contributed in his turn to the happiness, the information and improvement of others.

The Adventures of Telemachus, almost forgotten now, was one of the most popular books of the eighteenth century, and an indirect but influential critique of the corrupt French monarchy. It is said that it influenced the French Revolution of 1789. Should you save such a benefactor to humanity in preference even to your own mother?

Here is another, more recent dilemma, from the moral philosopher Philippa Foot (1920–2010):

> Suppose that a judge or magistrate is faced with rioters demanding that a culprit be found for a certain crime and threatening otherwise to take their own bloody revenge on a particular section of the community. The real culprit being unknown, the judge sees himself as able to prevent the bloodshed only by framing some innocent person and having him executed. Beside this example is placed another in which [a man is] the driver of a runaway tram which he can only steer from one narrow track to another; five men are working on one track and one man on the other; anyone on the track he enters is bound to be killed. In the case of the riots the mob have five hostages, so that in both the exchange is supposed to be one man's life for the lives of five. The question is why we should say, without hesitation, that the driver should steer for the less occupied track while most of us would be appalled at the idea that the innocent man could be framed. (Foot, 1978, p. 23)

Both of Foot's examples involve the sacrifice of one person to save five. In the framing case we are horrified at the prospect, but in the tram case it just seems obvious that this is the right thing to do. What explains the difference? Foot's example, renamed "the trolley problem," has been refined by others and has generated a vast body of literature, including websites where you can test your own responses to modified examples and tangle yourself up in knots.

Notice, though, that neither Godwin nor Foot took themselves to be describing a situation anyone had ever encountered in real life, or would be likely to. Rather, these cases are regarded as **thought experiments** in which a situation is described in order to stimulate people to think deeply. Although science has the luxury of performing experiments, which rarely happens in philosophy (we will look at some examples toward the end of this book), scientists use thought experiments, too. For example, Einstein asked what you would see if you traveled at the speed of light. Although this experiment could never be done in practice, it is a fascinating question that could lead to new ideas and discoveries.

Why engage in thought experiments in moral philosophy? There are at least two different, though related, reasons. Godwin is using his example to illustrate his approach to moral philosophy, which is a form of **utilitarianism** (a theory we will explore in much more detail later) arguing that the right thing to do is to bring about as much happiness as possible. Given that saving Fénelon will, in Godwin's view, bring about more happiness in the world than saving your mother the chambermaid, the theory requires you to save Fénelon.

But do you agree with Godwin? The thoughts that occur to you when thinking about moral cases such as this are known as your **moral intuitions**. A moral theory that is in line with people's moral intuitions is usually regarded as having a great advantage. In the present case some people will completely disagree with Godwin, thinking that the right thing to do is to abandon the archbishop and save your mother. If you do, then you think that Godwin's theory has **counterintuitive** consequences. A theory with counterintuitive consequences can be hard to accept because it likely requires us to reject at least some of the moral beliefs that we have acquired. But in any case we can see one use for thought experiments: as a way of testing a moral theory by considering how it fares against our moral intuitions. If it agrees with your moral intuitions, then for you it is intuitive; if not, it is counterintuitive.

As is becoming a common theme, however, this test, while helpful, is far from infallible. Our intuitions can be wrong. Consider our intuitions about physics. Most people who haven't studied the theory of gravity assume that if you drop a cannonball and a baseball simultaneously from a high tower, the cannonball, being so much heavier, will hit the ground first. But according to the theory of gravity, the balls will hit the ground at the same time (or at least they would in a vacuum). The theory of gravity therefore predicts counterintuitive results. But that does not make it false, just rather remarkable. Similarly, just because a moral theory has counterintuitive results, that does not make it false either. However, in the case of morality, we cannot conduct the type of experiments that have been used to establish the theory of gravity. Hence, as we have noted, moral intuitions are often taken to be a significant source of evidence for a theory. But some moral philosophers are prepared to consider theories with counterintuitive results if the other reasons to accept them are good enough.

William Godwin used his thought experiment to present his moral theory; for the rest of us, it is more of a test than an illustration of the theory. Philippa Foot, in comparing two different ways that an innocent person could be sacrificed to save five others, is drawing our attention to the idea that most of us have clearly different moral intuitions about the two cases. Rather than using our intuitions to illustrate a theory, she is showing that our intuitions are complex, and it is not at all clear which theory best fits our intuitions. We can see that she is inviting us to try to produce a theory that is consistent with our intuitions. It is in fact a proposed application of the "inference to the best explanation" methodology. She is asking us to try to work out what moral theory best explains the apparently conflicting intuitions we have in these different cases. In this example, then, our intuitions do work rather like data in inductive arguments in science. The data, though, is not what we observe in the world, but the moral intuitions we have. The challenge is to work out how they fit into a theory. And sometimes we may have to abandon some intuitions to make this task even possible.

Special Moral Arguments

We began this section by looking at some general forms of reasoning that apply to all areas of inquiry. We then moved on to look at thought experiments that, although they are related to issues of wider application, have a specific use in the context of moral reasoning. We also looked at the related issue of moral intuitions. It is worth finishing the discussion of methodology by outlining two types of arguments that are commonly used within moral philosophy but are much more specific to it.

The first is the argument from **universalization**. It comes in many forms and variations, and we will consider it most thoroughly in relation to Kant's moral theory. But the basic idea will be familiar. Suppose you are considering some course of action that you know normally causes disapproval from those around you. One way of testing whether it is right or wrong is to ask, "What if everyone did that?" Suppose you live in a town that generally disapproves of cross-racial dating, but you and a potential date are thinking of breaking the custom. You could ask: What would happen if everyone did that? And you might think that nothing seriously bad would happen, even if it did surprise or upset a few people. If so, that might well give you confidence that nothing is wrong with what you propose to do.

To take a different example, suppose, you don't have the money you need to buy your college sweatshirt, and you realize that it would be possible to steal one without anyone ever knowing. Should you do it? Well, you can ask: What if everyone did that? Most likely, this shop, and others too, would go out of business; and if the example were generalized more broadly, commerce would break down. This is good evidence that stealing the sweatshirt would be wrong. This method of universalization requires a lot more discussion, but we can already see that it can be a good general guide to what you should do.

Finally, I want to return to an issue that has cropped up a couple of times already—firstly in relation to the distinction between the descriptive and the normative, and secondly when we looked at the possibility of collecting data to try to establish a moral principle. In both cases there seemed to be an important distinction between the type of "facts" that are involved in science and the "values" that we deal with in moral philosophy. And indeed the **fact/value distinction** is often regarded as an important line that should not be crossed. Whether this is correct is something that we will have to come back to, but in the meantime we should observe that it has played an important role in the history of moral philosophy. The Scottish philosopher David Hume (1711–76) put the point in terms of the difficulty of moving from an "is" to an "ought." Hume pointed out that many writers of his time would often start by describing various practices or situations, but "imperceptibly" they then began to moralize by using the language of what ought or ought not to happen. Hume correctly points out that this approach introduces something new into the discussion and needs to be explained. Hume simply issued the challenge that in each case an explanation is needed, although he is sometimes interpreted as setting out a hard-and-fast boundary. Whether or not there is such a boundary, we have to be alert to the possibility that some philosophers might try to deduce moral conclusions from factual premises. If we do observe such a form of argument, we need to be very careful as we try to understand how the transition is made.

THE PLAN OF THIS BOOK

Some people who come to the academic study of moral philosophy for the first time can be perplexed upon finding that it exists as a topic to be studied in a university. Because morality is always a part of our lives, and many people have reflected deeply on morality for themselves in sophisticated and imaginative ways, it is possible to come to the view that the truth about morality is clear and so there is little point in looking systematically at moral philosophy. People who argue in this fashion often state a particular philosophical view—for example, that all morality is subjective—as a challenge to the need for further reflection. If all morality is subjective, in the sense that anyone is free to believe whatever they wish, what else is there to discuss? In Chapters 2 and 3 of this book, we will discuss cultural relativism and then skepticism and subjectivism, each of which presents challenges to morality and to moral philosophy. In Chapter 4, we will also look at a different argument that threatens to make moral philosophy redundant: that we as human beings lack free will, and as a result do not have moral responsibility for our actions. The ideas in these chapters are often used, to different degrees, as ways of attempting to cut short philosophical discussion of morality. Instead I will try to convince you that they are all ways of entering into moral philosophy, and they all rely on philosophical assumptions that need detailed analysis and examination.

We then move to three chapters that combine some skepticism about the point or need for moral philosophy with more positive views. These chapters discuss, in turn, religious morality (Chapter 5), egoism (Chapter 6), and the social contract (Chapter 7). Following on, we will explore in some depth the main moral doctrines of the great philosophers: Jeremy Bentham, John Stuart Mill, Immanuel Kant, and Aristotle. It is hard not to notice, though, that these philosophers are all men—indeed, dead white European men—as are most of the philosophers we will discuss in this book. When examining these theories, we will also pay attention to some important feminist and race-based critiques, but I will end the book by looking in more detail at questions of gender and race, and at the positive accounts of moral philosophy that gender and race theorists can develop as alternatives to the philosophical mainstream.

CHAPTER REVIEW
Summary

In this chapter I have introduced the idea of moral philosophy as a reflection on the nature of morality and the moral problems we face, and suggested that part of the point of studying moral philosophy is to help you form your moral outlook on life, understanding what is important in thinking through the variety of life choices you and others inevitably will face.

I explained the distinction between (a) meta-ethics—questions about the nature and existence of value; (b) normative ethics—questions about what we should do and how we should live; and (c) applied ethics—questions about specific moral problems. I went on to introduce some techniques of reasoning that are commonly used in moral philosophy. I split these methodological issues into four types: (a) formal methods that apply to any form of reasoning; (b) less formal methods that also apply to all subject areas; (c) thought experiments and moral intuitions; and (d) some special moral arguments, including universalization and the is/ought distinction. While none of these methodologies provide infallible rules about how to engage in moral philosophy, they are all useful starting points. Finally, I explained the plan of the rest of this book.

Discussion Questions

1. Explain the distinction between meta-ethics, normative ethics, and applied ethics.
2. What is the difference between a valid argument and an invalid argument? When is a valid argument also sound?
3. What is a thought experiment? How can thought experiments be used in moral arguments?
4. What is meant by the fact/value distinction?

Key Terms

objectivity, p. 4

meta-ethics, p. 5

normative ethics, p. 6

applied ethics, p. 6

argument, p. 8

logical validity, p. 8

contradiction, p. 9

soundness, p. 9

logical form, p. 10

equivocation, p. 10

circular argument, p. 10

begging the question, p. 10

analogy, p. 11

induction, p. 11

inference to the best explanation, p. 12

abduction, p. 12

thought experiment, p. 14

utilitarianism, p. 15

moral intuition, p. 15

counterintuitive, p. 15

universalization, p. 16

fact/value distinction, p. 17

Key Thinkers

Epicurus (341–270 BCE), p. 1

Aristotle (384–322 BCE), pp. 1–2,3

Plato (429?–347 BCE), p. 2

Immanuel Kant (1724–1804), p. 3

Jeremy Bentham (1748–1832), p. 3

John Stuart Mill (1806–73), p. 3

Friedrich Nietzsche (1844–1900), p. 3

William Godwin (1756–1836), pp. 13–16

Archbishop François Fénelon (1651–1715), pp. 13–14

Philippa Foot (1920–2010), pp. 14–15

David Hume (1711–76), p. 17

Further Reading

▪ Epicurus's *Letter to Menoeceus* can be found online: www.epicurus.net /en/menoeceus.html (retrieved December 23, 2016).

▪ Many editions of Aristotle's *Nicomachean Ethics* are available. The text quoted in this chapter is from the Oxford World's Classics edition (Oxford University, 1980, 2009).

▪ Susan Moller Okin's book *Women in Western Political Thought* (Princeton University Press, 1979) is an excellent account of how women have been marginalized in the work of some of the greatest philosophers.

▪ *An Introduction to World Philosophy: A Multicultural Reader* (Oxford University Press, 2009), edited by Daniel Bonevac and Stephen Phillips, contains a wide array of texts, including selections from moral philosophers in the Chinese, Indian, Arabic, and African traditions.

▪ A good introductory guide to the many methods of arguments mentioned here, as well as numerous others, is *The Philosopher's Toolkit* (2nd ed.) by Julian Baggini and Peter Fosl (Wiley-Blackwell, 2010).

▪ William Godwin is quoted from his *An Enquiry Concerning Political Justice* (Oxford University Press, 2013), edited by Mark Philp. (Original work published 1793)

▪ You can test your intuitions in a variety of "trolley problems" at www .philosophyexperiments.com/fatman/

▪ The quotation from Philippa Foot is from her collection of essays, *Virtues and Vices* (Oxford University Press, 1978).

▪ Others who have discussed trolley problems in detail include Judith Jarvis Thompson, "The Trolley Problem" (*Yale Law Journal*, 94, 1985: 1395–1415); Frances M. Kamm, *The Trolley Problem Mysteries* (Oxford University Press, 2016); and David Edmonds, *Would You Kill the Fat Man?* (Princeton University Press, 2013).

▪ Selections from the works of many of the philosophers mentioned in this chapter are included in Jonathan Wolff (ed.), *Readings in Moral Philosophy* (W. W. Norton, 2018).

CHAPTER 2

Cultural Relativism

If anyone, no matter who, were given the opportunity of choosing from amongst all the nations in the world the beliefs which he thought best, he would inevitably, after careful consideration of their relative merits, choose those of his own country. Everyone without exception believes his own native customs, and the religion he was brought up in, to be the best; and that being so, it is unlikely that anyone but a madman would mock at such things. There is abundant evidence that this is the universal feeling about the ancient customs of one's country. One might recall, in particular, an account told of Darius. When he was king of Persia, he summoned the Greeks who happened to be present at his court, and asked them what they would take to eat the dead bodies of their fathers. They replied that they would not do it for any money in the world. Later, in the presence of the Greeks, and through an interpreter, so that they could understand what was said, he asked some Indians, of the tribe called Callatiae, who do in fact eat their parents' dead bodies, what they would take to burn them. They uttered a cry of horror and forbade him to mention such a dreadful thing.

HERODOTUS, HISTORIES, BOOK 3

THE VARIETY OF MORAL PRACTICES

One reason that history can be so interesting, and so shocking, is its ability to lead us to compare customs from the past with our current practices. Things taken for granted in one era are considered morally horrendous in another. For example, in the ancient world of Greece and Rome, some forms of slavery were regarded as morally acceptable. The great philosopher Aristotle himself argued that some people were "slaves by nature." Over time slavery became less prominent, without ever disappearing completely, but it was revived again on a mass scale in the plantations of the southern United States, the Caribbean, and Brazil. The American Civil War was fought to cement the abolition of slavery in the United States, although the practice is still with us today, illegally, in many forms throughout the world. Even if slavery still exists, its moral evaluation has changed dramatically over the centuries. Or consider practices of erotic love in the Ancient Greek world, where it was common for wealthy middle-aged men to have sexual relations with boys in their early teenage years. What was considered normal in Ancient Athens would lead to a person's being denounced as an outcast and serving a long spell behind bars today. Similarly, until the rise of modern medicine, the profession of nursing was sometimes considered morally equivalent to that of prostitution. In the theater of Shakespeare's time, the same was thought of actresses, which is why boy actors took female roles.

Not only do moral evaluations change over time, but different practices exist at the same time. Even in the ancient world, travelers returned home with outrageous tales of cultural difference. At the start of this chapter, I quoted one such account from the ancient historian Herodotus (484–425 BCE) on the difference between funeral practices of the Greeks and the Callatiae.

Contemporary theorists have documented wide variety in cultural practice. Here is the important American anthropologist, Ruth Benedict (1887–1948), on the issue:

> Standards, no matter in what aspect of behavior, range in different cultures from the positive to the negative pole. We might suppose that in the matter of taking life all peoples would agree in condemnation. On the contrary, in a matter of homicide, it may be held that one is blameless if diplomatic relations have been severed between neighboring countries, or that one kills by custom his first two children, or that a husband has right of life and death over his wife, or that it is the duty of the child to kill his parents before they are old. It may be that those are killed who steal a fowl, or who cut their upper teeth first, or who are born on a Wednesday. Among some peoples a person suffers torments at having caused an accidental death; among others it is a matter of no consequence. Suicide also may be a light matter, the recourse of anyone who has suffered a slight rebuff, an act that occurs constantly in a tribe. It may be the highest and noblest act a wise man can perform. The very tale of it, on the other hand, may be a matter for incredulous mirth, and the act itself impossible to conceive as a human possibility. Or it may be a crime punishable by law, or regarded as a sin against the gods. (Benedict, 1934, p. 45)

But we don't have to survey exotic works of anthropology to see great variety in what counts as acceptable and unacceptable behavior. Even in recent decades, practices have changed dramatically. I'm old enough to remember a time in the United Kingdom—the late 1960s—when it was common practice for jobs to be advertised with two rates of pay; a higher one for men, a lower one for women. There was no pretense that women were doing a different job, or couldn't do it so well. They were just paid around 15 percent to 20 percent less. (Of course, we have yet to achieve equal pay for equal work, but at least it is illegal to advertise different rates.) Until the last few decades, same-sex relations between men were illegal in much of the world, and many people—including the playwright Oscar Wilde (1854–1900) and the mathematician, computing pioneer, and Second World War code-breaker Alan Turing (1912–54)—were tried and found guilty.

Furthermore, even now there is a good degree of variation in ordinary social practices. In some countries you drive on the right-hand side of the road, in others the left. In some countries owning a handgun is an ordinary part of life; in others it is a horrifying prospect. You could grow up thinking there is only one correct way of driving or only one correct rule about gun ownership; but as you become more experienced, by watching television programs from other countries or traveling, you realize there are different ways of doing things. And customs of personal conduct differ too. On my first trip to the United States as a graduate student in the 1980s, I was given a leaflet by my sponsor explaining some aspects of expected behavior in the country. My favorite example was the suggestion that North Americans feel uncomfortable if you stand very near to them when you are having a conversation. Some people from Southern Europe and Latin America prefer to come close when talking, and North Americans will tend to back away; this kind of push-pull interaction might repeat itself indefinitely, to comical effect. Obviously the person who wrote this leaflet noticed that conventions of good manners or etiquette differ in different parts of the world.

Norms of personal conduct differ from culture to culture, and it seems oddly dogmatic in the examples just cited to insist that one culture has the right idea and another got it wrong. But if one culture permits every capable adult to drive, and another—as in the case of contemporary Saudi Arabia—refuses to allow women this ordinary privilege, are we really prepared to brush this off as an idiosyncrasy of cultural difference, or is one country making a moral error? Still, some will insist that no culture has the right to judge what happens in another, proposing that just as rules of etiquette vary from culture to culture, so do moral norms.

OBJECTIVISM OR CULTURAL RELATIVISM?

There are, then, at least two attitudes we can take—two types of **moral intuition** we can have—about these facts of moral variation. One is to insist that a certain set of practices is the true or correct moral standpoint, and all others are in error. Or we can say that moral truth is in some way relative to a particular culture or tradition, and there is no basis for saying that one is the superior to others. The first view is often called **objectivism** and the second **cultural relativism**. This is a dispute in meta-ethics, concerning the nature of moral value. Are moral values objective, at least in the sense that the same values are valuable for all people, in all places, at all times, or do they vary from culture to culture? Which is correct? The facts of variation are impressive, but they are not enough to show that cultural relativism is true, for that would commit the fallacy (discussed in Chapter 1) of deriving an "ought" (a moral conclusion) from an "is" (a statement of how things are) without explaining how the derivation is possible.

Some philosophers have argued that objectivism is the intuitive view built into our ordinary moral thought. Most people naturally find themselves making assumptions about meta-ethics without having much of a sense that this is what they are doing. Just as our language has a grammar that most of us know but couldn't describe without extensive training, our moral thought also makes underlying assumptions that we may not be aware of and that we have to work hard to articulate. Here are some of the commonly made assumptions about meta-ethics that infuse **commonsense morality**, by which I mean the morality we tend to use in everyday life.

- Some things are morally wrong, such as harming an innocent child simply for the pleasure of doing so.
- Statements such as "It is wrong to harm an innocent child simply for the pleasure of doing so" are straightforwardly either true or false, and, in this case, the statement is true.
- It is possible to know that some things are morally right and some things are morally wrong.
- If someone does something he or she knows to be wrong, then it is right to blame or criticize him or her for doing so.
- It generally would have been possible for those who have acted wrongly to have acted in some other way.

Although these assumptions are part of our ordinary moral belief system, some of them are challenged even in ordinary moral life. For example, some people are often reluctant to blame others for morally bad behavior, putting their actions down to a bad start in life or difficult circumstances. Others may doubt whether moral beliefs really are capable of being true, preferring the view that they are, in some sense, subjective judgments. But the idea that there are objective truths of morality—some things are just right or wrong, whatever people think about it—is a powerful one.

Nevertheless, even if it is common to believe that some things are right and some things are wrong, philosophically it can be hard to understand what this really means. Take the statement that "being kind to strangers is good." "Good" is a value, and objectivism in ethics seems to presuppose that values are "real" and therefore in some sense exist in the world. The view that values exist in the world, independently of what human beings think of them, is also known as **moral realism**, and many philosophers have defended it. But it is easy to be puzzled about what it means for values to exist in any objective sense. Table and chairs exist "objectively." I can see them, or bump into them, and you can see and bump into the same ones if you are in the same room as me. But if values exist, where are they? Can I see them? If not, how do I know about them, or interact with them? Asking these questions tends to lead us away from objectivism to a different, more subjective, view that values are somehow invented by human beings and are dependent on us for their existence. Those philosophers who believe in objective values therefore have the difficult burden of saying what it is that they believe in.

Plato (429?–347 BCE) is probably the first recorded philosopher who attempted to explain in detail what it would be for values to be objective. He believed that we can discover the nature, and even the existence, of objective values by the use of reason. But what, exactly, is it that we will discover if we are successful? Plato uses the idea of the **form of the good**, which needs to be examined carefully. As a first step, we can think of the form of the good as what it is that all good things have in common, just as the form of a circle is what it is that all circles have in common. A circle is the set of points in a two-dimensional plane equidistant from a single point. To a first approximation, then, the "form of the good" seems to be something like a definition of *good*. But Plato pushes the analogy with geometry even further. It is commonly said that it is impossible to draw a perfect circle. Any representation of a circle will have slight bumps or imperfections in the line, even if you need a microscope to see them. Therefore any actually existent circle is only an approximation of a perfect circle, which is the true "form of a circle." Similarly Plato argues that we will never experience pure good on earth, because any good action or person will have some imperfection. But just as there is an ideal form of the circle, there is also an ideal form of the good, which exists although not in the physical world.

There is certainly something very plausible in the idea that good things, just like circles, have something in common that is not to be found in perfect form in anything in the world. But when we reflect on this idea it can seem very hard to make sense of it. What is it to exist, but not to exist in the physical world? Plato concludes that the forms must exist in some other-worldly realm. Plato strives throughout his work to make sense of what this means and how we can come to have knowledge of something we cannot directly experience. He tells a number of myths about human preexistence in something like heaven where we become acquainted with the forms not just of the good, but of other equally difficult philosophical concepts such as beauty and truth. Whether he intended this literally is hard to know, but it does show that although we can easily be drawn to the view that there must be objective values, that idea is not straightforward.

Other philosophers have taken comfort in an analogy we have already mentioned between values and numbers. Take the simple arithmetical truth $2 + 2 = 4$. The commonsense view, of course, is that this is an objective truth, true in all times and all places, and for all people. Its truth predated human existence, although, of course, our knowledge of the truth could not. Yet, you might wonder, what are the numbers two and four? Where do they exist? How can we understand them? When we start to think about it, they are pretty mysterious things. The mystery does not, though, undercut our belief in the objective truth of mathematics. And so, perhaps, the mystery of what values are need not undercut our belief that they exist in whatever sense is necessary to make the truths of morality objective. For all these philosophical difficulties, the objectivity of morality is for many people the highly intuitive view.

Nevertheless, the social and anthropological evidence of moral difference we looked at in the last section puts objectivism under pressure, and cultural relativism will, for many people, be an attractive alternative to objectivism. Practices elsewhere and in other times sometimes differ from what we are used to, but what basis do we have for saying that we are right and they are wrong? How can people who follow one set of practices criticize those who follow another? The cultural relativist argues that each of us has to see things from the perspective of our own culture. Everyone will naturally think that their own culture has the superior moral code. But in fact, says the relativist, there is no ultimate right or wrong here, and it is exceptionally arrogant to think that you and your culture have the truth, and everyone else who thought and acted in a different way, now living or dead, is wrong. Difference is difference, and that is all. We must respect the fact that we live in a particular point in space and time, and we have no basis for regarding ourselves as superior to those who lived in different times or in different places. Hence there can be great appeal in cultural relativism, and many people find it to be more intuitive than objectivism. But as we discussed in the last chapter, moral intuitions can be questioned. We must dig deeper, especially when our moral intuitions conflict with those of other people, or, indeed, when we find ourselves conflicted.

RELATIVISM AND PSEUDO-RELATIVISM

The central claim of cultural relativism is that the ideas of "right" and "wrong" can be understood only within a particular cultural or social context, and what is right in one context may well be wrong in another.

Consequently we must respect divergence in moral practice. However, philosophers have commented on the strangeness of the argument that because values are relative, societies must keep out of each other's business. Consider how we might formulate the argument with two premises and a conclusion:

Premise 1: *Right* and *wrong* means "right for a given society" and "wrong for a given society."

Premise 2: What is right and wrong in one society may differ from what is right and wrong in another society.

Therefore

Conclusion: It is wrong for one society to impose its ideas of right and wrong on another.

This may look like a valid argument, in the sense that the conclusion follows from the premises, although strictly speaking some missing steps need to be filled in if the argument is to be formally valid. But the oddity is that if the conclusion is true, then the first premise must be false. After all, the conclusion "It is wrong for one society to impose its idea of right and wrong on another" is a claim with *universal* scope, applying to all societies, not just one. Therefore it is not relative to a particular society, and so it contradicts the claim that all ideas of right and wrong are relative. It says that all people, of all cultures, have the right to act according to their local customs, without the threat of interference from outside. In the terms introduced in the last chapter when discussing fallacies in reasoning, it seems that this argument suffers from **equivocation** because it uses the same word, *wrong*, in more than one sense.

Perhaps what happened is that cultural relativism has been confused with a form of **liberalism**, understood in the sense of calling for the toleration or even encouragement of diverse ways of living. Liberals have some views in common with cultural relativism. They accept that diverse moral views are held in society or between societies. For example, people follow different religions—or none. They also generally acknowledge that unless one person or group threatens another, they should be allowed to live according to their own values. Therefore, liberals will often argue that cultural self-determination has value. But, and here is the important point, acknowledging each society's right to self-determination is a universal value, not a local one. Let's call this liberal, highly tolerant, universalist position **pseudo-relativism**. Rather than denying the existence of universal values, it asserts the existence of at least one universal value: that each culture has the right to moral self-determination.

Again this seems like an enlightened view; but before returning to the discussion of relativism, it is worth considering whether pseudo-relativism really is so attractive. Consider an analogy in international relations. In 1648 the Treaty of Westphalia was signed as a result of discussions between many of the states of Europe. Its purpose was to recognize the principle of state sovereignty: that each state had the right to determine its own affairs, without outside interference. But 300 years later—in the aftermath of the Second World War—it became clear that the Treaty of Westphalia effectively had given too much power to states. If states have sovereignty over their territories, what do we say when they start to turn on their own citizens? Do we have to stand by and watch when states commit genocide as long as it is within their own borders? The Universal Declaration of Human Rights (adopted on December 10, 1948) was a response to the recognition that states can do horrendous things to their own citizens.

In looking closer at examples of apparent moral differences, we can see that in other times and places people often followed practices that appear to oppress disadvantaged or powerless groups: slaves, people of unfavored races, women, and those who engage in same-sex relations. Is the liberal policy to be tolerant of extreme discrimination, or to stand up for the human rights of the vulnerable? As the contemporary Ghanaian American philosopher Kwame Anthony Appiah (b. 1954) remarks, the two ideals of respect for difference and concern for all can clash. The tolerant liberal position, then, has somehow to get the balance right between leaving certain things to societies to determine for themselves while at the same time setting down some lines that cannot be crossed in order to protect individuals. So there is a difference between being someone who, like the liberal, is happy to tolerate or encourage many different ways of life and being someone who refuses to criticize any of the practices of another society . A liberal can regard many different ways of life as acceptable, even admirable, but at the same time can judge some to have crossed a line.

In our own time, the practice of what has been called genital cutting in young girls is a good example of something that most people think falls beyond the tolerable. Some societies engage in a practice of removing part of the genitals of young girls, or practice other surgical techniques that are intended to ensure that a girl will remain a virgin until she is married. This practice has, for example, been very common in parts of Africa for centuries and is not associated with any particular religion. Critics point out that because of the surgery, a girl may experience reduced sexual pleasure for the rest of her life, often suffers considerable pain and discomfort, and also risks infection and even possible death as postsurgical complications. Is the tolerant position to regard genital cutting as a matter of acceptable cultural difference? Or is the correct stance to argue that these young women are being oppressed and dominated by obsolete, sexist practices and that we should campaign for reform or even the criminalization of the practice, not just in our own country but throughout the world?

You may be surprised that I have used the term *genital cutting*, because you are probably much more used to referring to the practice as female genital mutilation (FGM). But it is clear that the moral relativist, or anyone who wished to defend the practice, could not accept that label. Naming it a form of mutilation presupposes that it is harmful and probably morally illegitimate. It would be equivalent, it could be said, to referring to male circumcision as male genital mutilation. Now many will want to argue that there is a key difference, suggesting that for boys and men circumcision is beneficial, but for girls and women genital cutting is harmful. But not all agree that there is such a difference; and in any case it needs to be established by looking at the evidence, not prejudged by the use of names. Interestingly, then, how we name practices can already embody assumptions about their permissibility.

For the opposite extreme, consider the words of Jomo Kenyatta (c. 1891–1978), the first president of Kenya (1964–78). In 1938 Kenyatta wrote an important work of anthropology called *Facing Mount Kenya*. In that book, he describes the Giyuku tradition in which he was raised. He defends male and female circumcision by showing their centrality to Giyuku ritual and ceremony, especially concerning initiation into adulthood and full membership of the group. At one point he refers to the practice as "trimming the genital organs," making it sound no more troublesome than having a haircut. Unlike Kenyatta, or the critics, I will continue to use the term *genital cutting* to avoid biasing the discussion in either direction, even though some people will regard my doing so as an appalling example of "political correctness." But political correctness is really just the awareness that we should not sidestep serious moral debate by using morally "loaded" language to prejudge issues. Prejudgment, of course, is the origin of the term *prejudice*.

The question we have been considering, then, is whether genital cutting crosses a moral line and thereby shows the limits to cultural self-determination. But cultural self-determination, as we saw, is not moral relativism proper, for it imposes a universal value: self-determination of groups. It is actually much harder to understand what pure cultural relativism is as a thesis. It is not the same as universal tolerance for group practices. It is also not the same as the view known as **individual subjectivism** (see Chapter 3), in which the truth of a moral claim depends on each person's preferences or judgment. Rather, cultural relativism locates the truth of a moral claim in the traditions or judgments of a cultural group.

Consider again some of the examples from anthropologist Ruth Benedict. Let's take suicide. In some countries or groups, especially those strongly influenced by Catholic religion, suicide is a terrible, mortal sin and an offense against God's purposes. In other countries, such as Japan, it is a noble and respected way of responding by, say, a military leader or even the head of a major corporation who has made a disastrous decision. Are we to say that one of these societies is right and the other is wrong, or should we say that they are both simply to be understood within the context of their own societies, and what is right in one place can be wrong in another? But as soon as we add "and therefore we must not intervene or criticize," we have superimposed a universal value and abandoned the relativist position.

The cultural relativist, it seems, has to stop short of making any universal moral claims. Rather, being an explicit cultural relativist seems to require adopting two standpoints on morality. On the one hand, as a member of a culture that has its own morality, the relativist, like everyone, will perceive the world through the values of that society. For example, those of us who live in societies that regard suicide as morally wrong will, at least in the first instance, condemn it as wrong not just in our society but everywhere we see it, for that is what our morality says. It would be rare for a morality to have relativism "built in." Yet at the same time, the relativist must adopt another, more abstract standpoint—that of the anthropologist or philosopher—and say, "But that is just the way we think about it here; others in different cultures may have different moral views." This does seem to be a possible and consistent position, allowing you to have a moral view while also achieving a type of critical distance from it. But it is an interesting question whether you can see that there are alternatives to your own moral view and still hold on to your view as firmly as you did before. Consider again the Greeks who heard about the funeral practices of the Callatiae. Their natural reaction was to condemn eating dead bodies as morally horrendous. But Darius, the king, had clearly adopted the abstract standpoint of the philosopher or anthropologist and was able to see that practices differ in different societies. Our question is whether, once he had understood cultural variation, he would be able to continue endorsing the view that the Greek practice of burning dead bodies is morally the right thing to do. Or would his moral faith be weakened? Would he begin to see the issue as a matter of custom that can differ from place to place rather than as moral rules?

Cultural relativism seems to require us to hold fast to our moral beliefs while also recognizing that had we been brought up under different circumstances, we would just as firmly hold different moral beliefs. This view is certainly possible, but at the same time it could be psychologically difficult and might lead some to question the tradition in which they were brought up.

Problems for Relativism

Cultural relativism is often presented as a sophisticated position, but certain arguments may make it less appealing than it seemed at first. Indeed the contemporary African American philosopher Michele Moody-Adams has argued that moral relativism has to make a number of very implausible assumptions. First of all, it assumes that it makes sense to assign each person to his or her particular, hermetically sealed group. But can this be right? Consider yourself. What is your group? You may be of a particular religion that means a lot to you, or a citizen of a particular country with which you strongly identify. Or alternatively, your family may mean more to you than your religion or country. Or perhaps you identify most with people on your sports team. Furthermore you may have left one country and find yourself living in another, or perhaps your parents or your grandparents did (to flee oppression in their country of birth). For many people in the modern world, it is not a straightforward matter to say which group they belong to. And if different groups have different and conflicting practices, and you belong to more than one group, what should you do? Which culture should your moral beliefs be relative to?

Second, Moody-Adams points out that cultural relativism assumes that within each group there is a single agreed-on moral standpoint. But this is absurd. Any culture will include a wide variety of views, some of them the direct opposite of each other. What, for example, is the agreed-on U.S. position on gun control? On legalization of marijuana? On state-funded health care? Those tempted to the view that every society has an agreed-on set of values should spend some time listening to U.S. political debate. And to return to the topic of genital cutting (which we will talk about again shortly), the philosopher Martha Nussbaum (b. 1947) points out that it is illegal in many of the countries where it is practiced. This example, it seems, shows a diversity of views within a single country—although the position is complicated, especially in countries that only recently gained political and legal independence, as is common in Africa. In these countries formal legal frameworks are often based on international standards and sometimes conflict with the customary law of different groups.

Moody-Adams's third point is that cultural relativism seems to assume that any individual's moral beliefs are a direct consequence of the values of their group. But surely it is not always true that individuals simply absorb and reproduce the values of their group, even if this is often the case. Free, critical thinking can lead anywhere. People brought up in the United States sometimes convert to Buddhism or Islam. There are Baptists in Japan. Although cultural relativism is often presented as a refined and enlightened moral theory, it seems, paradoxically, not to reflect the complexities of our moral lives.

MODEST RELATIVISM

For all that has been said so far, nothing rules out the possibility that one approach to morality is correct and all conflicting practices are mistaken. Nevertheless, in the face of the diversity of moral practices throughout the world and human history, it is worth thinking about how far it is possible to acknowledge and accept at least some of this diversity. Another approach to incorporating the possible insights of relativism is to start by distinguishing two levels to morality: a level where there must be unity, and a level that accepts diversity.

One way of developing this approach starts with reflection on the general point of morality. Many philosophers will agree that without morality life would be intolerable, riven with conflict. One point of morality (and there may be many) is to settle conflicts in a peaceful fashion, for the benefit of everyone. On this account, then, morality helps us find ways of avoiding or dealing with disputes, or, more positively, to find ways of regulating cooperation for mutual benefit. Morality is a set of rules of adjudication, by which, to use a phrase from the political philosopher John Rawls (1921–2002), we allocate the benefits and burdens of social cooperation.

To say this much is to give an account of part of the nature of morality. But it does not yet tell us what those rules are. This is where differences between different cultures can enter the picture. Although all societies need rules, it may well be that more than one set of rules could serve broadly the same general purpose. Consider again the example of road safety. Every country has rules about whether to drive on the right- or the left-hand side of the road. It doesn't seem to matter which convention is adopted, as long as everyone in the same country drives on the same side of the road. As a result of scientific studies, we may find out that it is safer to drive on one side than the other (perhaps having something to do with the great majority of humans being right-handed). Nevertheless, the correct side to drive on is the one adopted in your country, even if it turns out that your country has adopted the marginally more dangerous convention. And it would be recklessly immoral for anyone to decide to drive on what is for your country the wrong side, on the basis of scientific studies. Or consider the example of the funeral practices of the Greeks and the Callatiae, as described by Herodotus. You probably have observed already that although their practices may differ, at a deeper level both sides agree that the dead must be honored in an appropriate and dignified ceremony that also takes into account the social need to dispose of dead bodies safely. The differences are at the level of details, highly significant though they are.

A relatively modest form of moral relativism argues by analogy to these examples. While the general point of morality is to avoid conflict and harness cooperation, and although sets of rules are needed for this purpose, no single, unique set of rules is always best for these purposes. The moral rules, like the color of mailboxes—or a better example, the rules of language—can vary from society to society, even though they serve the same general purposes. A view of this sort has been defended by David Wong (b. 1949). Wong is a Chinese American philosopher who, through his upbringing, found himself exposed to two rather different value systems. The American system pays a great deal of attention to individual autonomy, privacy, and independence, whereas the Chinese system gives great weight to loyalty to community and family. It is not that in America the community has no value, or that in China the individual is ignored. Both cultures take these values seriously. However, conflicts between these values are sometimes resolved in different ways in the different societies. Jomo Kenyatta detected the same difference between African and European societies, finding that Africans give much more weight to traditional values of community and family. Extending this example, we can see that societies might possibly evolve different moral codes to deal with the different problems they face. And here is a space where cultural relativism can operate.

An interesting feature of Wong's account is that although we can recognize a different society's morality as distinct from our own, we can also, very often, see value in it. Indeed, we might even admire another society's values and wish we had been brought up their way, meanwhile accepting there is no real possibility to change what we do now. Wong's position seems reasonable, although some will challenge it. One opponent will be the philosopher, or perhaps religious thinker, who believes that a single true set of detailed moral rules apply in all times and places. Wong suggests that morality has a type of universality, but this allows for relativism at a societal level, as we have seen. And this does seem to reflect the anthropological evidence of the sort we quoted above from Herodotus and Ruth Benedict.

Some, however, will question whether this really is a form of cultural relativism as generally understood—or just another form of liberalism, which rejects the meta-ethics of relativism but retains some of its practices. The test, perhaps, is what it says about the more troubling type of example we explored earlier where a group is exploited, oppressed, or harmed. How does modest relativism judge slavery, ancient and modern, or oppressive gender practices such as genital cutting? Are we compelled to say that the difference between those societies that accept genital cutting and those that find it outrageous is just like the difference between those societies that drive on the right and those that drive on the left, or those that speak French and those that speak Portuguese? This would be a troubling result, and it is why so many people worry about moral relativism, thinking it is tantamount to giving up moral standards altogether.

Genital Cutting and Cultural Relativism

Wong does discuss the practice of genital cutting, in the context of how a hospital in Seattle faced the dilemma of knowing that if it refused to offer the procedure, then families would still go ahead with it in a far more radical and dangerous way. Hence without taking a moral stance, a hospital might offer a "safe" and very minor, almost symbolic, version of the procedure drawing a single drop of blood in hygienic conditions. Assuming that the families involved considered this to be an acceptable form of genital cutting, it would protect young girls against the serious harm of the very invasive procedures that would have been pursued otherwise (Wong, 2006, pp. 260–263). This is similar to an argument often given in support of legalizing abortion. In countries where abortion is illegal, the practice of dangerous "backstreet" abortion springs up, along with a significant proportion of deaths or permanent damage to fertility. By this argument legalized abortion is simply the lesser evil, which is why some people who morally oppose abortion nevertheless accept its legality.

Wong's discussion of genital cutting is not really directed to the question of how people in one society should view practices in another society, for he focuses his discussion on multicultural society that contains a variety of moral practices, some of which are regarded as morally outrageous by the majority culture. However Wong's "modest relativism" provides a way of discussing the more general questions of how one society should respond to the practices of another, and it will be useful to continue to use genital cutting as our example. We first should recall Wong's distinction between the two levels of morality. First is the "moral core" that all moralities share: the value of cooperation, conflict resolution, and providing ideals of a good life. Second are the particular practices of society, which provide detailed rules and may vary from society to society. The question, then, is whether genital cutting violates the moral core. And here different versions of modest relativism may disagree, depending on how the practice is viewed, and how exactly the distinction is drawn between the core and the particular rules.

The standard liberal discussion of genital cutting sees it as an exercise of brutal male power over female freedom and pleasure: Male dominance runs so deep that often women are implicit in, and even strongly approve of, the practice. This is why it is regarded as so objectionable, but so difficult to eradicate. Yet Wong points out that "in some communities the practice is regarded as rendering the body fertile, as a rite of passage, and a test of courage and endurance to pain that binds together the community of women who practice it" (Wong, 2006, p. 263). Jomo Kenyatta makes similar comments about the role of genital cutting in Gikuyu society. If these claims about the practice can be taken at face value, it can be liberating rather than oppressive, though deep anthropological work will be needed to be sure. However, to understand the practice in the context of Wong's theory, we first have to understand how it may relate to the fundamental moral core shared by all societies.

Generally, genital cutting and other similar practices are undertaken to increase the likelihood that a woman will be a virgin on her wedding day (or if she is not, that it can be detected easily) and will remain faithful during marriage, for if, as a result of the procedure, a woman becomes less capable of sexual pleasure it is thought she will be less likely to be unfaithful. Opposition to sex outside marriage is hardly an eccentric value. It has long been the teaching in the Islamic and Judeo-Christian traditions. Of course practices have changed over time, and sex before marriage now has little stigma in many communities, but still infidelity is generally a subject of wide disapproval even though it is common. Consider how the revelation of infidelity, even the suspicion of it, can ruin a politician's career in many countries. The high-level moral core—that a good life involves sexual fidelity in marriage—is shared across many moral codes. The difference is how it is enforced: in some societies by taboo, moral disapproval, and marriage contract; in other societies by all these means but also through surgical intervention.

The question is whether surgical intervention goes too far. One worry is that it seems so starkly unjust and oppressive that women have to undergo a burden to ensure marital fidelity when men do not—although we should remember that in many societies, men do have to go through their own painful and difficult rites of passage for other purposes. Nevertheless the extreme sexism of the practice is deeply troubling. And this alone may lead us to conclude that genital cutting violates the moral core, just as other ways of protecting fidelity seem a clear violation. Consider, for example, the practice of stoning to death women who have been unfaithful, whether through choice or, in the most horrendous cases, after having been raped. Most two-level relativists will be extremely uncomfortable and say that although stoning the unfaithful may be in accordance with one important core value (fidelity), nevertheless it violates others of far greater importance, such as individual autonomy and freedom from harm. Hence societies that stone unfaithful women can be condemned, even by the two-level relativist, for ignoring part of the core that all moralities must share if they are to be moralities at all.

A similar argument can be made with respect to genital cutting, arguing that even though it serves the value of marital fidelity, and also, perhaps, helps with group bonding and marking the passage to adulthood, these values fall far short of providing a justification. For it also violates the much more important core moral norms of autonomy and, freedom from harm, as well as violating equality, and must be condemned. We can see, then, that everything depends on two key issues: whether autonomy, freedom from harm, and equality are to be regarded as core values that all moralities must share, and the degree to which genital cutting violates these values. Practices differ, and so the same theorist may accept some minor forms but not others (this seems to be Wong's position). But theorists also differ, and so the same practices may be accepted by some modest relativists but condemned by others. However, we need to bear in mind that the notion of "acceptance" is not itself entirely straightforward. For example, the contemporary African philosopher Godfrey B. Tangwa has argued that while genital cutting below the age of consent for both girls and boys is morally wrong, it should not be made illegal. Although this may seem strange, in fact many things are widely believed to be wrong but are not against the law. Marital infidelity, an example we have already used, falls into this category in many countries. Broadly, however, the two-level theory at least provides a way of conceptualizing the issues, even if, on its own, it does not solve all of them.

And we can supplement Wong's and Tangwa's analyses with a suggestion from another contemporary philosopher, Miranda Fricker (b. 1966). When we do view other cultures and want to criticize the practices, it does not follow that we should blame the people who carry them out. For example, we saw that although genital cutting surely exists as a consequence of male domination, that domination runs so deep that the practice is carried out and encouraged by women. We can certainly criticize the practice from our point of view, but many argue that it would be wrong to criticize or blame the particular people involved. They are following what seem to them to be the right values. And the same is true of ancient slavery or perhaps even more recent intolerance of same-sex relations. People can act wrongly, in perfectly good faith.

CHAPTER REVIEW

Summary

When we observe the moral diversity we find in the world today, and even more so when we look back through history, it is easy to believe that values must be in some way relative to each particular culture or society. But as we saw, many people have moral intuitions that support objectivism rather than cultural relativism, and so it is not possible to settle the question by appealing to intuition.

Some people who are attracted to relativism wish to argue that one society should not interfere with the values of another society. But to draw this conclusion is to state that there is a universal value of cultural self-determination, which is a form of liberalism, or what I called pseudo-relativism rather than relativism proper. And we must also face up to the question of whether it is true that all moral traditions are deserving of respect—or whether, on the contrary, sometimes a moral system is a way of camouflaging oppression and needs to be challenged from outside. One difficulty, then, in the idea that we should respect the traditions and practices of each group is that the practices of a group may have evolved to favor one subgroup over another, most often men over women or one race over another. This does not mean we should abandon ideas of "self-determination of groups," but it turns out to be a much more subtle and difficult idea than we first thought.

We have also seen that stating a genuine moral relativist position requires you to step outside your own values and adopt a more abstract perspective. I raised the question of whether it is psychologically difficult to believe your moral values while at the same time accepting moral relativism. Yet we also saw that moral relativism has difficulties coping with the complexity of the modern world, in which it is not true that individuals automatically adopt the moral values of their culture.

The more modest two-level view of moral relativism—distinguishing a moral core, held by all societies, and a culturally relativist element that may vary from society to society—is a possible compromise. We can recognize that although some hard moral constraints must be respected by all societies, how those constraints are translated into particular practices varies from society to society, none of which has a unique claim to being correct. But like any compromise, this position can be attacked from both sides: those who favor cultural relativism will say that there is no shared moral core; those who think there is a single moral truth will not be prepared to accept social diversity. To conclude, although moral relativism presents itself as a highly sophisticated and enlightened position that promises to explain away apparent moral disagreement, on examination it draws us into a new range of conceptual and moral puzzles.

Discussion Questions

1. How should the cultural relativist position be formulated?
2. What considerations support cultural relativism?
3. What considerations oppose cultural relativism?
4. What is the distinction between cultural relativism and liberalism?
5. What is two-level cultural relativism?

Key Terms

moral intuition, p. 23

objectivism, p. 23

cultural relativism, p. 23

commonsense morality, p. 24

moral realism, p. 25

form of the good, p. 25

equivocation, p. 27

liberalism, p. 27

pseudo-relativism, p. 27

individual subjectivism, p. 30

Key Thinkers

Herodotus (484–425 BCE), pp. 21–22, 33

Aristotle (384–322 BCE), p. 21

Ruth Benedict (1887–1948), pp. 22, 30

Oscar Wilde (1854–1900), p. 22

Alan Turing (1912–54), p. 23

Plato (429?–347 BCE), pp. 25–26

Jomo Kenyatta (c. 1891–1978), pp. 29, 33, 35

Michele Moody-Adams, pp. 31–32

John Rawls (1921–2002), p. 32
David Wong (b. 1949), pp. 33–35
Godfrey B. Tangwa, p. 36
Miranda Fricker (b. 1966), pp. 36–37

Further Reading

- Herodotus's *Histories* is available in many editions. I have used the Penguin Classics version, revised edition, published in 2003.

- Aristotle's views on slavery are set out in Book 1 of his *Politics*. A helpful edition, also containing some of his other political writings, is published by Cambridge University Press (1996) edited by Stephen Everson.

- For a detailed discussion of same-sex relations in Ancient Greece, see Kenneth J. Dover *Greek Homosexuality* (Harvard University Press, 1978).

- The quotations from Ruth Benedict are from her *Patterns of Culture*. I have used the 1989 Houghton Mifflin reprint (original work published 1934). A selection is included in Jonathan Wolff (ed.), *Readings in Moral Philosophy* (W. W. Norton, 2018).

- The argument that cultural relativism is self-defeating comes from Bernard Williams in his book *Morality: An Introduction to Ethics* (Cambridge University Press, 1972, pp. 22–25).

- Jomo Kenyatta's *Facing Mount Kenya* was published in an edition by Vintage Books (1962). (Original work published 1938)

- Michele Moody-Adams's arguments are developed in her *Fieldwork in Familiar Places* (Harvard University Press, 1997).

- John Rawls' *A Theory of Justice* was first published in 1971, with a revised edition in 1999. It is published by Harvard University Press with selections in Jonathan Wolff (ed.), *Readings in Moral Philosophy* (W. W. Norton, 2018).

- The discussion of David Wong is based on his *Natural Moralities* (Oxford University Press, 2006).

- Godfrey B. Tangwa's arguments appear in "Circumcision: An African Point of View." In *Male and Female Circumcision: Medical, Legal, and Ethical Considerations in Pediatric Practice* (Kluwer/Plenum Publishers, 1999, pp. 183–193), edited by George Denniston et al.

- Miranda Fricker's discussion of blame and moral relativism is contained in her book *Epistemic Injustice* (Oxford University Press, 2007).

CHAPTER 3

Skepticism and Subjectivism

What humanity has hitherto deemed important are not even realities, but merely illusions, more strictly speaking lies born of the bad instincts of sick natures.

FRIEDRICH NIETZSCHE, ECCE HOMO

MORAL NIHILISM

In the previous chapter we looked at the view known as **cultural relativism**, which takes as its starting point the fact that there has been great moral diversity over time, and at different places at the same time. These facts of relativism have led some people to push the argument even further, to suggest that, while there are different customs in different times and places, in a deeper sense there is, strictly speaking, no such thing as morality. Although people find it important to follow the traditions of their society, it has been said that they are nothing more than traditions—in many ways, they are arbitrary and could have been quite different. This is a very radical criticism of morality. It contends that there is simply no such thing as morality—or, to put it another way, nothing can be morally wrong. This view is sometimes called **moral nihilism,** and the person who holds such a view is known as a moral nihilist. Moral nihilists may nonetheless do what morality is said to demand, either because they happen to want to do what is normally done in their society (either generally, or in the particular case), or because acting immorally often leads to legal or social punishment. But the nihilist's position is not so much about what to do or not do. Instead, the nihilist simply denies that morality has any fundamental justification.

It could be suggested that the moral nihilist is merely someone who follows their own self-interest, supposing that instead of obeying some sort of code of conduct, the rational, moral, or the only possible thing to do is pursue pleasure and avoid pain. These views are known as forms of egoism (directed toward self-interest), and we will look at **psychological egoism** and **moral egoism** in detail in Chapter 6, "Egoism." And it is true the nihilist could be an egoist of some form. Interestingly, however, the moral nihilist need not be. If there is no valid code of behavior, why should I somehow be forced to follow self-interest? I can do what I like, whether it is in my interest or against it. After all, many people seem prepared to engage in behavior that harms them (smoking, drinking too much, overeating, getting into fights) for no one's benefit. The nihilist just acts as he or she feels, arguing that there is no good argument for anyone to do anything else.

If asserted on its own, though, the nihilist position seems intellectually unsatisfying. Societies have developed complex moral codes. Was all of that simply some sort of intellectual mistake, rather like astrology? If so, why does it persist? (We could ask the same question about astrology.) Now, the nihilist could refuse to answer; but if morality can be explained away somehow, the nihilist position looks stronger.

Who, then, are the moral nihilists? Friedrich Nietzsche (1844–1900), a trenchant critic of the morality of his day, is sometimes considered to be a nihilist. Nietzsche is a radical figure in moral philosophy: He is one of the most exciting, terrifying, and diversely interpreted philosophers of any age. Consider the title of one of his most famous works: *Beyond Good and Evil: Prelude to a Philosophy of the Future* (1886). This title in itself seems to suggest that morality is a relatively superficial phenomenon: something we can—something we should—get beyond, as a therapist might tell you to get beyond some of your hang-ups.

Yet what is it to get beyond good and evil? It sounds like it is to throw off the shackles of morality, and that is how Nietzsche is often read. However, Nietzsche is a philosopher who, while exhilarating to read, is notoriously difficult to interpret. The nihilist reading of his works is encouraged by Nietzsche's description of himself not only as "The Antichrist" but also "the first immoralist" (*Ecce Homo*, III UM 3). But an alternative reading is preferred by many, though not all, scholars. In this alternative view, getting "beyond good and evil" means that the terms *good* and *evil* are to be replaced by *good* and *bad*—a subtle, but as we shall see, vitally important shift. In this reading, Nietzsche's project may not have been so much to reject morality but to call for what he terms a **revaluation of all values**, generating a new type of morality. We will look at this view further shortly.

Perhaps a clearer example of the nihilist is Thrasymachus. He is a character in Plato's dialogue *The Republic* who argues with great force at the opening of the book that "justice is the interest of the stronger," but his position is one that Plato sets out to refute rather than defend. Fiction also provides examples, such as the character Meursault in *L'Estranger* (*The Stranger*, 1942), a novel by the French philosopher and novelist Albert Camus (1913–60). Meursault kills another man, someone he barely knows, but feels no emotion. If we read a news story about a modern Meursault, we would imagine that he is a psychopath; and indeed, in cases of severe psychopathy it is common to suppose that the sufferer lacks the type of moral response that others have. So perhaps here we have stumbled on the real-life moral nihilist: the psychopath. Understandably few, if any, philosophers have recommended the psychopath's position as one that captures the truth about morality.

MORALITY AND CUSTOM

A more reasoned position, which can lead to a form of nihilism, returns with full force to the question of whether the rules of morality have an independent justification or are simply customs or habits that we find hard to break. It is a thought that must have occurred to many people. It is the theme, for example, of Fyodor Dostoyevsky's (1821–81) masterful novel *Crime and Punishment* (1866), in which an impoverished Russian student named Raskolnikov convinces himself that moral action is, for a certain sort of person, essentially a form of cowardice and that the truly strong person will, in the appropriate circumstances, rise above it. In support of his case, he argues that it can be right to ignore conventional morality in pursuit of higher goals:

> It is my view that if the discoveries of [German astronomer Johannes] Kepler and [English physicist Isaac] Newton could not on any account, as a result of certain complex factors, have become known to people other than by means of sacrificing the life of one person, the lives of ten, a hundred or even more persons, who were trying to interfere with those discoveries or stand as an obstacle in their path, then Newton would have had the right, and would even have been obliged . . . to *get rid of* those ten or a hundred persons, in order to make his discoveries known to all mankind. (Dostoyevsky, 1866/2003, pp. 308–309)

Raskolnikov, however, stops short of the wish to overturn all conventional morality. For example, he goes on directly to say it doesn't follow that Newton has the right to kill anyone he wants or to steal at the market every day. Nevertheless Raskolnikov brings himself to believe that he, Raskolnikov, should ignore ordinary morality and is perfectly justified in robbing and killing a wealthy old woman; though, as we can imagine, when he puts his theory into practice it doesn't work out so well for him. Raskolnikov's position, perhaps reflecting his status as a psychologically disturbed individual in a work of fiction, is not entirely clear; but he seems to think that conventional morality is a type of conspiracy of those who are not strong or willful enough to survive through their own efforts and so need artificial rules to hold others in place. Morality is a device to protect the weak from the strong. In some circumstances the truly strong person has the right, or even the duty, to ignore the rules if the opportunity is presented. As soon, however, as it is stated that the strong person has the "right or duty" to break conventional rules, one conception of morality has been replaced with another. This is not a form of pure nihilism after all, but rather a form of morality that gives the strong special rights. To understand it better, it is worth looking briefly at Nietzsche's more philosophical presentation of a similar position.

Morality as a Device to Curb the Strong

Raskolnikov's view that splits society into "the herd" and "the elite" is also associated with Friedrich Nietzsche, mentioned earlier as presenting the thesis that we need to "revalue" our values. Nietzsche's key idea is that we must subject contemporary morality—the morality we currently find ourselves with—to scrutiny and examine its nature and the justifications we give for it. For Nietzsche, writing in nineteenth-century Germany, contemporary morality was the morality of the Christian church, which had its own categories of **virtues** and **vices**, justified by human belief in God's will. To be a good Christian and therefore a "good person," you need to be humble, pious, and meek. But to be like this, says Nietzsche, is to accept what he calls a **slave morality**—a term that clearly provides a clue about how attractive he finds it. Nietzsche's revaluation question can be put like this: Is it good to be a good person? Or, indeed, is it a bad thing to be an evil person, if to be evil is to be the opposite of humble, meek, and pious? The question had been raised before, by the Scottish philosopher David Hume (1711–76), as early as 1751:

> Celibacy, fasting, penance, mortification, self-denial, humility, silence, solitude and the whole train of monkish virtues . . . are rejected everywhere by men of sense. . . because they serve no manner of purpose. . . . We justly, therefore, transfer them to the opposite column, and place them in the category of vices. . . . A gloomy, hair-brained enthusiast, after his death, may have a place in the calendar; but will scarcely be admitted, when alive, into intimacy and society, except by those who are as delirious and dismal as himself. (Hume, 1751/1983, pp. 73–74)

To put it another way, we can ask whether Christian morality is "fit for purpose." Of course, defenders might point out that it is perfectly well suited for Christian purposes. But then is that the right test? How would Nietzsche have us judge? For Nietzsche the key test seems to be whether these values are "life-promoting, life-preserving, species-preserving, perhaps even species-cultivating" (*Beyond Good and Evil*, 1886/1989, part 1, section 4, p. 11). Under the conditions of the original formation of Christianity, when Christians were a ruthlessly persecuted minority, these virtues allowed the survival of the religion, even at great sacrifice for individuals. But for Nietzsche that time had passed, and it is necessary to replace one set of obsolete values with a more positive set suitable for our time.

In sum, although in a sense Nietzsche did believe that morality is purely a device used by the weak to curb the strong, his immediate target was the Christian morality of his day. But in the reading we are considering, Nietzsche's view seems to be that despite its strong grip on modern life, Christian morality is out of date and now does more harm than good. There is a deeper form of morality—the morality of good and bad rather than good and evil—that is not a device used by the weak to curb the strong. Instead, it is a morality the strong can use to assert themselves. And that, in turn, may be why many people find Nietzsche's approach to morality disturbing: his admiration for the small minority of the strong and talented at the expense of "the herd," the ordinary people, which includes the great majority of us.

As I have said, although Nietzsche attempts to undermine conventional morality, by the interpretation we have been considering he is not really a moral nihilist, because he seeks to establish a different morality. However, other philosophers—such as the twentieth-century philosopher J. L. Mackie (1917–81)—have argued for views that are similar to the moral nihilist position, and we will return to Mackie's views at the end of this chapter. But it will be illuminating to approach it through another route, looking at a number of other ways in which morality has been reinterpreted as not being what it seems.

INDIVIDUAL SUBJECTIVISM

In our "commonsense" approach to morality, we tend to assume that some moral judgments are straightforwardly true and others false. For example, most of us will assume it is straightforwardly true that it is wrong to shoot a man "just to watch him die," in the words of the old Johnny Cash song "Folsom Prison Blues." But we have also seen our common sense about morality challenged. For example, we looked in Chapter 2 at cultural relativism, which is the view that morality is relative to each person's culture. One of the difficulties we noted with cultural relativism is that even within a culture, people often disagree deeply about morality. That thought might push us into a more individualist direction: There is no general truth about morality, even within a culture. Rather, in this view, each person's code of ethics is subjective in the sense of being unique to that person. This position, often called **individual subjectivism**, is something that many people suspect to be true about morality—especially when they meet and argue with someone who holds a different view, and the arguments get more and more heated. It is tempting at that stage to withdraw from the argument, perhaps saying that "Everyone is entitled to their own opinion." Of course that is not what you would say to someone who insists that 2 + 2 = 5, or that the earth is flat, unless you are simply being polite or want to get away as quickly as possible. When people disagree on an objective matter of fact, at least one of them is wrong. Some other issues are purely subjective, where the notion of right and wrong seems out of place. The question we face is where morality fits.

We can all agree that different people can have different views. But we should be aware that, as so often in philosophy, the same name—in this case, subjectivism—can cover a variety of distinct positions. Subjectivism, of course, contrasts with **objectivism**; and the basic issue is whether values are objective and there to be discovered, or subjective, meaning created in some way by us. And if we do create them, is this something we do in the context of humanity as a whole, or within each group or culture, or for each of us as an individual? We discussed cultural subjectivism, better known as cultural relativism, in the Chapter 2. In this section we will look in particular at the last issue, individual subjectivism.

Our question is whether we should treat disagreement about morality in the way we treat disagreement about basic matters of fact, or in some other way. Consider another area of apparent disagreement: two children arguing about whether chocolate or vanilla ice cream is better. One says, "Chocolate is much better than vanilla." The other says, "You're wrong; vanilla is so much better than chocolate." No doubt it looks like there is an argument here, and it could get intense. But as an onlooker—an older brother or sister, say—you might feel that it is possible to defuse the situation if you have the patience. You might try to persuade the children that there is no real disagreement. When the first child says, "Chocolate is better than vanilla," you could argue that she is talking about her own preferences rather than about the ice creams. That is, she is really reporting, "I prefer the taste of chocolate to vanilla." Similarly the other child is really saying, "I prefer the taste of vanilla to chocolate." Once these views are restated, something remarkable has happened. There is no disagreement any more. Both statements can be true. Unless one of the children is misrepresenting his or her preferences just for the sake of having an argument (which can happen, of course), by this interpretation they are both effectively saying something true. Of course they have different preferences, and they may find it hard to believe that the other child really can have the preferences he or she claims, but still there is no contradiction. It is not like one of them saying that chocolate is made from cocoa beans and the other claiming it is made from the shells of turtles. Unless there are two sources of chocolate, in that argument only one child can be right. But when arguing about which is the better flavor, there is a sense in which both children are right and another sense in which neither of them is.

This proposal for dissolving the disagreement suggests that statements apparently attributing values to objects, such as "Chocolate ice cream is lovely," really express something about the person making the statement, perhaps "Eating chocolate ice cream gives me great pleasure." And it is easy to see how to apply this to moral judgments: "Nelson Mandela was a good person" would mean something like "I strongly approve of the character and actions of Nelson Mandela." In this view, moral judgments do state facts, but different facts than we first thought: facts about the person making the judgment rather than about Nelson Mandela. And again we can analyze apparent moral disagreement as we did disputes about taste: One person approves, the other person disapproves, end of story. Subjectivism has the appeal that it dissolves moral disagreement. But this comes at a cost. Are we ready to say that moral disputes are no more important than disputes about the better ice cream, where both parties can state their view and simply move on? In other words, subjectivism dissolves moral problems without resolving them. Is that acceptable?

Expressivism

The view we have been considering proposes that apparent moral judgments state facts about the person making the judgment: the fact that he or she has an attitude of approval. However, some philosophers adopt a subtly different form of individual subjectivism known as **expressivism**. The modified view suggests that moral judgments *express* attitudes without *stating* that you have them. This may seem a fussy distinction: What is the difference between expressing a preference and stating you have it? Well, there is a difference. Consider an analogy. Imagine you are watching your favorite team take the lead, and along with the rest of the crowd instantly start to cheer and applaud. It would be odd to say that your cheering should be analyzed as a sentence in English that really means "I am happy that my team has gone into the lead." Rather, we might say that your cheering expresses your happiness rather than states that you are happy.

This analogy gives rise to a range of theories in moral philosophy which have at their core the idea that moral statements express our attitudes or our emotions. These views are variously known as **emotivism** or expressivism, although, irritatingly, not everyone uses the terms in exactly the same way. The heart of these views, though, is the claim that saying "Nelson Mandela is a good person" is rather like saying "Nelson Mandela!" in a particular tone of voice that expresses strong approval. As in the previous version of subjectivism, this view denies that the judgment says something about Nelson Mandela. But in the expressivist view, it doesn't literally say anything about the person making the judgment either. What it does is express their attitudes or emotions rather than stating that they have them.

In the philosophical literature the view that moral judgments express emotions rather than state facts is known as **noncognitivism**. Cognitivism, by contrast, is the view that moral propositions express "genuine" beliefs, like the beliefs of science, that will be true or false, even if it may be difficult to tell which. (Beliefs are also known as cognitions, hence the name *noncognitivism*.) Noncognitivism, naturally, denies that moral propositions express genuine beliefs. Rather, they express something about the agent: tastes, preferences, emotions, or something else that is subjective to the person expressing the judgment. Like many technical terms, *cognitivism* and *noncognitivism* mean different things in different parts of philosophy. But in moral philosophy, they are concerned primarily with whether moral statements express genuine beliefs.

Could the expressivist theory—ridiculed by its opponents as the "boo-hurrah" theory of ethics—possibly be correct? To repeat the problem for subjectivism mentioned above, it is disturbing to think that moral disputes are like children squabbling over which ice cream is better, or rival sports fans cheering on different teams. And there are obvious disanalogies with these cases. In moral argument we often give reasons for our views, sometimes in elaborate and detailed fashion. And occasionally we convince another to change his or her view, or we even change our own. How could that be if the noncognitivist is right, and a moral judgment is a mere expression of an attitude?

The philosopher A. J. Ayer (1910–89), a prominent expressivist, was fully aware of this criticism, and he pointed out that most moral disagreement concerns background information rather than the judgment itself. Suppose, for example, you are convinced that a friend is unkind, while I strongly hold the view that he is kind. To convince me of your view, you might tell me about episodes when he told damaging lies. Coming to know this might lead me to change my mind because I didn't know all the background facts. Preferences or attitudes can change. But exactly the same is true regarding ice cream. For example, a child might come to change her preferences about vanilla and chocolate ice cream by tasting a particularly delicious sample of vanilla ice cream. This is a way of improving background knowledge—that vanilla ice cream can be much tastier than previously thought—rather than merely changing the judgment.

Ayer's point is that apparent moral disagreement is often a result of one person not having all the facts available and that, once there is agreement on the facts, his or her moral judgment may change. Yet, as Ayer asks, if there is agreement on the facts but the disagreement in moral judgment remains, what happens next? It looks like there is nothing else to do except make your point again and again, raising your voice and losing your temper. This, he believes, is a consideration in favor of the expressivist view.

Still, there is another problem lurking. Moral judgments have a special role in our lives and conversation. Moral judgments are not used merely to vent our feelings. Rather, we use them to communicate and try to persuade others of our position. This recognition led the American philosopher Charles Leslie Stevenson (1908–79) to propose a more complex theory. Stevenson's view is essentially that moral judgments do not merely express our emotions, but also include the further element that they are an invitation to others to share in them too.

We can see why Stevenson has done this. Making a moral judgment is not the same as cheering your team on, for normally when you make a moral judgment you expect—or at least hope—that other people will see things the way you do. Making the judgment can even be part of your strategy to bring others to share your view. By contrast, when you cheer your team you are not trying to change the allegiance of the rival supporters, to get everyone in the stadium to cheer for your side. In fact you would be rather disturbed if this did happen, and you would think that the opposing supporters were being ironic or making some sort of protest against their team. It is wrong, then, to think of moral judgments as merely expressing personal emotions, for they are also ways of trying to persuade others to share them. Stevenson adds this element of intended persuasion to his analysis of moral judgments: They are an expression of your emotions, and an invitation to others to adopt the same emotions. This extended form of expressivism fits better with how we use moral language in real life. Between them, Ayer and Stevenson have presented a significant challenge to an objectivist, universalist position based on their philosophical analysis of moral language.

Can we accept some version of a subjectivist position? Clearly it has some intuitive pull. It would explain why moral disagreement exists, and why it is so difficult to resolve. It also explains how we can be motivated to act morally, for we already have the attitudes that support our moral judgments and therefore are more likely to act in what we see as the morally correct way. But at the same time it is rather troubling, for it seems to leave morality completely unconstrained. If we diagnose moral disagreement as in any way like stating or expressing difference in preference or taste, then what do we say about someone who holds moral views that most of us consider outrageous, such as the view that there is a moral duty to persecute members of a different religion or race? In the subjectivist view, it seems that this person simply has unusual emotions or preferences, like those who enjoy eating the sort of chili peppers that burn most people's mouths. Can we really accept such a view?

It is tempting to say that anyone who has attitudes or emotions that lead them to express approval for racism is simply a bad person. However, on the expressivist view, by saying this I am simply expressing my disapproval of people who state racist views and am encouraging others to disapprove of them too. But this expressivist analysis of the negative moral judgment is very frustrating. When I say that someone who expresses racist views is acting badly and ought to stop, I take myself to be talking about the racist, not about myself. In cases like this it is hard to resist the thought that at least some elements of morality are more objective than the expressivist allows. For all their appeal, subjectivism and expressivism hit an intuitive barrier; they have many counterintuitive implications.

OBJECTIVE MORAL CONCEPTS

To understand some of our resistance to subjectivism, it is worth returning to the discussion of objectivism in Chapter 2. There, in contrast to cultural relativism, I suggested that the objectivist believes that a certain set of practices is the true or correct moral standpoint. It is easy to be suspicious of such a bold and perhaps arrogant and exclusionary view, and this is why many people look for alternatives such as cultural relativism or subjectivism. But it will be helpful to look in a bit more detail at how versions of objectivism have been developed to make this idea sound less grandiose and more down to earth. If more modest versions of objectivism are available, they may turn out to be an intuitively appealing alternative.

Some forms of objectivism start by paying close attention to the language we use when we make moral judgments. So far in this book, I haven't said much about this. I have used the words *good* and *bad* and *right* and *wrong*, but it is worth pausing to think about how we tend to praise and criticize people in ordinary life. I have used examples such as "Nelson Mandela was a good person," but when was the last time you said of a man or woman that he or she was good or bad? This is what we say when we are training our dogs—"good dog," "bad dog"—or perhaps our children, but it is less common to apply these terms to adult human beings. It is true that we do often wonder about what is the "right" thing to do for ourselves, but stop to think how you praise and blame other people. We often use terms like *kind, generous, friendly, welcoming, thoughtful, considerate, open,* or *brave* to praise people, and we criticize them with terms like *mean, cruel, two-faced, dishonest,* or *thoughtless.*

Let's consider the first term in the list—*kind.* What is it to be kind? This is an interesting and subtle question. It must involve taking another person's feelings or concerns into account and giving the person attention, time, or money without making them feel that you are doing something especially burdensome. No doubt there is more to it, but that gives us a core understanding. If someone says that a woman who has just stubbed out her cigarette on your bare arm is kind, something odd has gone on. Perhaps they were being sarcastic. Perhaps there is some complicated story that puts the action in a different light (perhaps they were helping you remove a parasitic insect that had to be burned out). But if nothing like this applies, then it simply seems to be untrue that this is a kind act or a kind person. In other words, morality does seem to involve some objective truths, such as this: Stubbing out your cigarette on someone's bare arm is not kind.

The philosopher Bernard Williams (1929–2003) used the distinction between what he called **thin and thick ethical concepts** to help make this point (Williams, 1985). Thin concepts—such as right, wrong, good, and bad—are called thin because they often seem to do little more than communicate moral approval or disapproval. But the concepts of everyday ethics, such as kind, brave, and considerate, are much thicker than this: They also have what is called a descriptive content, as we saw in the example of *kind.* From this it follows that in some circumstances, it is simply false to call someone kind. The key point is that the approval or disapproval seems to be connected to the descriptive element: Unless the action meets the conditions for being kind (or for some other positive ethical concept), we will not approve of it. This is why the concept appears to be objective, after all.

Subjectivists are, of course, aware of this type of example, and they can agree that some moral judgments have a descriptive element as well as an evaluative side. But it may be that the descriptive and evaluative aspects could be separated, with moral judgment remaining with the evaluative element. The point of this attempted analysis is to be able to insist that morality remains subjective. To test this idea, imagine an anthropologist from Mars, where—let us suppose—there is a moral nihilist culture. This anthropologist simply has no moral concepts. Could this visitor to earth write an anthropological report on human practices, pointing out that human beings have the concept "kind" that they use on certain occasions and precisely analyzing its use? This should be possible if the descriptive aspect is separable from the evaluative. The subjectivist needs to argue that in the thought experiment, the Martian can use the word *kind* just as we do. Objectivity, in this view, attaches to the descriptive part—the part that the Martian grasps—but not to the subjective evaluation, which the Martian does not share or even understand. The subjectivist claim comes down to this: It is one thing to be able to identify kind acts, but quite another to know that society approves of them.

Is this account plausible? Could you really identify kind acts, or brave acts, or generous acts without approving of them? Some contemporary philosophers, such as John McDowell (b. 1942), have argued that the descriptive and evaluative elements cannot be detached. The Martian anthropologist's task is impossible: You could not identify acts as kind unless you knew that they were the sort of thing that is found valuable. This would mean that at least some of our moral concepts are objective: If you are to have the concept "kind," you must acknowledge that people who are kind are morally good, in that respect at least. Others disagree, arguing that you could know what counts as kind without holding any views that are related to morality. This remains an area for debate.

ETHICS, LANGUAGE, METAPHYSICS, AND EPISTEMOLOGY

Many of the subjectivist views we have looked at so far make an interesting claim about moral language. They argue that, in a sense, it is deceptive. Take a simple example: "Hitler was evil." The apparent logic of this sentence is that it attributes a property—"evil"—to an object, the person Hitler, just as in the sentence "Hitler had black hair" we attribute the property "black hair" to him. As we have already seen, some subjectivists say that this is not the real underlying logic. In reality, they say, in uttering the sentence I am expressing my own feeling, or emotion. For example, in the simplest expressivist analysis, which claims that moral judgments have more in common with cheering on a sports team than stating a fact about the world, the statement that "Hitler is evil" is equivalent to "Hitler—boo!"

In these views, the apparent or surface logic of the statement is misleading. Thinking that the way to understand morality is through the analysis of language was popular in the mid-twentieth century, when much of philosophy concerned itself with linguistic analysis.

But things move on, and probably the most significant strand of skepticism in the current debate is known as **error theory**, from the philosopher J. L. Mackie (1917–81). Mackie's most important work on the topic is *Ethics: Inventing Right and Wrong* (1977), a book with a title giving a strong hint about what we will find in it. Mackie does not try to reanalyze our ordinary moral language. He accepts that our ordinary moral language presupposes that values are objective—that in saying "Hitler was evil," I am attributing an objective value, albeit a strongly negative one, to an object. But Mackie argues that all statements involving the attribution of objective values to objects are false because, unlike black hair, objective values do not exist. In this sense, then, Mackie's view can be understood as a form of moral nihilism, which we encountered at the start of this chapter. True, Mackie writes that his view could be called subjectivism; but he is not completely comfortable with that term, and nihilism may be closer. Error theory is the name that has stuck. Error theory has the consequence that strictly speaking, it is not true that Hitler was evil. But this is not to say that he was a good man, for that would equally be false. Both claims are false because they have a false or erroneous presupposition: that there are objective values. Hence the name *error theory*.

The Argument From Queerness

Why take error theory seriously? Well, Mackie wants us to share his puzzlement about the "essence" of objective values, especially the thin moral values without descriptive content, such as good, bad, right, and wrong. Mackie, we noted, subtitles his book *Inventing Right and Wrong*. As we have seen, the alternative to the view that our value system is invented is that it is discovered: an objectivist position. Mackie puts this question to the objectivist: "What is it that you think you can discover?" Plato, as we saw in the last chapter, believed that there are objective values, and that these objective values underpin the objectivity of morality. But Mackie wants us to think hard about what these objective values are. Where are they? How can we know about them? Plato, we noted, used the idea of the form of the good—the perfect idea of the good—that we will never encounter in the actual world but that exists in some otherworldly realm. If this really is what it means for values to exist in an objective sense, it is understandable to begin having doubts.

The difficulty of making sense of objective values is the basis of Mackie's argument. He claims, "If there were objective values they would be entities or qualities or relations of a very strange sort, utterly different from anything else in the universe" (Mackie, 1977/1991, p. 38). This, which he calls the **argument from queerness** (using *queer* in its old-fashioned sense, as in "odd" or "strange") raises a fundamental question of **metaphysics**, which is the study of what there is in the world. Here, the question is essentially "What would an objective value be?" Animal, vegetable, or mineral? Where is it? What does it look like? And this argument also raises a question of knowledge: How can we come to know these strange objects? In the philosophical jargon, questions about how we know things are questions of **epistemology**. Mackie's argument also raises an important question of motivation. How can any fact about the world have "built-in to-be-doneness," in the sense that my recognition of its existence somehow automatically requires me to pursue it?

When we raise these deeper philosophical questions, we understand the advantages of the subjectivist view. The subjectivist answers the metaphysical question by saying that values are ultimately preferences or emotions that are perfectly ordinary things we encounter in the world, indeed inside ourselves, and nothing mysterious. And we can know these things in the way we know anything in our own minds, through introspection. Admittedly introspection does raise a puzzle: How is it that I know the contents of my mind? But the point is that in the subjectivist view, knowing that something is bad is no more difficult to understand than knowing that being poked with a sharp stick is painful. Finally, I am motivated to pursue values because they are *my* values—my preferences or emotions—rather than something imposed on me by an independent objective reality.

Mackie's argument can be formulated in simple terms:

Premise 1: If objective values exist they would have to exist, but not in physical realm, and also have "built-in to-be-doneness."

Premise 2: Nothing can exist, but not in physical realm, and also have built-in to-be-doneness.

Therefore

Conclusion: Objective values do not exist.

This argument is based on his reflections on the strangeness of objective values: how odd they seem to be, and how odd it is that we can come to know anything about them, or be motivated to follow them if they exist. Of course, not everyone shares Mackie's puzzlement. One response that

Mackie mentions himself is to deny the second premise in the argument above by pointing out that the universe includes many odd things: Should we say there is no such thing as the perfect circle for the same reason? And what about numbers, quarks, the Higgs boson, and consciousness? Values don't seem much stranger than these.

However, anyone responding in this way does have an important challenge to explain what objective values are. Do we have to accept Plato's theory of forms, as just outlined? Or is it possible to build a different form of objectivism, perhaps using the idea of objective moral concepts explained above? Mackie's argument presupposes that if morality is objective, then values must somehow be things in the world. But perhaps this is the wrong way of thinking about objectivity, and we should deny the first premise in the argument. Another alternative could be that some sort of nearly universal agreement in judgment is a sufficient form of objectivity. But is there near universal agreement? Probably not. This is the topic of cultural relativism, which we explored in Chapter 2. Mackie suggests that cultural relativism also supports his error theory about values.

In sum, Mackie's argument does seem to be valid. But its soundness is not so obvious. Each of the premises of the argument can be questioned. I have not shown that they are false, but it is reasonable to say that they are at least controversial.

RESPONDING TO NIHILISM, SUBJECTIVISM, AND ERROR THEORY

We have considered a number of different ways of undercutting objectivism, each of which raises some plausible lines of argument. Subjectivism, for example, has much to be said for it. It seems to preserve the important human freedom of being able to form your own moral views. It also makes the metaphysics and epistemology of morality easy. The question is whether anyone, in their heart of hearts, really believes that subjectivism is true. Is it really true that morality allows you to think whatever you want? When you describe a killer as evil, are you really merely expressing your own strong disapproval (and perhaps inviting others to share your judgment)?

But perhaps the most challenging difficulty for all of the views that question the objectivity of morality is knowing why it is that you approve or disapprove of an action or person in the first place. Consider again the flavors of ice cream. I enjoy vanilla ice cream and prefer it to chocolate ice cream. Why is that? It isn't that I have just made up my mind to have these preferences, although of course some people do make up their mind to have particular preferences (for instance, training themselves to prefer fine wine to beer, perhaps for snobbish reasons). But in the ordinary case, my preferences about ice cream are based on the sensations of taste, and perhaps smell and texture, I receive from eating the different ice creams. I simply find one more pleasant than another, and possibly even something can be said about my physiology that would explain my preferences.

Consider, though, the case where I approve of a kind action. Why do I do so? It doesn't seem that it is some sort of brute fact about my physiology. Rather, I have noticed that someone has made a special effort to do something that improves the situation of someone else in some way. Certainly I approve of it. But the critic of subjectivism will say, "Why should I approve of it unless I recognize that it is good to help other people?" But if we agree with this point, then it seems that subjectivism ultimately rests on objectivism: an understanding that some things are good and some are bad, which is why I approve and disapprove of them. Objectivism is harder to reject than it may have appeared. But the critics of objectivism can leave us less sure that we know what objectivism is.

CHAPTER REVIEW

Summary

In this chapter we have looked at a number of challenges to conventional views of morality. I began with the nihilist view that there is nothing to morality at all, but soon moved on to Nietzsche's idea that it is necessary to "revalue" our values, as distinct from rejecting all values as the nihilist argues. I then explored a number of versions of individual subjectivism, including the view that morality can be reduced to individual preference. I also looked at forms of expressivism, which claim that moral judgments express attitudes of approval and disapproval, or express our emotions, and invite others to share them.

I then outlined a form of objectivism that claims that when we use objective moral concepts, our moral judgments can be straightforwardly true or false. Next I examined Mackie's error theory, which states that our ordinary moral judgments are all false because they presuppose the existence of objective values. This seems to be a form of nihilism, as discussed earlier in the chapter. Finally, I looked at some objections to subjectivism. Subjectivist views may be hard to refute, but it is hard to see why we would retain any interest in morality if subjectivism were true. It seems that the attempt to short-circuit moral philosophy, this time by adopting a subjectivist analysis, simply returns us to some of the deepest questions about morality.

Discussion Questions

1. What is moral nihilism?
2. Does subjectivism reduce morality to individual preferences?
3. Explain the expressivist position.
4. What are objective moral concepts? Can they be used to provide a reply to the subjectivist?
5. What is the error theory of morality?

Key Terms

cultural relativism, p. 40

moral nihilism, p. 40

psychological egoism, p. 40

moral egoism, p. 40

revaluation of all values, p. 41

virtue, p. 43

vice, p. 43

slave morality, p. 43

individual subjectivism, p. 44

objectivism, p. 45

expressivism, p. 46

emotivism, p. 47

noncognitivism, p. 47

thin and thick ethical concepts, p. 50

error theory, p. 52

argument from queerness, p. 53

metaphysics, p. 53

epistemology, p. 53

Key Thinkers

Friedrich Nietzsche (1844–1900), pp. 40–41

Plato (429?–347 BCE), pp. 41, 52

Albert Camus (1913–60), p. 41

Fyodor Dostoyevsky (1821–81), pp. 42–43

Johannes Kepler (1571–1630), p. 42

Isaac Newton (1643–1727), p. 42

David Hume (1711–76), p. 43

A. J. Ayer (1910–89), pp. 47–48

Charles Leslie Stevenson (1908–79), p. 48

Bernard Williams (1929–2003), p. 50

John McDowell (b. 1942), p. 51

J. L. Mackie (1917–81), pp. 52–54

Further Reading

▪ Friedrich Nietzsche's views are set out throughout his writings, although *Beyond Good and Evil* is the most important text from the viewpoint of issues covered in this book. It is available in a 1989 edition from Vintage, edited by Walter Kaufmann. (Original work published 1886)

▪ A good selection of Nietzsche's other writings is *The Portable Nietzsche* (Penguin, 1954), edited by Walter Kaufmann. *Ecce Homo*, from which the opening quote is taken, is published by Oxford University Press (Oxford World's Classics, 2007), translated by Duncan Large. (Original work published 1888)

▪ Plato's *The Republic* is widely available, for example, in an edition from W. W. Norton (1999).

▪ Albert Camus's *The Stranger* is available in an edition from Vintage (1989). (Original work published 1942)

▪ Dostoyevsky has been quoted from the Penguin Classics edition of *Crime and Punishment* (2003), translated by David McDuff. (Original work published 1866)

▪ The quotation from David Hume's *Enquiry Concerning the Principles of Morals* is taken from the Hackett (1983) edition. (Original work published 1751)

▪ A. J. Ayer's *Language, Truth and Logic* is available in a Dover reprint (1952). (Original work published 1936)

▪ Charles Leslie Stevenson's *Ethics and Language* was published by Yale University Press (1944).

▪ Bernard Williams, *Ethics and the Limits of Philosophy* was published by Fontana (1985).

▪ J. L. Mackie's *Ethics: Inventing Right and Wrong* was published by Penguin (1991). (Original work published 1977)

▪ Selections from Plato, Hume, Ayer, and Mackie are included in Jonathan Wolff (ed.), *Readings in Moral Philosophy* (W. W. Norton, 2018).

CHAPTER 4

Free Will and Moral Responsibility

We ought then to regard the present state of the universe as the effect of its anterior state and as the cause of the one which is to follow. Given for one instance an intelligence which could comprehend all the forces by which nature is animated, and the respective situation of the beings who compose it—an intelligence sufficiently vast to submit these data to analysis—it would embrace in the same formula the movements of the greatest bodies of the universe and those of the lightest atom; for it, nothing would be uncertain and the future, as the past, would be present before its eyes.

PIERRE-SIMON LAPLACE, A PHILOSOPHICAL ESSAY ON PROBABILITIES

FREE WILL

In the previous two chapters we looked at a variety of challenges that try to disrupt our ordinary sense of morality. In this chapter we will look at a different set of arguments that some have found threatening to the existence of an important aspect of morality: the notion of moral responsibility and the associated concepts of praise and blame.

The idea is simply this: that human beings lack **free will** and that all of their behavior is predetermined in some way. In this view, known as **determinism**, we are like sophisticated machines or robots. If this is so, it is claimed, then there can be no morality, for we are not responsible for anything we do. And if we are not responsible, then we cannot be praised or blamed for our actions. And what is morality if it is not a system for praising and blaming? In this chapter we will explore the determinist challenge to moral responsibility, and consider some replies and alternative views.

The ideas just expressed amount to a simple argument that can be formulated in the following way:

Premise 1: Moral appraisal requires us to be able to hold people responsible for their actions.

Premise 2: If human beings are to be held responsible for their actions, then they must have free will.

Premise 3: Human beings do not have free will.

Therefore

Conclusion: Human beings are not subject to moral appraisal.

If the three premises are correct and it really does follow that human beings cannot be assessed morally—in other words, if the argument is sound in the technical sense introduced in Chapter 1—then, it seems, that would be the end for human morality.

Like many apparently simple arguments, this one needs considerable further exploration. The first two premises lead to the sub-conclusion that without free will, human beings are not subject to moral appraisal; premise 3 states that human beings do not have free will. Let's start with the partly scientific question of the third premise: Do human beings have free will?

Here are some quick terminology points. First, sometimes the view that human beings have free will is known as **libertarianism** because it claims we have the liberty to make free choices. I prefer to avoid that term, for it is also the name of a theory in political philosophy that defends individual liberty to the point where it questions the justification of government, taxation, and welfare benefits. That theory is also interesting and important, but the two uses of the term are not connected. Second, another way of stating that human beings have free will is to say there is such a thing as **agent causation**: that human agents can cause their own actions. In contrast, determinism suggests that actions are caused by factors outside the agent's control. The term *agent causation* is a useful reminder of what seems to be at stake in the debate.

Intuitive Belief in Free Will

Intuitively, the premise that human beings lack free will seems absurd. You are presently reading a paragraph of this book. A short time ago, when you finished the last paragraph, you made the decision—most likely an unconscious decision, but if you are finding the book a struggle, possibly a fully conscious one—to carry on reading at least for a bit longer. Those seconds ago, you could have stopped. You could have shut the book, stood up, and gone out with friends. Yet you did not. You chose—you freely chose, even if under a bit of pressure—to carry on reading. Every day you are faced with hundreds if not thousands of decisions, and the actual course of your day is one of countless millions, possibly billions, of ways it could have gone if you had made different choices. Some of the differences put you back on the same track—Which of my teeth should I clean first?—but others could change the course of your day or even your life. Hence our intuitive belief is that we have free will.

And yet there may be nagging doubts. Consider again the decision to carry on reading. Perhaps, after all, you had no choice: The interest of the topic and the compelling nature of my writing made it simply impossible for you to stop. Slightly more realistically, the combination of a pressing deadline and your well-drilled scholarly habits made it unthinkable for you to stop, at least for the time being. Could these compulsions extend back in time, all the way to your birth, so that your life is simply a chain of events that couldn't have unfolded in any other way? From the earliest days of philosophy, many philosophers have been convinced that something drives our behavior and that free will is an illusion. True, we assume that we do have free will and can make any number of choices. But then we used to assume that the earth was flat, and the sun went around the earth. Perhaps, just as our understanding of the cosmos was turned on its head by the Polish astronomer Nicolaus Copernicus (1473–1543), who showed that the earth goes around the sun, our common view of free will is on the cusp of being shown to be an illusion.

Certainly, as Arthur Schopenhauer (1788–1860) argues, our conviction that we have free will shows nothing:

> Let us think of a human being who, while standing in the street . . . might say to himself: "It is six o'clock in the evening, the day's work is ended. I can now go for a walk; or I can go to the club; I can also climb the tower to see the sun going down; I can also go to the theatre; I can also visit this friend, or again that one; yes, I can even run out of the gate into the wide world and never return. All of that is solely up to me, I have total freedom over it; and yet I am doing none of that now, but am going home with just as much free will, to my wife." That is exactly as if water were to speak: "I can strike up high waves (yes! in the sea and storm), I can rush down in a hurry (yes! in the bed of a stream), I can fall down foaming and spraying (yes! in a waterfall), I can rise freely as a jet into the air (yes! in a fountain), finally I can even boil away and disappear (yes! at [212] degrees of heat); and yet I am doing none of all that now, but I am staying with free will calm and clear in the mirroring pond." Just as water can do all of that only when the determining causes to the one thing or the other occur, so that human being can in no way do what he imagines he can do except under the same condition. (Schopenhauer, 1841/2009, pp. 62–63)

Schopenhauer shows that the notion of free will is highly problematic. True, he says, to act freely is to be able to act in accordance with your will. But, he asks, what causes your will? Do you will how you will? That would lead to an **infinite regress**, in which every act of willing has to be preceded by another act of willing. At the start of the chain, it seems, there must be an "unwilled willing," which, being unwilled, was not free. If the first action was unfree, then how can anything that follows it be truly free? Something must cause us to will the way we do, and ultimately that cause must lie outside of us and determine our actions.

Sociological Determinism

Determinism—the denial of free will—comes in many forms. Perhaps the most common version is sociological: we are formed by our upbringing, and there are severe limits to how much we can break free. In the earlier discussion of cultural relativism (Chapter 2), we observed that there are many moral systems in the world, and the values you are likely to hold will depend in some way on the circumstances of your birth and upbringing. If you had been adopted and brought up in a different family, especially one of a different religion and with different political views, you would most likely have reached adulthood with a rather different set of values. This can be an alarming thought because it makes holding even our deepest beliefs seem like some sort of accident.

In ordinary life when we talk about the limits of free will, we often mean that the facts of an individual's upbringing will strongly influence how he or she will act later in life. For example, many people who abuse children, it is said, were abused themselves as children. With a different childhood, perhaps their adult patterns of behavior would have been quite different. And this consideration is sometimes reflected when some child abusers receive punishment: Those who were brought up in unfortunate circumstances are sometimes shown mercy and given a lighter sentence.

The thesis that we are determined by the circumstances of our upbringing and other social pressures and forces has plausibility, but we need to understand its limits. Many people seem to overcome their circumstances, throwing off the patterns of behavior and values that were part of their upbringing. Even those who do not fully overcome their circumstances nevertheless seem to have free choice over a whole range of parts of their life. Determination, in this case, is at best "great influence" rather than "full determinism." It does raise a challenge for free will and moral responsibility in that, as we have seen, it doesn't always seem fair to punish people for behavior that has been caused by their upbringing; but this sociological version of the thesis is limited in the degree to which it denies free will. In effect it says that we have less free will than we have traditionally thought; not that we have none. And while this realization will have moral consequences, it does not write off morality entirely.

Psychological and Physical Determinism

The second challenge to free will is psychological. We will look at this theory in greater detail in Chapter 6 when I discuss psychological egoism. The psychological egoist claim in its most extreme form is that all we are constituted to do is constantly seek pleasure and avoid pain. From this, then, it follows—so it appears—that we have no free will. We are built to seek pleasure and avoid pain, and that is what we must do. I will postpone discussion of this theory until Chapter 6, for it requires detailed investigation.

A third, and perhaps most sophisticated, type of challenge to free will comes from science; and there are several different versions. One comes from genetics: Each of us is born with a genetic code that determines us to act in various ways. We are therefore like preprogrammed computers, determined to act by our genes. Again, we will look at this argument in more detail when we discuss egoism and altruism; but the point to note here is that no serious geneticist claims that we are fully determined by our genetic inheritance. Rather, as with the sociological argument, the idea is that our genes strongly influence our behavior. If this is true, as it surely is, then once more we have less free will than we might have thought; but it doesn't follow that we have none.

An apparently more powerful scientific argument requires a sub-argument of its own. The general idea is that ultimately, human beings are only complex physical systems; we are nothing more than atoms and molecules in an incredibly intricate arrangement. If we are physical systems, then we must obey the laws of physics. And the laws of physics, so it was claimed for a long time, are fully deterministic. The quotation at the start of this chapter by the French mathematician and astronomer Pierre-Simon Laplace (1749–1827) sets out the case. Laplace argues that if you knew the current state of the universe and all the laws of physics, you could predict all of its future states with absolute precision. Human beings are, of course, part of the universe, and our "states" are "states of the universe." Hence it follows that human beings are entirely predictable, at least in theory. Even if we can't predict everything in practice—if the methods of making such predictions are beyond our mental capacities—that fact doesn't invalidate the theoretical possibility of such predictions. And if we are predictable, then how can we have free will? What passes for free will is simply ignorance of the laws of physics and our inability to make predictions. But a godlike intellect would see it all laid out to eternity.

Now anyone who knows anything about modern physics will know that the argument just given is faulty. It is not true that everything in the physical world is determined; rather, the consensus among physicists is that at the smallest known level—the quantum level—there is indeterminacy or randomness. So it is not true that all future states are predictable. Of course much does remain predictable, for generally the randomness cancels out, and the laws of physics hold at the macro level despite micro indeterminism. But still there is a sliver of light, for not *everything* is predictable. How much comfort, however, does the believer in free will feel on learning that not everything is determined because some things are random? The defender of free will needs to be able to explain how it is possible that sheer acts of the human mind can, apparently, overcome the laws of physics. Agent causation, as required by the believer in free will, does not seem to be supplied by quantum indeterminacy. Being told that not everything is determined because some things are random does not provide support for the believer in free will.

With the development of brain scanning and experimental techniques in recent years, neuroscience has produced further ammunition for the defender of scientific determinism, in the form of some interesting experiments. The neuroscientist Benjamin Libet (1916–2007) suggests that while we believe that we first make a decision to act and then our brains and bodies react to the decision, in fact—at least in the experimental situation—the brain and the body start to act before we are conscious of having made the decision to do so (Dennet, 2003; 2015). Just as we blink before we know, in other cases too we "make" the decision after the physical body has already started to act. This is a fascinating observation: The body seems to act before the mind tells it to do so. The social psychologist Jonathan Haidt (b. 1963) likens the human mind to a "rider on an elephant" (Haidt, 2012). We may be able to do some things to nudge or cajole the elephant to move one way rather than another, but our control is extremely limited and may not be there at all.

We cannot settle the question here of whether not human beings have free will. Indeed, however much time we had, we would be unlikely to settle the question. The dilemma—the philosophical puzzle—is stark. On the one hand, it just seems obvious that we have free choice over a whole range of decisions. On the other hand, how can we? Even if human beings are more than physical systems, even if we have some sort of ghostly mind, or even a soul, how could that mind or soul intervene in the physical world to change the course of physics? The problem of free will and determinism is one of the most fascinating and intractable problems in philosophy.

DETERMINISM AND MORAL RESPONSIBILITY

Rather than trying to resolve the question of free will, let's move on to the other key step in the argument: premise 2, as laid out in the argument at the start of this chapter. It stated that without free will, there can be no moral responsibility. In the philosophical jargon this is known as **incompatibilism**: the idea that determinism is incompatible with moral responsibility.

Incompatibilism may seem to be obviously true. If the way that I act is determined by forces outside my control, then how can I be held responsible? Suppose that you hold me down and force a gun into my hand. You then push my finger, which presses the trigger, and the bullet kills another person. It would seem absurd to hold me morally responsible for murder. No aspect of the act of killing was under my control, and I would have a complete moral and legal defense against the idea that it was in any way my fault. Well, if determinism is true, then all our actions are like this. If determinism is true, we must, it seems, escape moral and legal liability.

Compatibilism

Many philosophers, however, claim to believe in **compatibilism**. A compatibilist argues that determinism is, remarkably, compatible with moral responsibility. The relation between free will and determinism has been particularly important in theology, and compatibilism was designed as a solution to a deep theological puzzle; but it also has application in nonreligious discussion of free will. The theological puzzle is this. In many religious views, God has perfect knowledge. If so, then he already knows what I am going to do. But if God can know what I am going to do, then my future must already be determined. And if my future is already determined, then I could not act differently. Yet if I could not act differently, then I don't have free will. Therefore God's perfect knowledge seems to rule out human freedom. In most religious views, though, human freedom, and with it moral praise and blame, is central to religious doctrine and, for example, to an individual's prospects in the afterlife. Hence it has been important to argue that God's perfect knowledge does not rule out moral responsibility.

Although the problem of freedom and responsibility presses heavily for those who believe in God's foreknowledge, the same issue can arise for anyone who is convinced by the arguments for determinism but does not want to give up on moral responsibility. The compatibilist must argue that even if we lack free will and all our behavior is determined, nevertheless we still have moral responsibility for our actions. Now this view may be hard to understand: It seems to suggest that even if we are not responsible for our actions, we are still responsible for our actions—which seems an obvious contradiction. But we can make the contradiction disappear, at least on the surface, by realizing that two different senses of *responsible* are in play. The thesis of determinism is that human beings ultimately lack causal responsibility for their actions. But causal responsibility is not the same as moral responsibility. Imagine someone walking along a country path in a hot, dry summer, and her shoes strike up a spark that eventually leads to a devastating forest fire. Assuming there was no way of knowing that this could have happened, and hence no negligence, then we may well agree that this person is causally responsible for the fire but not morally responsible. And suppose you are walking a little behind that person, and you notice that a small fire has started. You could easily put it out, but you ignore it and walk on. In this case we are likely to say that you are morally responsible for the devastation, which was a predictable consequence of the small fire, even though you played no role at all in its causation and thus were not causally responsible.

These examples show that causal responsibility and moral responsibility are not the same thing, and they can come apart: It is possible to have causal responsibility without moral responsibility, and moral responsibility without causal responsibility. Yet ordinarily the two will go together: If I am not causally responsible for something, normally I am not morally responsible for it. And the incompatibilist—the philosopher who believes that determinism rules out moral responsibility—relies on this ordinary case. If determinism is true, then there is a sense in which I am not causally responsible for anything at all. It's like the shooting example, where I had no control over whether my finger pulled the trigger. Therefore, the incompatibilist argues, if I am not causally responsible for anything I do, then I am not morally responsible for it either. How can the opponent of this argument, the compatibilist, present a competing picture?

Well, consider ordinary life. If determinism is true, then it is true for us here and now. That stands to reason. But in everyday life we hold people morally responsible for their actions. In the worst case we send people to prison, or even to their death, because of what they have done. But if the determinists are right, then we have been acting with horrendous inhumanity in the practices we take for granted. We should be ashamed of ourselves. Now, it is easy to tangle yourself up in knots at this point. If determinism is true, and if as a result there is no moral responsibility, then we have neither causal nor moral responsibility for our unfair behavior: we are determined to act as we do. We can't help ourselves any more than the murderer, and we can't be blamed. True, we send innocent people to prison, but we can't be blamed because determinism made us do it.

Rather than sink into this morass, the compatibilist argues that even if determinism is true we should hold on to our ordinary practices of praise and blame. Why should we hold on to them? One reason is that we just can't imagine what life would be like otherwise. Even if determinism is true as a deep and ultimate fact, on a more superficial level we do make a distinction between when something is someone's fault and when it isn't. If someone really couldn't help themselves on this superficial level—"I was pushed," "I'm a kleptomaniac," "I was sleepwalking"—then we are prepared to excuse them. But if none of these conditions apply, we hold them morally responsible. In practice what we do is say that you are morally responsible if your actions are caused in some ways, but you are not morally responsible if they are caused in other ways. Typically we will hold you responsible if your actions are caused by your ordinary beliefs, desires, or intentions; but we will excuse you if your actions are caused by physical compulsion, mental coercion (such as brainwashing), or psychological disorder. In these later cases, we are likely to think there is a sense in which those "actions" were not yours at all. We must concede, though, that the distinction is not absolutely clear. We are prepared to blame people for negligence, or thoughtlessness, as in the case of the person who ignored the forest fire, even though strictly these are not actions either.

The distinctive element in the compatibilist position is the idea that even if we have no alternative to how we act, we can still be held morally responsible for our actions. The argument just given is that we find, in ordinary life, that we cannot stop holding people responsible for their actions; and so if determinism is true, then we are already compatibilists. But the lingering doubt here is in this question: How can I be morally responsible for doing something if I could not have acted otherwise?

But consider this case, introduced by the contemporary philosopher Harry Frankfurt (b. 1929), concerning a person called Jones. Unbeknownst to him, another person—Black—has managed to implant in Jones's brain a physical device that can be controlled by radio signals. Black wants Jones to commit a particular crime, and he is ready to send radio signals to control Jones's brain so that he commits the crime. However, as it turns out Jones decides to commit exactly that crime and goes ahead and does so. Black doesn't have to do a thing. The question now is whether Jones is morally responsible for the crime. Most people will say, without hesitation, that he surely is. But notice that Jones could not have acted otherwise; for if he had tried to do something else, Black would have intervened and set him back on his dastardly course of action. From this case it follows that we are prepared to say that people can be morally responsible for what they do even if they could not have acted otherwise. And that is the compatibilist case. What matters, it seems, is the reasons that you act and not whether you were free to act in some other way. When someone puts a gun in your hand and then physically forces you to pull the trigger, then you are not acting for reasons at all—you are not even acting. But in the ordinary case we do act for reasons, for there are things we want our actions to achieve. And, the compatibilist says, in many of these cases we are morally responsible for what we do, even if we could not have acted in a different way.

Law and Determinism

For another attempt to reconcile a form of determinism with moral responsibility, it is worth briefly considering the views of Jeremy Bentham. Bentham believed that we have two "sovereign masters," pleasure and pain, and in everything we do we seek pleasure and avoid pain (Bentham, 1789/2011, 2018). This is a version of psychological egoism, which we will discuss shortly (Chapter 6). Yet throughout his writings, Bentham clearly assumed that some actions are morally required and others morally prohibited. How can he combine the two? For if "nature has constituted us" to seek pleasure and avoid pain, then how can we respond to the demands of morality, or be blamed if we fail? Bentham's task is to show how we can, in fact, set up a moral and legal system so that pleasure and pain become aligned with right and wrong. If we suffer pain, either through legal punishment or through the disapproval of others, in proportion to the badness of our actions, and if we are rewarded in some way for good actions, then morality and determinism will be in harmony. The trick for the legislator is to set up a system that gives people the right incentives to act morally. The point of punishment, for example, is not to exact retribution for past acts, but to deter future acts. Problem solved.

This is a neat solution, at least on the surface, but it raises another question: What are the legislator's motivations? The legislator is, after all, just another human being and therefore also constituted to seek pleasure. Why should the legislator pass the right laws, rather than, perhaps, corrupt ones that advance his or her own interests? As Bentham got older, wiser, and more cynical, this problem troubled him more and more. There is an obvious answer and an obvious problem: The answer is that the legislator has to be placed in a system where approving good laws leads to pleasure and bad laws pain. But the problem repeats itself: Who can set up that system? And this problem seems to recur ad infinitum, another case of infinite regress.

Bentham, I think, would say there is another way of looking at it. While the legislators set laws for the people, the people also need to have a check on the legislators, through regular democratic elections. By these means, if all goes well, everyone is kept in check. Bad behavior, whether by the citizens or the legislator, is punished: Citizens will be fined or go to jail, and the legislator will not be reelected. If we are thoughtful and careful, self-interest will bring us collectively to develop the rules that tie together morality and self-interest.

It is also worth keeping in mind that even if we truly are determined to seek pleasure, we might nevertheless have considerable freedom of action. After all, very often in life we find ourselves in situations where the options open to us are either equally pleasurable or equally unpleasant. In such cases Bentham's theory seems to offer nothing to stop us from choosing directly on moral grounds, or on the basis of any other consideration that comes to us. This is an important difference between the theory that we are constituted to seek pleasure and avoid pain and the type of scientific microphysical determinism in which human beings are little more than sophisticated robots following the laws of physics.

The arguments we have considered do not prove the truth of compatibilism; they show us only that such a view is possible to hold. And it is an important option for those who are convinced by one or more of the arguments for determinism but are unable to give up the idea of human freedom or moral responsibility. But it could be, of course, that being unable to shake a view tells us not that the view is true, but that we are flawed creatures, condemned to dwell in a world of illusions, and not strong enough to live with the truth.

CHAPTER REVIEW
Summary

Intuitively we believe that we have free will. But this intuitive view can be challenged by a series of arguments—sociological, psychological, and scientific—in favor of determinism, which is the view that our actions are ultimately caused by factors outside our control. And it seems that if determinism is true, we not only lack free will but also, as a consequence, have no moral responsibility.

The compatibilist replies that even if determinism is true, we still should hold people morally responsible for their actions. Causal responsibility and moral responsibility are two different things. Of course, in some cases we recognize that people are not morally responsible; they might suffer from duress or compulsion, for example. But in the ordinary case—when people's actions align with their beliefs and desires—then, whether or not determinism is true, we should continue to hold people morally responsible for their actions. This view can be hard to accept; yet if determinism is true, then remarkably, it describes our actual practice.

Discussion Questions

1. What arguments are available to challenge the intuitive view that we have free will?
2. If determinism is true, does it follow that human beings lack moral responsibility?
3. What is the difference between causal responsibility and moral responsibility?
4. How should a compatibilist position be formulated?

Key Terms

free will, p. 58

determinism, p. 58

libertarianism, p. 59

agent causation, p. 59

infinite regress, p. 60

incompatibilism, p. 63

compatibilism, p. 64

Key Thinkers

Nicolaus Copernicus (1473–1543), p. 60

Arthur Schopenhauer (1788–1860), p. 60

Pierre-Simon Laplace (1749–1827), p. 62

Benjamin Libet (1916–2007), p. 63

Jonathan Haidt (b. 1963), p. 63

Harry Frankfurt (b. 1929), p. 66

Further Reading

▪ The opening quotation is from Pierre-Simon Laplace, *A Philosophical Essay on Probabilities*, in an edition by Dover (1995). (Original work published 1814)

▪ Arthur Schopenhauer's essay, "On the Freedom of the Will," is included in his *Two Fundamental Problems of Ethics* (Cambridge University Press, 2009). (Original work published 1841)

▪ Benjamin Libet's experiments are discussed by Daniel C. Dennett in *Freedom Evolves* (Viking, 2003), which also extensively discusses the topic of free will, as does Dennett's *Elbow Room: The Varieties of Free Will Worth Wanting*, revised edition (Bradford Books, 2015).

▪ Jonathan Haidt's ideas are set out in his book *The Righteous Mind: Why Good People Are Divided by Politics and Religion* (Random House, 2012).

▪ Selections from Jeremy Bentham's *Introduction to the Principles of Morals and Legislation* can be found in his *Selected Writings* (Yale University Press, 2011), edited by Stephen G. Engelmann (original work published 1789), as well as in Jonathan Wolff (ed.), *Readings in Moral Philosophy* (W. W. Norton, 2018). That edition also includes Harry Frankfurt's "Alternate Possibilities and Moral Responsibility," first published in *The Journal of Philosophy,* 66 23(1969): 829–839.

CHAPTER 5

Religion and Natural Law

And the LORD said unto Moses, Come up to me into the mount, and be there: and I will give thee tablets of stone, and a law, and commandments which I have written; that thou mayest teach them. And Moses rose up, and his minister Joshua: and Moses went up into the mount of God.

EXODUS *24:12–13*

RELIGION AS A BASIS FOR MORALITY

Consider some of the most difficult moral questions that people could face at some point in their lives. At what point should someone decide that a terminally ill relative should not receive further treatment? Should a couple divorce, or remain together in an unhappy marriage for the sake of their children? Should you take up the career that your parents have encouraged and pressured you to follow, or should you pursue your own goals? For many people, for much of human history, guidance on these and similar questions would be sought from religious sources. Some people would have consulted religious texts for themselves; but in preliterate cultures, and probably in all cultures on the hardest questions, individuals would turn to their religious leaders for help. For most of human history, religion and morality have been inextricably linked, almost as if they were the same thing. We are now moving into a secular age in which morality is discussed as a topic apart from religion. Is that a mistake? Should I do whatever my religion (if I have one) tells me to do? That is probably what the vast majority of people have believed over time.

In many interpretations of the Judeo-Christian tradition, for example, God is the source of all morality. A short statement was set out in the Hebrew Bible in the form of what are traditionally called the Ten Commandments. The last six, which make no direct reference to God or religion and hence can be thought of as purely moral commandments, are as follows: (5) honor your mother and father; (6) do not kill; (7) do not commit adultery; (8) do not steal; (9) do not bear false witness against your neighbor; and (10) do not covet your neighbor's wife, servant, donkey, or other property. Many other religions also have a summary statement of their fundamental moral views, supplemented by much more complex and detailed rules as well, such as the dietary rules of Judaism, Islam, or Hinduism, or the rules about sexual morality that are found in virtually all religions. Morality, in these traditions, stems from God's command, as stated in the holy texts and interpreted by religious leaders: holy men and, here and there, holy women.

Those who have a strong religious belief seem to have little option but to follow the morality of their religion. Moral rules are part of the religious doctrine, and following something else would seem heretical. Nevertheless many religious people disagree with some of the moral teachings of their church. For example, some Catholics accept that abortion can be permitted under some difficult circumstances such as rape or incest; others approve of, or themselves use, artificial contraception. Many religions have had strict prohibitions against homosexuality, but today branches of some religions now completely accept same-sex relationships and will give approval to same-sex partnerships. Hence religious doctrine is not necessarily fixed and can be reinterpreted over time. Still, many religious people will continue to follow the guidance of their religion unless an official change is decreed, even when they think it could be questioned.

From a philosophical point of view, finding a religious basis for your morality seems to give it a firm foundation: What could be stronger than God as a basis for ethics? It is not unusual to encounter the argument that without belief in God, or some other religious basis for morality, there is no morality at all. As a character in the novel *The Brothers Karamazov* (1880), by Fyodor Dostoyevsky (1821–81), says, "If God is dead then everything is permitted." And the belief that religion and morality are intimately connected certainly has had its influence in law and policy. For example, John Stuart Mill (1806–73), in *On Liberty* (1859), complained about the policy that then did not allow atheists to give evidence in court. To give evidence you first had to swear an oath on the Bible that you were telling the truth. But if the Bible meant nothing to you, then it was assumed that neither did the oath; and you might as well tell lies. The official view, then, was that atheists were not to be trusted because they had no fear of God's wrath. Mill argued that this stance was insulting both to nonbelievers and believers. The insult to nonbelievers is obvious, but believers should feel insulted too, for they were assumed to tell the truth only out of fear of God's punishment. Yet even now, many people around the world believe that religion is essential to morality. For example, a study conducted in 2014 found that more than half of the Americans surveyed agreed with the statement that belief in God is essential to morality.

Nevertheless, some religious believers wish to develop a morality that is not based on God's command. For example, the English moral philosopher and theologian Bishop Joseph Butler (1692–1752) suggested that the view that God punished immorality could be, if not insulting to God, nevertheless "very presumptuous." Butler asked what basis we had "to assert, that the end of divine punishment is no other than that of civil punishment, namely, to prevent future mischief" (Butler, 1983). As I understand this passage, Butler is pointing out that it is rather arrogant for religious believers to presume to know God's purposes. Perhaps God has another plan for human beings and punishing people for their misdeeds on earth may be too trivial or even counterproductive in the context of his plan. The implication of Butler's observation is that human beings need to sort things out for themselves.

The idea that God enforces morality through punishment and reward in the afterlife raises an awkward point. If people obey the moral code because they fear that God will punish them in this or a future life, then ultimately they are acting out of self-interest, at least in the long term. If that is right, then we have something quite paradoxical. Rather than being the only true foundation for morality, the belief in God, and in particular God's retribution, seems to reduce morality to self-interest. A purer religious morality would attempt to avoid this trap, downplaying the motivation to seek rewards and avoid punishments whether in this life or the next. One suggestion is that we should follow God's commands simply out of our love for God rather than any thought of punishment or reward. We will return to the question of the relation between morality and acting out of self-interest in Chapter 6. In the remainder of this chapter, we will look at ways of developing a religious morality and some of the problems that could be encountered.

DIVINE COMMAND AND THE EUTHYPHRO DILEMMA

So far we have been considering the view that morality is a code of behavior set out by God, and therefore morality has its authority over us because it is God's command. This is commonly known as the **divine command** theory of morality. There is, however, a well-known philosophical problem for the divine command theory. Its significance can be appreciated by looking at a more general problem for religious morality, one first set out by the Ancient Greek philosopher Plato (429?–347 BCE) in his dialogue, *The Euthyphro*. In this work, Plato refers to "the gods" rather than "God," for in the Ancient Greek world people believed there were many gods who were often at war with other. But the argument, known as the *Euthyphro* dilemma, has equal force in the context of contemporary monotheisms, which advocate belief in only one God. The dilemma starts with the idea that we must obey God's commands because they are morally correct. Well, we can ask the question, "What makes God's commands morally correct?" It seems there are two possible answers. One is that God has discovered the moral truth, the other that he has invented it (this is the divine command theory). But both answers are problematic for a religious morality. This is the **dilemma**.

Consider the possibility that God has discovered the moral truth. But for him to discover it, then it already must have existed independently of God. If so, morality does not seem to be God's command after all. True, God could *pass it on* to human beings as a command, but the basis of morality must have been something else. Otherwise God could not have discovered it. Therefore, it seems, a wise human being could discover it too, at least in principle, without God's help. In conclusion, if God discovered morality, then the basis of morality cannot be God's command. This strand of the dilemma has been developed into what has been called **natural law** theory. Natural law theory has the consequence that morality is not God's command after all, or at least not in any straightforward sense. (We will explore natural law theory later in this chapter.)

We seem forced to the conclusion that if God is the foundation of morality, then he must have created or invented morality rather than discovered it. So let's suppose that God invented morality. From a religious point of view, this may seem to be the right option to choose. But there is a problem lurking here. Even though God invented morality a particular way, with the moral rules that are familiar to us, he presumably could have invented it some other way, with completely different commands. Suppose God had invented what seems to us an immoral set of rules. Would we be obliged to follow them? For example, the medieval philosopher William of Ockham (c. 1287–1347) argued that if God had ordered us to perform those acts we call "theft," "adultery," or even "hatred of God," then these would be the morally right things to so (Adams, 2003, p. 463). In this view, then, anything God tells us to do is right. But can the religious believer accept that God could turn morality upside down? In fact, the eighteenth-century German philosopher Immanuel Kant (1724–1804), though a strong religious believer, argued that it would be a serious mistake to base morality on God's revealed will:

> The concept of [God's] will ... made up of the attributes of desire for glory and dominion, combined with dreadful representations of power and vengefulness, would have to be the foundation for a system of morals that would be directly opposed to morality. (*Groundwork* 4:443; 1998, p. 49)

Kant presumably has the idea of God as depicted in the Hebrew Bible in mind here. Nevertheless William of Ockham would have replied that our duty is to follow God's will, whatever it happens to be.

The ultimate question, then, is whether God's command could make something morally right (or wrong) that would not have been right (or wrong) without God's command. Could God simply create moral rules by saying so? But is this so difficult? Think of the dietary restrictions of many religions. Orthodox Jews may not cook or eat milk and meat together. Presumably this is a command from God and would have been a matter of individual choice without that command. So God, it seems, can make things wrong just by saying so. In reply, however, it seems important to distinguish religious and moral duty. Certainly for those Jews who believe in God, God can create—indeed has created—religious duties. It is easy to imagine that God could have created a completely different set of rules about dietary restrictions, or, within limits, even about sexual morality. But could he have created a world in which cruelty, murder, and torture are moral duties?

Responding to the Dilemma

A religious believer could of course accept the position that whatever God commands is right, just as Abraham (in the book of *Genesis* in the Hebrew Bible) after great personal struggle accepted God's command to sacrifice his son Isaac—though thankfully, God used the command merely as a test of Abraham's commitment, and Isaac was spared. Perhaps the defender of the divine command theory of morality would say that morality is a matter of following God's commands; and if there are commands we don't understand or don't agree with, we simply have to accept that "ours is not to reason why" and that God's infinite intellect must know better than our limited minds. But on reflection, this reasoning backfires. For if we assume that God knows morality better than we do, then we seem to be assuming there is something to know, and this pushes us back to the thought that morality must exist, in some form, independently of God.

A similar problem arises if one instead says that although God could command us to do anything and that would make it right, God's goodness means that he would not command us to do anything abhorrent. The difficulty is again obvious: This view assumes that a standard of good and bad character exists independently of God, which is exactly what the position sets out to deny. It is also worth noticing that any constraint on what God can command also becomes a limit on his power, which is a problem for the Christian conception of God, which assumes that God is omnipotent (all-powerful).

In sum, the *Euthyphro* dilemma is that if God discovered morality, then there is an independent, nonreligious foundation for morality; but if God invented morality, then nothing is stopping it from being an arbitrary set of rules. If that is the case, why, from a moral point of view, should we follow these rules? In either case the religious basis of morality is in trouble. Can the religious philosopher reply? It would be surprising if religious morality could be undermined so easily, given that for most of human history, religion and morality have been so closely related. Then again, it was surprising to find out that the earth was not the center of the universe but in fact orbits the sun, which itself is a rather insignificant celestial body.

The Logic of the Dilemma

It is worth reflecting on the logic of the *Euthyphro* argument. It is presented, of course, as a dilemma: a forced choice between two options, neither of which is acceptable, hence the philosophical expression "caught on the horns of a dilemma." However, not everything presented as a dilemma really is one. You might, for example, be wondering about whether to go out tonight to the movies or to stay in and have an early night. That may seem like a dilemma, but it is not a dilemma in the logical sense we are considering. It might be possible, for example, to do both: go to an early movie and still get to bed in good time. It is also possible to do neither: go out for a late meal, or stay in but go to bed late. For a dilemma to be genuine, first of all, the two options have to be truly distinct from each other (in the philosophical jargon, they have to be **exclusive** in the sense that one excludes the other); and second, they have to cover all the available possibilities (they have to be **exhaustive** in the sense that they must exhaust all of the options). We have seen that going to a movie and having an early night are neither exclusive (you could do both) nor exhaustive (you could do other things). If a supposed dilemma fails to be both exclusive and exhaustive, then it can be called a **false dilemma** because it may allow a possibility of escape, either by taking both options together or finding a third option.

Is, then, the choice between God inventing morality and God discovering morality a genuine or a false dilemma? First, is it exclusive? There are obviously clear cases of both categories of discovery and invention: Fire was discovered in prehistoric times; the programmable computer was invented in the mid-twentieth century. Yet can something be both an invention and a discovery? This is a subtle question. Consider the wheel. Was that a discovery or an invention? In one sense it seems obvious that it was an invention, dreamed up by an unknown human's ingenuity. Yet it may well have been "invented" by many people at many different times, which makes it sound more like a discovery. And it also seems obvious that its design was severely limited: A triangular or square wheel never would have caught on. Hence the wheel seems to combine elements of both invention and discovery.

Perhaps the moral laws could be like the wheel: invented by God, but under severe constraints. Does that help solve the dilemma? Unfortunately, it is hard to see how; as soon as we say there are constraints, we seem to be saying there are limits to God's commands—which seems to suggest some sort of independence for morality and limitation of God's omnipotence. So let's move on to the next question. Is the distinction exhaustive? Are the alternatives that God invented morality or that he discovered it the only possibilities for religious morality? Maybe not. Perhaps morality could have a religious basis in other ways. But it is not easy to see what the candidates are. In sum, the dilemma does appear to be genuine.

But still, how serious is this dilemma? We have said that if God discovered morality, or at least part of it, then he cannot be the (only) source of morality. On the other hand, if he created morality, then it seems that nothing is stopping it from being an arbitrary code of conduct. This dilemma may seem powerful, but a religious moralist can simply accept one of the options. This, we saw, is what William of Ockham did in saying that we must follow God's commands whatever they are and however they absurd they may seem. Alternatively, we could return to the first horn of the dilemma. How problematic is it to suppose that God discovered an independently existing morality? Does this really undermine the idea of a morality based on religion? Let's explore this question by turning now to the theory of natural law, which we have noted is the option of taking the first horn of the dilemma.

RELIGION AND NATURAL LAW

The term *natural law* is widely used in moral philosophy. Usually it refers to a form of universal objectivism that insists morality is not merely a human invention, but that human beings are able to come to understand a moral law that is in some sense natural. Many versions of natural law theory include it as part of a religious view, but it needs to be distinguished from divine command theory. Divine command theory, as we have seen, is the view that morality is created by God's command. In contrast, natural law theory pays much more attention to God's purposes rather than mere commands. One way of making this point is to say that the natural law is part of a rational plan for the universe. Hence the basis of natural law morality is God's plan, but human beings must discover how to accomplish that plan—the rules of morality. The theory that morality is based on some sort of purpose or meaning in the world is sometimes called a **teleological view**, based on the Greek word *telos*, meaning "purpose" or "end" (in the sense in which "end" contrasts with "means"). Hence natural law theory is a teleological morality, seeing the moral rules as the way in which we will accomplish God's (or some other) purposes. In its religious version, to come to understand the natural law we have, first, to understand God's purposes for humankind, and then to consider the rules of behavior that would best enable us to fulfill those purposes.

Proponents of a religious version of natural law theory sometimes suggest that to assist us in this task, just as God has given us the five senses of perception, he has implanted in us a moral sense that is based on reason or conscience. In coming to understand what our moral duties are, we use these capabilities. For example, it could be argued that God is concerned to ensure that human beings achieve happiness; that they live in a harmonious society; and that they pay due respect to their maker. The natural law theorist will add that God has given us mental capabilities so that we can, by using our **natural reason** or our **conscience**, derive for ourselves the natural law that is also God's law—though not merely God's command, because it has a particular purpose.

There are in fact two different theories here. One is that God has given us natural reason that allows us to discover the moral law; the other, that he has given us a conscience. Reason and conscience are not the same things. Reason concerns analysis, deduction, and problem solving, whereas conscience is more about feeling or emotion. If you act against reason, you can be accused of being irrational; if you act against conscience, you are likely to feel guilty. Basing the natural law on reason is the more common approach, so we will start there and then take up the topic of conscience.

Natural Law and Reason

The medieval philosopher and theologian St. Thomas Aquinas (1225–74) was one of the great theorists of natural law. He inspired many later figures, such as the civil rights campaigner Martin Luther King Jr. (1929–68), who followed Aquinas in adopting the dictum of St. Augustine (354–430) that "an unjust law is no law." Aquinas believed that all of creation was ordered by God, according to a benevolent plan, and governed by what he called "the eternal law." The natural law is the part of the eternal law specifically directed toward human affairs and aimed at the common good. Because the natural law is based on human nature, it will be the same for all human beings, at all times and places; for Aquinas assumed that we all share the same human nature. Hence the natural law is objective and universal. Yet at the same time, it is unwritten, which is why reason is needed for its discovery. The French Catholic philosopher Jacques Maritain (1882–1973), an important twentieth-century defender of natural law theory, quotes the character Antigone, from the play of the same name by the Ancient Greek playwright Sophocles (497/6–406/5 BCE). Of the unwritten laws, Antigone says, "But they live always and forever, and no man knows from where they have arisen" (205). Maritain regards these words as an excellent summary of the natural law tradition.

Natural law theory can be traced back to the Ancient Greek philosophers. Aristotle (384–322 BCE), who we will discuss in detail in Chapter 12 of this book, has often been considered one of the founders of natural law theory, influencing the later development of Christian thought. As an approach to morality, this theory still survives today. Because of its long tradition, it comes in many varieties. The distinctive idea of natural law theory is its assumption that reflection on human beings and our place in the world will allow us to come to conclusions about the human good, from which we can then draw particular moral conclusions. However, it is fair to ask how this is different from other ways of thinking about morality. After all, many moral philosophers use reasoning of some sort to derive moral conclusions. What, then, puts some forms of moral reasoning, but not others, in the natural law tradition? At the heart of natural law theory is what we called its teleology, assuming that knowing the purpose of human life will allow us to use our mental capacities to derive the rules of morality.

It is easy to see how natural law theory supports many of our core moral beliefs. God's purposes for human beings could not reasonably be thought to allow us to murder or steal from each other, or to deceive or coerce for individual advantage. It "stands to reason" that a natural moral law designed to help us pursue God's purposes would oppose these actions, and therefore would classify them as immoral. And indeed the appeal to what is "natural" will have much intuitive resonance and appeal.

Yet relying on ideas of what is "natural" has its dangers, too. Throughout history, for example, it has been common to object to sex between people of the same sex as "unnatural." The natural human family, it is supposed, consists of a husband and wife and their children, with the husband as head of the household and, in many traditions, the wife in a subservient role. This was the teaching of the church, and Aquinas argued that it was the natural law ordained by God and conducive to the common good. Sex between people of the same sex, in such a view, was a serious sin—though not as serious, thought Aquinas, as bestiality (sex with animals); but more serious than masturbation, which was also condemned.

Interestingly, Aquinas also considered the question of whether virginity was a sin. After all, if human beings have been put on earth to reproduce, as the Bible and "right reason" both suggest, how we can defend those who choose not to do so? And this was no trivial issue, given that the Catholic Church demanded celibacy for priests as well as for monks and nuns. Aquinas's answer starts with the claim that human beings have a higher purpose of contemplating the divine, and bodily pleasures can distract from calm contemplation. He supplements this view by interpreting the duty to procreate as a collective duty falling on all human beings together rather than a duty for each person. Therefore, so long as the human race is not in danger of dying out, it is better to have a division of labor where some people make the choice of "holy virginity" and contemplate the divine even at the expense of normal family life.

An obvious problem, however, is that there can be disputes about God's purposes, or about the purpose of a particular activity. Consider again the examples of homosexuality raised by Aquinas. In the Christian tradition it is sometimes asserted that the sole purpose of sex is procreation within the confines of marriage. On this basis a wide range of sexual practices are deemed immoral: contraception, sex outside of marriage, masturbation, and same-sex relations among them. Jeremy Bentham (1748–1832), in writings he dared not publish in his own lifetime, took a different view. He thought that at least one of the purposes of sex was to bring pleasure. On this basis, as long as all parties involved are consenting, and no adverse consequences are to be expected, virtually everything the church rules illegitimate is to be welcomed.

Nevertheless, defenders of Aquinas will continue to insist that homosexuality is "unnatural." This raises the difficult question of how we know what is natural. Several philosophers, including David Hume (1711–76) and John Stuart Mill, have argued that everything that happens on earth must be natural in some sense, and therefore it is impossible to say that some things that happen are unnatural. This is a powerful point, yet most of us are unable to shake the intuition that some things are "more natural" than others; think, for example, what we say about food, or the materials used to make our clothes.

Natural law theory, understandably, can also be criticized by those who do not believe in God. If there is no God, there are no "God's purposes"; therefore, it seems, the theory cannot get off the ground. This critique may seem devastating, but in fact many natural law theorists do not appeal to the existence of God. Rather they say that we can work out the purposes, or the nature, of humans from "natural reason." Jacques Maritain, while a believer in God, set out a form of natural law theory that was based on human nature rather than God's purposes. Maritain argues that just as pianos have a function—the production of sounds—and a piano is defective if it cannot produce the right sounds at the right time, human beings also have a function and will be considered defective if they do not follow the rules that allow them to achieve the function that is true to their essence.

But what is the function of human beings? Maritain argued that it is much more complex than that of a piano, and in fact is not entirely known to human beings. If it were known, then we could straightforwardly deduce the natural law of morality. We do have some knowledge, and also some theories, that we dispute among ourselves; and this explains why there is moral disagreement. Nevertheless, in reflecting on this disagreement and trying to resolve it, we need to focus on our human nature and purposes and generate those moral rules that will best help us achieve those purposes. Understanding the purpose of human beings, and the natural law, is therefore a work in progress.

Although the idea that human beings have a purpose may seem plausible, some have argued that making such as assumption amounts to smuggling in a theological premise. Of course you and I have our individual "purposes": My purpose at the moment is to finish writing this chapter; yours, presumably, to finish reading it. These small-scale purposes fit into a broader plan of life. But these are intentions or goals we have formed for ourselves, not something "given to us" by nature. On many contemporary scientific views, human beings have come to exist by complete accident. It is a matter of tiny chance that human beings evolved at all, and no purpose can be read into it. Natural law theory makes much more sense if it is based on a religious foundation, in which God has purposes for us. In such a view, a teleological morality—a purpose-driven one—makes sense. But the obvious cost is that it then has no appeal to those who do not share the religious assumptions.

The Fact/Value Distinction

Another difficulty often raised for natural law theory concerns a rather technical question in moral philosophy, which I drew attention to in Chapter 1. Many people believe there is an important **fact/value distinction**. In outline, the distinction is probably a familiar one. On the one hand is a world of scientific facts that can be confirmed or disconfirmed by evidence. And on the other hand are values, such as "good" and "bad" or "beautiful" and "ugly," that are not assessable in the same way; no amount of scientific evidence on its own can establish that something is good or beautiful. Indeed this is another way of making the point introduced earlier—that "normative" or value questions are not subject to proof or disproof by the same means that factual claims are. Given this distinction, many people also often argue that it is illegitimate to move from claims about facts to claims about values. Sometimes this view is put in terms of the claimed logical mistake or fallacy of deriving an "ought" (a value judgment) from an "is" (a matter of fact). And it is sometimes argued that natural law theory makes exactly this mistake. Consider, for example, the argument that because the purpose of sex is procreation, contraception is morally wrong. This appears to move from a fact (the purpose of sex is procreation) to a value judgment (contraception is wrong). Hence it would follow that natural law theory has a fatal flaw because it is based on faulty reasoning.

The general argument against natural law theory can be set out as follows:

Premise 1: To say that God or nature has purposes is to make a claim about a matter of fact.

Premise 2: Natural law theory derives claims about what human beings ought to do from God or nature's purposes.

Premise 3: Claims about what human beings ought to do are claims about values.

Therefore

Conclusion: Natural law theory derives claims about values from claims about facts.

However

Premise 4: It is a logical mistake to derive claims about values from claims about facts.

Therefore

Conclusion: Natural law theory is based on a logical mistake.

Now, we can agree that in many cases we cannot derive statements about values from statements about facts. It is a fact, for example, that more than 300 million people live in the United States. But what is meant to follow from that? Is this a good thing or a bad thing? If we were to try to make the argument one way or another, we would have to say something like this: Having such a large population leads to diversity and vibrancy, which are valuable, and therefore having such a large population is a good thing. Or: Such a large population leads to environmental unsustainability and social division, which are undesirable, and therefore having such a large population is a bad thing. But notice that in both cases, to deduce conclusions about values, more values had to be added to the argument: that vibrancy is good, or that social division is bad. Therefore it is commonly said that to get a value out, you need to put a value in; but natural law theory fails to do this. If that is right, then there is a problem right at the heart of natural law theory.

But you might wonder if this argument is as clear-cut as it seems. The argument, in its religious form, starts from premises about God's purposes for human beings. Of course there would be a problem if the argument moved to a value judgment from an ordinary scientific fact about human beings, such as that human beings typically have 23 pairs of chromosomes. Nothing would follow about right or wrong from that. But facts about God's purposes seem rather different. It is as if God's purposes already have a mix of fact and value about them that could make the move arguably legitimate. Hence this objection is not as decisive as some suggest, at least not against religious forms of natural law theory. And even in nonreligious versions, the criticism is not completely compelling. After all, if we base the idea of "natural" on reasoning about what is needed to fulfill the purposes given by human nature, arguably we are starting with a value judgment, or perhaps a combination of factual and value judgments. It is not, therefore, so easy to dismiss natural law theory on the grounds that it moves from an "is" to an "ought."

Natural Law and Conscience

I said earlier that natural law theory comes in at least two forms, based on whether we come to know the natural law by our reason or by our conscience. So far we have been discussing the idea that natural law is derived from reason, which is the dominant strain in natural law thinking. We should, though, briefly consider the conscience form, which is well expressed in Romans 2:15, translated in the New American Standard Bible as

> in that they show the work of the Law written in their hearts, their conscience bearing witness and their thoughts alternately accusing or else defending them.

Here, then, the idea is that, unlike the "reason" version of natural law, which tells you to follow your head, the "conscience" version tells you to follow your heart. The idea is that we all have a well-developed moral sense, and if we pay attention to it we will find, in our heart of hearts, that we already know what to do. Often we are tempted by self-interest—or desire, as Adam was tempted in the Garden of Eden—but just as Adam really knew he was doing wrong, so do we.

How defensible is this theory? It is in many ways an attractive approach, and we do often know that some proposed action is wrong by realizing that we would feel bad about doing it. Nevertheless, we have to face the question of how our consciences get formed. In the religious view, our conscience reveals what God has written on our hearts. It is likely, though, that for many people what their conscience tells them to do will simply be the result of the accumulated moral lessons they have had since childhood. Therefore the question arises about how we know whether what our conscience tells us is right or wrong. If we have been brought up to believe prejudiced views, our consciences will also be infected with prejudice. As we saw, for example, Bentham in effect argued that throughout history many people have been crippled by their conscience not to satisfy their same-sex desires, leading to torment and misery.

To illustrate the point further, philosophers have been interested in a story by Mark Twain (1835–1910) in *Adventures of Huckleberry Finn* (1885). In it Huck helps his friend Jim, a slave, run away from his owner Miss Watson. However, Huck's conscience troubles him deeply and prompts him again and again to consider handing Jim back over to Miss Watson. In the end Huck's compassion for Jim overcomes his conscience, and so while "knowing" that he acts badly, Huck resists his conscience not out of principle but, he thinks, out of weakness. This story brilliantly illustrates an argument made by the twentieth-century philosopher Elizabeth Anscombe (1919–2001) concerning the views of Bishop Butler, mentioned above: "Butler exalts conscience, but appears ignorant that a man's conscience may tell him to do the vilest things" (Anscombe, 1958, p. 2). Hence basing a moral philosophy entirely on conscience seems highly problematic. This, of course, relates closely to the discussion about moral intuitions in Chapter 1. Your conscience is very likely to inform, and be informed by, your moral intuitions. Moral intuitions can be a good way of responding to a moral question or dilemma, but to suppose that your intuitions are beyond question is to lapse into dogma, not insight. And the same can be said for your conscience.

CHAPTER REVIEW
Summary

The main focus of this chapter has been the attempt to base morality on religion, considering the view that the morally good person needs only to follow his or her religion. Of course this argument would not appeal to atheists, but in this chapter we have seen that it has difficulties even for devout religious believers. The *Euthyphro* dilemma posed a serious problem: If God discovers morality, then why cannot human beings discover it independently of God? If God invents morality, then it would seem we would have equal reason to follow "immoral" rules if that is what God decreed.

I explored the response that takes up the first horn of the dilemma, by means of natural law theory. According to this approach, God has implanted in us natural reason so that we can work out what is required of us if we are to fulfill God's purposes for human life on earth. In this and similar views, God reveals morality to us by creating human reason so that we can work it out for ourselves. Alternatively, God equipped us with a conscience so that we could follow His morality for ourselves, by consulting our hearts. It is also possible to develop a form of natural law theory that starts from assumptions about human nature, rather than God's purposes.

While it may be appealing to think that religion can solve our moral problems for us, in fact natural law theory makes moral philosophy inescapable. It makes us ask these questions: Are human beings on earth for a purpose? If so, what purpose, and how do we know? And finally, if we do have a purpose, how should we treat each other—and ourselves—so that purpose can be advanced?

Discussion Questions

1. What is the *Euthyphro* dilemma, and what does it show?
2. What is natural law theory?
3. Is it possible to have a nonreligious version of natural law theory?
4. Does the claim that it is not possible to derive an "ought" from an "is" present a difficulty for natural law theory?

Key Terms

divine command, p. 73	false dilemma, p. 76
dilemma, p. 74	teleological view, p. 77
natural law, p. 74	natural reason, p. 78
exclusive, p. 76	conscience, p. 78
exhaustive, p. 76	fact/value distinction, p. 81

Key Thinkers

Fyodor Dostoyevsky (1821–81), p. 72
John Stuart Mill (1806–73), pp. 72, 80
Bishop Joseph Butler (1692–1752), pp. 73, 84
Plato (429?–347 BCE), p. 73

William of Ockham (c. 1287–1347), pp. 74, 77

Immanuel Kant (1724–1804), p. 74

St. Thomas Aquinas (1225–74), pp. 78–80

Martin Luther King Jr. (1929–68), p. 78

St. Augustine (354–430), p. 78

Jacques Maritain (1882–1973), pp. 78–81

Aristotle (384–322 BCE), p. 79

Jeremy Bentham (1748–1832), pp. 80, 84

David Hume (1711–76), p. 80

Mark Twain (pen name of Samuel Langhorne Clemens [1835–1910]), p. 84

Elizabeth Anscombe (1919–2001), p. 84

Further Reading

▪ *Exodus*, from which the opening quotation is taken, is the second book of the Old Testament, or Hebrew Bible. Here it is quoted from the New American Standard version, which is also the source of the later quotation from *Romans*.

▪ Fyodor Dostoyevsky's *The Brothers Karamazov* is available in many editions, including Penguin (2013). (Original work published 1880)

▪ The survey regarding belief in God referred to in the text is a Pew Global Report (March 13, 2014): "Worldwide, Many See Belief in God as Essential to Morality: Richer Nations Are Exception." Retrieved October 22, 2016, from www.pewglobal.org/2014/03/13/worldwide-many-see-belief-in-god-as -essential-to-morality/

▪ John Stuart Mill, *On Liberty*, is widely available in many editions, and is included in a collection of his writings, *The Spirit of the Age, On Liberty, and The Subjection of Women* (W. W. Norton, 1996), edited by Alan Ryan. (Original work published 1859)

▪ The passage from Bishop Joseph Butler's *Sermons* is from the preface of his *Five Sermons* (Hackett, 1983), edited by Stephen L. Darwall.

▪ Plato's *Euthyphro* is available in *Plato: Complete Works* (Hackett, 1997), edited by John M. Cooper.

- William of Ockham's views are quoted in Robert Merrihew Adams, "A Modified Divine Command Theory of Ethical Wrongness." In Charles Taliaferro and Paul Griffiths (eds.), *Philosophy of Religion: An Anthology* (Blackwell Publishers, 2003).

- The Immanuel Kant quotation is from *Groundwork of the Metaphysics of Morals*, edited by Mary Gregor (Cambridge University Press, 1998), p. 49.

- A useful selection of the works of St. Thomas Aquinas is *St. Thomas Aquinas on Politics and Ethics* (W. W. Norton, 1987), edited by Paul E. Sigmund.

- Martin Luther King Jr.'s writings include "Speech from Birmingham Jail," reprinted in Jonathan Wolff (ed.), *Readings in Moral Philosophy* (W. W. Norton, 2018), which also includes selections from Plato, Kant, and Aquinas referred to in this chapter.

- Jeremy Bentham's writings on sex are published in his *Selected Writings* (Yale University Press, 2011), edited by Stephen G. Engelmann.

- David Hume's discussion of the "natural" can be found in Book Three, Part 1, Section 2 of his *Treatise on Human Nature* (Oxford University Press, 2000), edited by David Fate Norton and Mary Norton. This treatise is available in many other editions. (Original work published 1751)

- John Stuart Mill's similar arguments can be found in his essay "On Nature." Retrieved October 22, 2016, from www.lancaster.ac.uk/users/philosophy /texts/mill_on.htm

- Jacques Maritain's book on natural law referenced here is *The Rights of Man and Natural Law* (Scribner, 1943).

- Many editions of Mark Twain's *Adventures of Huckleberry Finn* are available, including a critical edition published by W. W. Norton (1998; original work published 1885). An important discussion of the story discussed in the text is Jonathan Bennett's "The Conscience of Huckleberry Finn," first published in *Philosophy*, 49, 1974: 123–34.

- Elizabeth Anscombe's "Modern Moral Philosophy" was published in *Philosophy*, 33, 1958: 1–19.

CHAPTER 6

Egoism

Ask a man why he uses exercise; *he will answer,* because he desires to keep his health. *If you then enquire,* why he desires health, *he will readily reply,* because sickness is painful. *If you push your enquiries farther, and desire a reason,* why he hates pain, *it is impossible he can ever give any. This is an ultimate end, and is never referred to any other object.*

DAVID HUME, AN ENQUIRY CONCERNING THE PRINCIPLES OF MORALS

WHY BE MORAL?

One of the earliest systematic discussions of moral philosophy in the Western philosophical tradition occurs in the Ancient Greek philosopher Plato's great masterpiece, *The Republic* (c. 380 BCE). In that text, Plato defends his own view of the nature of morality, part of which we briefly looked at in Chapter 2 of this book. However, in an argumentative strategy that we all can learn from, Plato is not content with brushing aside his opponent's view. Instead he sets out the opposing view in its strongest possible form. We can understand why he does this: If he can find the strongest version of his opponent's view, and still refute it, then his own view is firmly defended.

Plato therefore tells us a story about someone who is able to get away with acting immorally but with no adverse consequences. This is the mythical story of the "Ring of Gyges." According to the story, Gyges was a shepherd who found a magic ring that, if twisted around, made its wearer invisible. Suppose you had such a ring. What would you do? In Plato's *Republic*, a character named Glaucon represents the skeptical view in a dialogue with Socrates; he suggests the following:

> No man is so unyielding that he would remain obedient to justice and keep his hands off what does not belong to him if he could steal with impunity in the very midst of the public market itself. The same if he could enter into houses and lie with whom he chose, or if he could slay—or release from bondage—whom he would, behaving toward other men in these and all other things as if he were the equal of a god. The just man would act no differently from the unjust; both would pursue the same course.
>
> One might argue that here is the great proof that no one is willingly just; men will be just only if constrained. This is because every man believes that justice is not really to his interest. If he has the power to do wrong, he will

*full
this*

do wrong, for every man believes in his heart that injustice will profit him more than justice.

These are the settled convictions of all those who choose to adopt them. They hold that anyone who acquires extraordinary power and then refuses to do wrong and plunder others is truly to be pitied (and a great fool as well). Publicly, however, they praise the fool's example, convinced that they must deny what they really think so that they will not encourage unjust acts against themselves. (1999, p. 56)

Who could resist using the Ring of Gyges? I think a lot of people would be tempted to use their new power to do such things as looking around the homes of the rich and famous; snooping and listening in on conversations, especially conversations about themselves; and doing other disreputable, slightly thrilling, things. But how far would you go? Steal? Kill? If not, why not? Is it because morality does have strong independent force after all? Or is it because we have been brought up not to harm others, and these rules are difficult to break whether or not we think they are ultimately justified? But perhaps, once you really were convinced that you could not be caught, you would kill if that were the only way of getting what you wanted. Or to put a rather different question: Would it be rational to stick with the moral rules if you knew that you could get away with breaking them?

Reflecting on this example suggests at least two different theories we need to consider. The first is what we could call a psychological claim, one about human behavior. This view suggests, as Glaucon presents it, that human beings cannot help pursuing their own self-interest. This theory has become known as **psychological egoism**; and if it is true, it would rule out the possibility of acting morally unless that behavior happened to coincide with self-interest. The second is a moral claim: Human beings have the right, perhaps even the duty, to pursue their own self-interest to the exclusion of the interests of others. For obvious reasons, this theory is often called **ethical egoism**. Although closely related, these theories are not the same. For example, some ethical egoists believe we are capable of acting altruistically, but we would be morally wrong to do so (strange though that may sound). Therefore, they deny psychological egoism. It is, though, possible to hold both views; and both have serious implications for morality and for moral philosophy. Let's turn first to psychological egoism.

PSYCHOLOGICAL EGOISM

Ultimately, in the psychological egoist's view, everything we do is aimed at making things better for ourselves. We are destined to seek pleasure, happiness, or even feelings of self-worth. Of course, we are often rather clever about it, making it look like we care about others or would sacrifice our own interests for the common good. But deep down, in this view it is always the same. All we do—all we can do—is follow our self-interest. But if that is true, then it seems that morality, properly speaking, is squeezed out from the start. For if you have no choice but to follow your self-interest, how can you also act morally? Surely morality, from time to time, requires genuine self-sacrifice.

This skeptical point about morality can be set out as consisting of an argument from two premises to a conclusion:

Premise 1: Human beings are constituted by nature to pursue their own self-interest.

Premise 2: Morality often requires self-denial (i.e., acting against your self-interest).

Therefore

Conclusion: Human beings are not capable of acting morally.

Those who are impressed by this argument sometimes draw the further conclusion that morality is somehow redundant or perhaps even deceptive—a myth we tell ourselves, perhaps to feel better about our selfishness.

Let's examine the logic of this simple argument more closely. The critic of morality holds premise 1, the psychological egoist claim that humans are constituted to follow our own self-interest, and premise 2—that morality often requires self-denial—and claims it follows that human beings cannot act morally. Is the critic right? One question is whether the conclusion really does follow from the premises. Is it a **logically valid** argument? If we look at it again, can we poke holes? Being maximally critical, is it possible to think of a situation in which the premises are true but the conclusion false? As we saw in Chapter 1, this is how philosophers normally attempt to determine whether an argument is logically valid: They test it to the point of attempted destruction. And in this case we can in fact question the argument. Look at the conclusion: Human beings are not capable of acting morally. Why is that? Because, according to the premises, we are constituted to follow our self-interest; and morality often requires self-denial. But does morality *always* require self-denial? Perhaps, but that's not what premise 2 says. It says that morality *often* requires self-denial. All that follows, then, is that *often* human beings are not capable of acting morally. And so we can see that the conclusion is ambiguous between

Conclusion a (modest version): Human beings are *often not capable* of acting morally.

Conclusion b (strong version): Human beings are *never capable* of acting morally.

The modest version of the conclusion does seem to follow logically from the premises, but the stronger version does not. That doesn't mean that it is false—it may be that human beings are never capable of acting morally. The point is that the argument we have been given so far does not establish such a claim. The argument allows that where morality is consistent with self-interest, we can in fact act morally. Suppose, for example, you have promised to look after your neighbor's dog for the day. So now you have a moral obligation to do so. But suppose looking after this particular dog is lots of fun and one of your favorite things to do. In this case morality and self-interest seem to coincide. Therefore, acting self-interestedly can be compatible with morality even if they can also clash. For example, you might also have promised to look after your neighbor's cat, which you view as a nuisance.

We can, though, push the discussion to a deeper level. If you are acting to pursue your self-interest, can it also be that you are acting morally, or is it just a happy coincidence? Let's take another example. Suppose you spend a great deal of time, effort, and energy helping a friend through a difficult time in her life simply because you miss going out with her and want to get back to how things used to be. Have you acted morally or not? This case relates to an important debate about **moral motivation**: Is an action "moral" only if it is done for moral reasons? We will return to this in a later chapter, for Immanuel Kant (1724–1804) claimed that an action has moral worth only if it stems from the appropriate moral motivation. But to stay focused on the main issue, recall that so far our central challenge is based on the claim that human beings are constituted to pursue their own self-interest, and nothing but their own self-interest. And we have conceded that morality often requires self-denial. From these premises it follows that human beings cannot always act morally. This is obviously a serious issue. So now let's directly evaluate the root of this argument: the psychological egoist claim that human beings must always act out of self-interest.

The Evidence for Psychological Egoism

Is it true that human beings are constituted to pursue their own self-interest and nothing else? Many intelligent and thoughtful people think so. And this is a good reason to take the claim seriously. But as we know, simply thinking something doesn't make it true. Neither does the fact that you (if you do), your parents, or some of your friends think it. None of us can make something true by thinking it is true (except in very special cases). We need reasons, in the form of evidence or arguments, to support claims to truth. What reason is there to believe that human beings are constituted to always follow their own self-interest? Psychological egoism is after all a psychological theory about human beings; it is something that should be supportable by evidence. It is a theory about human behavior. So what is the evidence that human beings are constituted to pursue nothing but their own interest?

Of course it is easy to find evidence of human beings acting in their own self-interest. If we look at the world of business, just reading the newspapers reveals breathtaking examples. But this isn't good enough. The theory is stated as a universal truth about all human beings and all of their actions. Logically, the claim "all human action is self-interested" is equivalent to the claim "no human actions are not self-interested." That is a bold suggestion indeed. The key issue, then, comes down not to how many positive instances can we find, but to finding proof that no negative instances exist: in this case, people engaging in genuinely self-sacrificing behavior. Compare the generalization that "all swans are white." We can come up with no end of examples of white swans, but nothing will prove the theory until we are somehow reassured that there are no swans of other colors (and famously, black swans were discovered in Australia eventually, thereby falsifying the previous theory).

Thus we need to turn the investigation on its head and look for examples of self-sacrificing, or self-denying, behavior among humans. Are there any? On the face of it, there are many. Maybe you've spent part of the weekend tidying up the apartment while your roommates were out enjoying the sun. Is this not a form of self-denying behavior?

The psychological egoist is not going to be very impressed by this example. Maybe you detest an untidy apartment so much that you would rather tidy it up than go out and enjoy yourself. Maybe you are tidying today in the attempt to guilt-trip your roommates into cooking for you next week. In either case the psychological egoist can say that you are taking a short-term loss for longer-term gain. The example does not show that long-term self-denying behavior exists.

But really, do we want to say that pure self-denying behavior is impossible? Here is the German philosopher Arthur Schopenhauer (1788–1860), actually a defender of something close to psychological egoism, on the topic:

> [There] are individual but undoubted cases where not only punishment by law, but also discovery, and even any hint of suspicion were totally excluded, and yet a rich man had what belonged to him given back by a poor man: e.g., where something lost and found, or something deposited by a third party who had then died, was brought to its owner, or where something secretly left with a poor man by someone fleeing the country was faithfully kept and returned. (Schopenhauer, 1841/2009, p. 186)

True, Schopenhauer goes on to say that such people are as rare as "four-leaved clovers," but at this point all we need is a single example to refute the case.

Mother Teresa (1910–97), who was made a saint in September 2016, is often mentioned as an inspiring example to us all and a refutation of the self-interest theory. She spent much of her life tending to the sick and poor in Calcutta, at great hardship to herself. Was this all part of a calculated plan to advance her self-interest in the long term? What did she hope to gain? In fact some critics have been skeptical about Mother Teresa's achievements. But even if the commonly believed story is correct, the particular case is easy for the psychological egoist. There is, of course, a straightforward calculation of self-interest. Mother Teresa was a Christian. Christian doctrine includes belief in the afterlife. To ascend to heaven a person has to do good on earth, and so all apparently moral behavior is really a form of hidden self-interest. As we noted in the last chapter, there is an interesting theological question here: Is religious belief in an afterlife, or even God's reward on earth, a way of reducing morality to self-interest? If moral behavior is rewarded and immoral behavior punished, and people are motivated by the reward and punishment, then morality is no more than enlightened self-interest after all. If Mother Teresa's plan was to do good simply to get into heaven, then her behavior is consistent with the self-interest theory. Still, we have to wonder whether she had to do *so much* good for others. Couldn't she have relaxed a little?

But let's imagine an atheist version of Mother Teresa. Admittedly, the self-interest theorist could jump on this suggestion and reply that an imagined example is irrelevant. After all, even though we can imagine a green swan, it doesn't show that not all swans are white: We need to find an actual, rather than an imaginary, nonwhite swan to show that. For the moment let's continue with the thought experiment, accepting that on its own it doesn't prove anything. I introduce it not as a direct counterexample to the self-interest theory, but as a stand-in for the many people who say they do not believe in the afterlife and yet also take a lot of trouble to do good for others. Let's use the idea of "Atheist Mother Teresa" to represent these people.

Once again, though, the self-interest theorist can make short work of Atheist Mother Teresa. True, Atheist Mother Teresa does a lot of good for others. But, so the theory goes, at some level she is acting this way because of the kick she gets out of it. It feels good to help, and those who help others do it to get a "warm glow" of righteousness. What looks like an act of self-sacrifice is an act of selfishness after all.

Well, is that right? How would Atheist Mother Teresa respond if you put this case to her? No doubt she would feel pretty hurt and insulted; she would vehemently deny that she has chosen a life of poverty, struggle, and sacrifice because, like a cocaine addict, she gets a rush from it. But you can press the point. Doesn't it feel good to do good? "Yes," she might say, "but that's not why I do it. If I didn't think it was the right thing to do, I wouldn't do it. And if I didn't think it was the right thing to do, I would not get a warm glow." In any case, the warm glow she feels barely registers on the scales compared to the pains suffered through a life of self-sacrifice. In other words, even if there is a warm glow, it is a small positive reward in comparison to the suffering she also experiences and not the main motivation of the action.

Here the critics might accuse Atheist Mother Teresa of deceiving herself. They could claim that no one would behave like this unless the warm glow more than compensated for the pain. But why should we believe this? Or, to use a simpler example, consider an atheist member of a resistance movement against a totalitarian regime who allows herself to be tortured to death to avoid betraying the movement. No warm glow, surely, would be enough to compensate for a prolonged and horribly painful death. Such cases seemingly refute the claim that humans are incapable of self-sacrificing behavior.

But the critic will be unbowed. These are fictional cases. In real-life cases, how do we actually know what is going on in someone's head? Perhaps the warm glow is ecstatic. Perhaps all atheist revolutionaries have a deathbed conversion and believe they are going to eternal bliss, or they believe the reputation of glory is enough to compensate for the pain. The self-interest theorist can dig in and insist: All action *must* be for the sake of self-interest. Notice, though, that once this move is made, the argument has changed significantly. Initially the critic made a psychological argument that drew on claimed empirical evidence: Anyone who appears to be self-sacrificing actually has, deep down, some selfish ulterior motive that we can discover. When faced with imagined counterexamples, the critic has changed to a theoretical argument: Self-sacrifice is simply not possible, and there *must* be an ulterior motive. But why must there be? Doesn't this argument assume that psychological egoism is true, rather than provide any grounds for believing it is true?

It is hard to see, though, how it could be possible to make a definitive argument for the self-interest theory, or indeed find a definitive refutation. The power of argument is sometimes more limited than we would hope. The psychological egoist, if utterly convinced of the truth of the view, can insist that the warm glow must outweigh any pain or sacrifice, even if this now sounds rather **dogmatic**. We can now appreciate, though, that the psychological egoist is simply someone who holds one theory—and perhaps it is not as plausible as it first looked. Psychological egoism needs support from evidence or argument, and so it is not obviously true. But even if the theory is not obviously true, that does not make it false.

Can Psychological Egoism Be Rejected?

Nevertheless, psychological egoism can be a hard view to shift. For example, in *The Republic*, Plato sets himself the task of trying to show that acting justly is not mad or foolish, even if you can get away with behaving however you want.

In a sense, though, Plato puts himself in a difficult position in the argument. What does he have to show? He thinks he needs to demonstrate that it is in people's interest to act morally, even if we can profit from immorality without fear of being caught and punished. How would you show that acting morally is in your interest even when you can get away with breaking the rules? We will not go through the details of Plato's argument because it depends on many other elements of Plato's philosophical system as a whole. Here we need to pay attention to one important claim he makes—that a certain special type of inner harmony comes from acting morally. A modern version of this view might be that if you acted very badly, you simply wouldn't be able to live with yourself, perhaps through the nagging and life-wrecking guilt or shame of having harmed others for your own benefit. If you act immorally, it will eat away at you and make you miserable. Suppose, for example, that you had the Ring of Gyges and went into a poor old couple's house—people who had only ever been kind to you—and took their last food because they live nearer to you than anyone else, and this is the easiest way for you to feed yourself. You know you will never be caught. Would you feel okay about it? If not, why not?

You might feel, however, that Plato's argument—or at least the modern version of it—reduces morality to something like self-interest. We have just seen the argument that the only reason people act morally is that doing so gives them a kick of some sort, a warm glow. Here we have an argument that is something like the opposite of the warm glow argument; what we might call the "cold chill" argument. It says that people avoid immorality because they don't want to suffer the cold chill of the remorse and guilt of having done something wrong. But then this theory also appears to reduce morality to self-interest, simply in a different way.

How might we avoid collapsing morality into self-interest? Think about the nice old couple whose food you stole when you had the Ring of Gyges. How would you feel if you had acted that way? Most of us, I believe, would feel awful and probably prefer never to think about it. Why? Is it because you have been brought up to obey ordinary moral rules and find them impossible to shake, like someone who automatically follows the rituals of the religion of their childhood even though they no longer believe? Or is it because the poor old couple will now find it hard to feed themselves in the coming days and will suffer real hardship as a result, unless someone else comes to help them? Knowing that other people can suffer, just as you would, seems to give you a reason to treat them well if you can. If that is your reason to feel awful when you break the rules, then the rules of morality seem to involve something beyond self-interest.

SELF-INTEREST AND EVOLUTION

Psychological egoists can try to find support from another quarter, evolutionary biology. The biologist J. B. S. Haldane (1892–1964) reportedly said, "I'd lay down my life for two brothers or eight cousins." This was a calculation based on what is now known as the **selfish gene** theory, as developed in detail by the contemporary evolutionary biologist Richard Dawkins (b. 1941). The idea is that old-fashioned self-interest theory is too crude. Human beings aren't selfish, our genes are. In this view, we might well sacrifice ourselves, but only if it is likely to lead to the greater preservation of our genes. Note, though, that the terminology can be confusing. Dawkins is not proposing that all human beings have a "gene for selfishness" (even if some people might have). Rather, he suggests that we are genetically programmed to try to preserve our genes. And we are programmed to do this whether we alone possess those genes or whether we have them in common with other people, in which case we will want to advance the interests of those other people.

Selfish Genes and Kin Altruism

The selfish gene hypothesis can seem powerful. When we think about the people in our world who are most self-sacrificing, mothers, caring for their children, are at the top of the list. A mother can be sure that her child contains half the genetic material that she has. So if, at some deep level, a mother's main motivation is to ensure the continuation of her genes, then she will do a good deal to help ensure that her children survive and reproduce. She will also care about her own brothers and sisters, who also have half her genes. Her nieces and nephews have a quarter of her genes, and her cousins have an eighth. This is why Haldane said he would lay down his life for two brothers or eight cousins; either way, the same amount of genetic material would be preserved. And indeed this type of self-sacrificing behavior is routinely observed in the animal kingdom, especially among what have been called the "social insects" such as ants and bees. In some examples sterile insects—incapable of reproduction—work tirelessly for the good of the group, all of whom are close relatives.

The selfish gene hypothesis is connected to the theory of **kin altruism** (although historically the idea of kin altruism predated the term *selfish gene*). Essentially, kin altruism supposes that your selfish genes lead you to act altruistically to those who are related to you. The more closely you are related to these people, the more altruistic you will be; conversely, you will be less altruistic toward people who are more distantly related.

In one way, though, the theory of kin altruism seems crazy. I do, of course, help my relatives from time to time. But I don't think I have ever reasoned that "I'd better help my brother, at some cost to myself, to make sure that my genes survive." We would be quite surprised, and possibly a little worried, if we came across someone who thought things through like that. The selfish gene hypothesis and the theory of kin altruism have to be understood as some sort of indirect motivation. One possible idea is that your genes cause you to love those who are closely related to you, and your love of family leads you to help them. The love is real, and it explains your behavior; but in this theory, your selfish genes strongly influence who you love. And we can concede, I think, that the kin altruism theory has some plausibility. We do seem to care most about those most closely related to us, and it would be no surprise if researchers found a genetic explanation for that phenomenon. In fact, the real surprise would be finding out this behavior has nothing to do with evolution or genetics.

What, though, is the scope of the theory? Is it intended to explain all altruistic behavior? It doesn't seem to explain why parents of adopted children devote such care and attention to them. Or why some people care much more for their cousins than for their brothers or sisters, or why others care for their friends much more than anyone who is related to them. Let's consider a husband and wife, who, we hope, are no more closely related than any two strangers taken at random. Kin altruism can explain why they care for each other if they have children together: If your husband or wife flourishes, this is likely to be good for your children and hence the survival of your genes. But suppose they have no children and are past childbearing age. Kin altruism can no longer explain why the spouses might make sacrifices for each other, although it might say that in all these cases our emotions are somehow tricked or hijacked. That may be true; but overall, kin altruism seems unable to directly explain a whole range of altruistic behavior, even if it seems to get a certain amount right. Worse still, kin altruism doesn't seem compatible with the behavior of family members who sometimes harm or neglect each other. Some will think that kin altruism gets things backward. What motivates us to help family members, they will claim, is not our genes but the love and close bonds we develop in growing up with our family. And the development of mutual affection will also explain why we make sacrifices for family members who are not genetically related.

The Mountain People

Besides the selfish gene theory, the evolutionary theorist has another card to play. We will begin discussing this next idea by looking at what was claimed to be a real-life example—although as we will see, we should be highly skeptical. In 1972 the anthropologist Colin Turnbull (1924–94) published a sensational book, *The Mountain People*, about a group called the Ik people who live in the mountains between Uganda, the Sudan, and Kenya. According to Turnbull, these people had virtually no compassion or feeling for each other. Some of his examples sound like cartoon horror stories, giving accounts of mothers laughing when their children burn themselves. Here is one of the most dramatic:

> The mother goes about her business [at the water hole or in the fields] leaving the child there, almost hoping that some predator will come and carry it off. This happened once when I was there—once that I know of, anyway—and the mother was delighted. She was rid of the child and no longer had to ... feed it, and still further this meant that a leopard was in the vicinity and would be sleeping the child off and thus be an easy kill. (Turnbull, 1972, p. 136)

The author gives us many other examples. Old people were neglected, abused, even killed. Food is taken from the mouths of the starving. The situation of the tribe seems unbearably bleak. But on reading the book, a question strikes you again and again. If this is how they behaved to each other, how did the society survive? Turnbull's answer is that this behavior is relatively new to the tribe. Since being forced off their traditional hunting grounds, which were turned into a highly protected nature reserve, the Ik people were now starving to death although they pretended not to be. Their egoistic behavior was an aberration; if it lasted, the tribe would not survive. Anthropologists now completely reject the credibility of Turnbull's account, arguing that his study was deeply flawed. Indeed it is said that upon hearing about the way Turnbull had represented them, the Ik people considered taking legal action against him, thus showing a level of sophistication that does not seem to fit with Turnbull's account. Rather than as a depiction of fact, then, let's treat Turnbull's book as another example of a "thought experiment." Could a tribe like the Ik ever have existed? Could they reproduce over the generations?

The answer is surely that such a tribe could not have survived. As Turnbull himself noted, he expected that the Ik tribe would soon die out. Group survival needs a measure of altruism, of individual self-sacrifice. Hence another evolutionary argument seems possible: Groups that don't develop cultures of altruism don't survive. And so a mechanism known as group selection has been suggested. This is Charles Darwin (1809–82) in his book, *The Descent of Man,* on the matter:

> A tribe including many members who, from possessing in a high degree the spirit of patriotism, fidelity, obedience, courage, and sympathy, were always ready to aid one another, and to sacrifice themselves for the common good, would be victorious over most other tribes; and this would be natural selection. (Darwin, 1871/2004, p. 157)

How, though, is this meant to work? Evolutionary biologists distinguish between three different possible moral evolutionary mechanisms. We have already discussed kin altruism (the theory of the selfish gene). The Ik and Darwin lead us to another possibility—**group altruism**: Groups die out if they don't develop altruism. And finally we need to look at the idea of **reciprocal altruism**: "If you'll scratch my back, I'll scratch yours." This is a fairly local, small-scale mechanism in which people implicitly agree to help each other. These three ideas—kin, group, and reciprocal altruism—seem to be closely related: Groups are likely to be made up of people who are related and who do mutual favors for each other. Group altruism suggests that individuals will engage in behavior that favors the group, even at a cost to themselves. Reciprocal altruism is rather more fine-grained; it occurs when individuals within the group cooperate with other particular individuals, but only when they also cooperate back from time to time.

Some evolutionary biologists, however, have questioned whether there is such a thing as pure group altruism, unless it is backed by kin or reciprocal altruism. It is plausible that groups with moral codes will survive and outcompete with groups without a moral code holding them together, but the problem is that a selfish and clever individual living with a group of altruists will have a tremendous advantage. He or she will be able to exploit others, and if this advantage turns into more offspring, the gene for selfishness (remember, not the same thing as the selfish gene) will be passed on and eventually dominate the group. Accordingly, some have argued that altruism within a group is not stable unless backed up with either kin altruism or reciprocal altruism (or both) to put a brake on **free riding**. Others have argued that in certain ways, group altruism can resist some level of noncooperative selfish behavior.

Reciprocal altruism, nevertheless, seems likely to be a stronger mechanism. It is the idea that I will look after you in the expectation that you will look after me. This can explain why nongenetically related individuals such as a husband and wife, or a group of friends, will help each other. Once more, this theory must contain a good deal of truth. People with a reputation for being selfish tend to get left out of group activities and are worse off for that. Therefore, we all have self-interested reasons for cooperating with at least the people we see regularly. On the other hand, it seems that what matters in the first instance is the reputation, not the reality. If you can be a free rider, pretending to be cooperative but slyly getting away with what you can when you can—as if you had the Ring of Gyges—then that's what self-interest says you should do. But in a small group, or a group that regularly interacts, free-riding often is detected and punished. (This may explain why villages are generally safer and more secure than large cities: Uncooperative behavior is much more easily noticed and dealt with.) In Chapter 7 we will return to the issues of free-riding.

To conclude the discussion of psychological egoism, even if it is true that morality can be reduced to self-interest, the task of the theorist of morality is not complete. The reason for this is that moral theory comes in many forms and varieties, and it is not clear which form of morality would best promote self-interest. Moral philosophy is needed even if in a somewhat different form than we normally suppose. It leads to the question of the optimum mix of short-term self-interest and altruism to preserve long-term self-interest.

ETHICAL EGOISM

So far we have been looking at varieties of what we called psychological egoism, which as I noted, is essentially, a scientific theory about human behavior. We have seen some arguments for the conclusion that human beings are somehow constituted or genetically programmed to pursue their own self-interest; and this, at least at first, raises the question of whether morality is possible. But we have also seen that once evolutionary arguments are taken into account, in some ways psychological egoism can generate behavior that looks very similar to ordinary morality.

But we need to explore another view, which I referred to above as ethical egoism. It says that whether or not psychological egoism is true, following your own self-interest is the *morally right thing* for you to do. Ethical egoism comes in many different forms, for "self-interest" can be understood in many different ways. Normally we think of self-interest in a relatively narrow form—getting what you most want, satisfying your desires, or perhaps achieving financial success and having a life of luxury. These are what we could call your "selfish" self-interests. But we can also take a broader view of self-interest by arguing that, for example, doing good things for others is part of an individual's self-interest if that is what she most wants to do. In this view a type of harmony exists between the person's self-interest and the good of others; and so by acting apparently selfishly, she is automatically acting morally. In Chapter 12 we will see that Aristotle held a view of this sort, and we will discuss his theory in detail. For now, however, let's restrict ourselves to what we could call "narrow ethical egoism," which claims that the morally right thing to do is to pursue your selfish interest. But can this really be right? Doesn't morality call on us to make, say, a small sacrifice to save a life? How could it be thought otherwise?

Private Vices, Public Virtues

Narrow ethical egoism comes in at least two versions. Consider this famous quote from the Scottish economist and moral philosopher Adam Smith (1723–90) from his book *The Wealth of Nations*:

> It is not from the benevolence of the butcher, the brewer, or the baker that we expect our dinner, but from their regard to their own interest. We address ourselves, not to their humanity but to their self-love, and never talk to them of our own necessities but of their advantages. (Smith, 1776/1982, p. 119)

Smith points out a remarkable fact about exchange in market economies. Economic agents are driven by self-interest: Both sides want the best deal they can get. But for butchers, as an example, it is in their self-interest to give customers good value so that they come back another time. In the longer term the butchers can get what they want—a regular profit—only by giving customers what they want—good meat. To pursue their self-interest, butchers have to give customers excellent service. In this way the pursuit of individual self-interest leads to the collective common good. As the Anglo-Dutch thinker Bernard Mandeville (1670–1733) pointed out, "private vices" lead to "public virtues" (Mandeville, 1714/1989).

This form of ethical egoism is, in a sense, conditional. It tells us to follow our own self-interest, but only because in this way, everyone's interest in the common good will be advanced. Some defenders of the capitalist free market economy have been impressed by this argument. Opponents of the free market, such as socialists, criticize capitalism because it encourages selfishness. But in reply, defenders say that capturing selfishness for the public good is actually the strength of capitalism. You can make a profit only by giving people what they want, so the greedier the capitalist, the better it is for the customer. Prices come down and quality goes up in attempt to capture more of the market. On this basis it is often argued that the way to advance the collective good is to allow the capitalist economy to function with minimal government intervention or regulation. This, it is said, will allow individual selfishness to flow for public benefit.

Unfortunately, as Adam Smith was himself aware, his argument has much more limited scope than some of his followers have suggested. Consider, for example, a financial agent selling you a pension plan. It is in the narrow self-interest of the agent to convince you that the right plan for you is the one that gives him the greatest commission. But if so much commission goes to the agent, it is rather likely that the product he is boosting will give you a poor deal. The same is true for agents selling subprime mortgages, product insurance, collateralized debt, or any other sophisticated financial product. Their interest is to lead you to buy whatever gives them the highest profit. If the product is no good, then, unlike the meat you bought from the butcher and eat that evening, it could be years before you find out. By that time the agent, most likely, will have moved on and be trying to sell something else. And this is no mere theoretical issue. In the view of some analysts, the root cause of the financial crisis of 2008 was a belief by some financial regulators that Adam Smith had shown that the pursuit of self-interest in an unregulated market would always work out in the common interest. But as we learned at enormous cost, Smith himself knew he had shown no such thing.

Pure Ethical Egoism

To recap, I said that ethical egoism comes in two forms. In the form we have been looking at so far, it states that pursuing your own self-interest is the best way of advancing the common good. I have given readers some reason to believe that, although this theory has merit in limited contexts, as a generalization it is highly problematic. But in any case, when understood this way, ethical egoism seems to fall short of being an "ultimate" moral theory: It presupposes that we can reach an independent "common good" by acting in our self-interest. It is a theory about how to achieve good results, understood in non-egoistic terms. Therefore, strictly speaking, it is not an egoist theory at all.

The second form of ethical egoism is uncompromising. Rather than arguing that we have a duty to act in a self-interested way because of the consequences, it suggests that it is right to act in our own interests, *whatever* the consequences for other people. This theory, sometimes associated with the influential Russian American thinker and novelist Ayn Rand (1905–82), has been described as arguing for the "duty of selfishness." This slogan reflects a striking and bold theory, apparently suggesting that it is your moral duty to be as grasping and selfish as you can be. But at least in some of her writings, Rand makes clear that her principal argument is against a type of joyless, altruistic self-sacrifice that requires individuals to put their own interests aside to promote the well-being of strangers. She clearly indicates that she believes a good life—a selfish life—can include generous behavior toward your family and friends, the enjoyment of which also contributes to your own self-interest. In this respect, her view allows a level of harmony between self-interest and action for the sake of others, rather than instructing everyone to follow a narrow, calculating path. Yet there remains a powerful element of self-concern in this view, given the strong stand Rand takes regarding some forms of self-sacrifice. Conventional morality, thinks Rand, is our "enemy," for we can only lose from it. In *The Virtue of Selfishness*, she says:

> By elevating the issue of helping others into the central and primary issue of ethics, altruism has destroyed the concept of any authentic benevolence or good will among men. It has indoctrinated men with the idea that to value another human being is an act of selflessness, thus implying that a man can have no personal interest in others—that *to value* another means *to sacrifice* oneself—that any love, respect or admiration a man may feel for others is not, and cannot be a source of his own enjoyment, but is a threat to his existence, a sacrificial blank check signed over to his loved ones. (Rand, 1964, pp. 49–50)

These are strong words. Yet we need to be careful. Rand is here rejecting a view of morality that claims moral value is found only in promoting the interests of others at your own cost. Certainly, some conceptions of morality do require such a level of sacrifice, such as extreme religious views. Or consider Mrs. Jellyby, a character created by Charles Dickens (1812–70) in his novel *Bleak House* (1853), to show how unappealing extreme altruism can be. Mrs. Jellyby lets her children go hungry and dirty while she devotes her time to setting up a mission in Africa. But rather than abject self-sacrifice, most moral views seek some sort of balance between the interests of the individual, their family, and other people. So rejecting such an extreme form of altruism is compatible with endorsing a wide range of approaches to morality, and not just Rand's own view. It would be a logical fallacy to think that rejecting extreme altruism results in establishing a form of ethical egoism, because intermediate positions do remain possible.

Nevertheless, the idea that pursuing your own selfish interests is the morally right thing to do has been discussed since the beginnings of moral philosophy. Ethical egoism, in this pure form, may look like the opposite of a moral theory because it seemingly instructs you to be indifferent to the plight of other people, especially strangers, however bad their situation is—or, indeed, whatever damage you do to them. Pushed to the extreme, this behavior would permit or perhaps require you to rob or even kill people in pursuit of your interest.

Ethical egoism is thus a highly counterintuitive theory. But its appeal is easy to see, at least in more moderate cases. It starts, most naturally, from facts about human existence. You have your own life, your own perspective on the world. And you will have only one life. No one else can feel your pleasures or pains, and you cannot feel those of anyone else. Although others may occasionally help you, or appear to do so, in the end the only person you can rely on is yourself. You should, then, do what you can to make your life as fulfilling and worthwhile as possible. This is an obligation to yourself; a moral duty to advance your own interests. Of course you can choose to help people, but you must not neglect yourself. You were given this one life to lead, and it is your duty to make the best of it.

Put like this, ethical egoism is not merely a type of convenient moral screen for selfishness. Instead, it seems to reflect a deep fact about human existence: Each of us has our own life to lead, and we are responsible for making our own life go well. This theory seems to respect individual responsibility, and in some ways seems to be of great rigor and integrity. However, its difficulties are also easy to see: First, although it is true that I have a life to lead, so do you; and so does everyone else. Why should my life take priority over yours? Rather than potentially crushing others in pursuit of our own interests, it seems we need to respect everyone's right to pursue a meaningful and fulfilling life. From this point of view, ethical egoism is a very one-sided position: It addresses only half of the moral problem. The moral dilemma we often face is how to reconcile our own interests with those of others. We ignore half the dilemma if we simply assume that we have a moral duty to pursue our own interests. And this point brings a second problem into focus: Even if we do have a moral duty to pursue our own interest, we can see how badly that can go by remembering the horror stories of the Ik. Perhaps, then, pursuing our own interests requires significant compromise, to avoid what Thomas Hobbes (1588–1679), in his book *Leviathan*, called "a warre ... of every man against every man" (Hobbes, 1651/1997, p. 61). We will return to this issue in Chapter 7, where we look at forms of social contract theory that attempt to build morality out of a type of agreement to moderate our pursuit of self-interest.

CHAPTER REVIEW

Summary

In the first section of this chapter, I explored psychological egoism, which argues that we are psychologically compelled to follow our own self-interest. I considered both defenses and criticisms of the thesis. I then looked at some approaches that tried to develop an argument for psychological egoism based on evolutionary theory, and we saw that, in evolutionary terms, self-interest may converge with some aspects of morality.

I moved on to examine two types of ethical egoism: one suggests that we have a duty to pursue our self-interest in order to advance the common good; the other, a purer form, contends that each of us has a duty to pursue our own self-interest whatever the consequences are for the common good. We saw reasons to question such a view, but we also considered what it would mean, in fact, to follow self-interest. To avoid a damaging war of all against all, we will have to compromise with others. Could the rules of compromise be a moral code? We will return to that question in the next chapter.

Discussion Questions

1. Explain and assess the theory of psychological egoism.
2. What are the distinctions between kin altruism, group altruism, and reciprocal altruism?
3. Are there good arguments for ethical egoism?
4. Does ethical egoism reject all concern for others?

Key Terms

psychological egoism, p. 89

ethical egoism, p. 89

logical validity, p. 90

moral motivation, p. 91

dogmatism, p. 94

selfish gene, p. 96

kin altruism, p. 97

group altruism, p. 99

reciprocal altruism, p. 99

free riding, p. 99

Key Thinkers

David Hume (1711–76), p. 88

Plato (429?–347 BCE), pp. 88–89, 95

Socrates (470/69–399 BCE), p. 88

Immanuel Kant (1724–1804), p. 91

Arthur Schopenhauer (1788–1860), pp. 92–93

Mother Teresa (1910–97), pp. 93–94

J. B. S. Haldane (1892–1964), p. 96

Richard Dawkins (b. 1941), p. 96

Colin Turnbull (1924–94), pp. 98–99

Charles Darwin (1809–82), p. 99

Adam Smith (1723–90), pp. 101–102

Bernard Mandeville (1670–1733), p. 101

Ayn Rand (1905–82), pp. 102–103

Charles Dickens (1812–70), p. 103

Thomas Hobbes (1588–1679), p. 104

Further Reading

- David Hume is quoted from *An Enquiry Concerning the Principles of Morals* (Hackett, 1983). (Original work published 1751)

- Passages from Plato's *Republic* are from the edition published by W. W. Norton (1999).

- The passage from Arthur Schopenhauer is from his essay "On the Basis of Morality," which forms part of his book *The Two Fundamental Problems of Ethics* (Cambridge University Press, 2009), edited and translated by David E. Cartwright and Edward E. Erdman. (Original work published 1841)

- Peter Singer's excellent discussion of evolutionary approaches to ethics is included in his book *The Expanding Circle*, revised edition (Princeton University Press, 2011). (Original work published 1981)

- Richard Dawkins's *The Selfish Gene* was published by Oxford University Press (2006). (Original work published 1976)

- Colin Turnbull's *The Mountain People* was published by Touchstone (1972).

- Charles Darwin's observation in *The Descent of Man* is quoted from the Penguin edition (2004). (Original work published 1871)

- The passage from Adam Smith's *The Wealth of Nations* is from the Penguin edition (1982). (Original work published 1776)

- Bernard Mandeville's *Fable of the Bees* is available in a Penguin edition (1989). (Original work published 1741)

- Ayn Rand is possibly best approached through her novels, such as *The Fountainhead* (1943; reprinted by Signet, 1996), also made into a 1949 film. *The Virtue of Selfishness* (Signet, 1964) is an introduction to her philosophical writings.

- Charles Dickens's *Bleak House* (1852) is widely available, including as a Penguin edition (2003). (Original work published 1852)

- Thomas Hobbes's *Leviathan* is widely available, including an edition from W. W. Norton (1997). (Original work published 1651)

- Selections from works by Plato, Singer, Rand, and Hobbes are included in Jonathan Wolff (ed.), *Readings in Moral Philosophy* (W. W. Norton, 2018).

CHAPTER 7

The Social Contract

Most men say that to be unjust is good but to suffer injustice is bad. To this opinion they add another: the measure of evil suffered by one who is wronged is generally greater than the good enjoyed by one who does wrong. Now, once they have learned what it is to wrong others—and also what it is to be wronged—men tend to arrive at this conclusion: justice is unattainable and injustice unavoidable.

Those so lacking in strength that they can neither inflict injustice nor defend themselves against it find it profitable to draw up a compact with one another. The purpose of the compact is to bind them all neither to suffer injustice nor to commit it. From there they proceed to promulgate further contracts and covenants. To all of these they attach the name of justice; indeed, they assert that the true origin and essence of justice is located in their own legislation.

Their lawmaking is clearly a compromise, Socrates. The compromise is between what they say is best of all—to do wrong without incurring punishment— and what is worst of all—to suffer wrong with no possibility of revenge. Hence they conceive of justice not as something good in itself but simply as a midway point between best and worst.

GLAUCON, IN PLATO'S REPUBLIC

MORALITY AS A COMPROMISE AGREEMENT

Thus far I have made several references to Plato's *Republic*. In this work the character Thrasymachus presents the view that "justice is the interest of the stronger," also known as the theory that "might is right." This is a skeptical view that ultimately morality is some sort of sham or trick—or, to put the point more radically, a form of ideology in which naked power cloaks itself in moral language to disguise its real nature. Naturally this is a view that Plato (429?–347 BCE), through the character Socrates, attempts to refute. Also in *The Republic*, the character Glaucon presents the story of the "Ring of Gyges," arguing that if any of us could get away with acting immorally, it would be irrational to resist. This is another part of the battery of attacks on morality that Plato unleashes before he settles down to the task of defending it. A further aspect of that attack is reflected in this chapter's opening passage, which Plato also put into the mouth of Glaucon (who in real life was one of Plato's brothers).

Glaucon presents the theory that justice is a compromise. By this he means that ideally, a person would act just as he or she liked without punishment or retaliation. But if one person could do that, then so could everyone else, and each of us would be powerless to protect ourselves. It would be catastrophic for all. So we all rather reluctantly agree to a system of justice that keeps us to a set of rules, for our mutual benefit. This position can be attributed to the **Sophists**, a group of philosophers who earned their living by teaching wealthy young Athenian men how to argue. It is said that the young aristocrats were more interested in winning the argument than getting to the truth, and the Sophists were thereby obliged to teach them the skill of making the weaker argument defeat the stronger, through the power of rhetoric. We owe the term *sophistry,* meaning "the presentation of false or dishonest reasoning," to the work of these philosophers; it is not a term they would have applied to themselves, of course. Some scholars suggest that history has been hard on the Sophists and that they were serious philosophers who sincerely made important arguments. Nevertheless, the term *sophistry* has stuck.

Whatever its origin, the account of morality as a compromise that allows us all to get on with our lives seems very powerful. It reduces morality to a type of implicit **social contract** that we have invented or evolved. If there were no morality, you could do whatever you wanted. But unfortunately for you, so could everyone else. You have more to lose than to gain from such a lawless situation. Even if you managed to protect your possessions, it would be at great cost. Life would be exhausting and full of fear. Indeed Thomas Hobbes (1588–1679), two thousand years after Plato in his book *Leviathan* gave an extremely colorful account of what life would be like in "a state of nature" without law (and therefore, in Hobbes's view, without morality):

> In such condition there is no place for Industry; because the fruit thereof is uncertain: and consequently no Culture of the Earth; no Navigation, nor use of the commodities that may be imported by Sea; no commodious Building; no Instruments of moving and removing such things as require much force; no Knowledge of the face of the Earth; no account of Time; no Arts; no Letters; no Society; and which is worst of all, continuall feare, and danger of violent death; And the life of man, solitary, poore, nasty, brutish, and short. (Hobbes, 1651/1996, p. 70)

In fact, this is not a bad depiction of the Ik society we discussed in Chapter 6.

Why oppose the view that morality is an external device or convention for mutual benefit? This concept of morality presents moral behavior as a type of agreement by which each of us indirectly pursues our self-interest. It also has the great advantage that it seems to base morality on human agreement and therefore does not need to raise the questions of objectivism that (as we saw in Chapter 2) can lead to metaphysical puzzles about the nature of value. A drawback of this position is that morality has **instrumental value** only, because it is valued solely as a means to self-interest. Therefore, in this view, morality has no **intrinsic value** or worth, in itself, and nothing is right or wrong until human beings have agreed to make it so. Morality is reduced to self-interest, or a means to an end. But then, those who could achieve the end—self-interest—without the means, would have no need for morality. As Glaucon puts it in Plato's *Republic*: "For anyone who is a real man with power to do as he likes would never agree to refrain from doing injustice in order not to suffer it. He would be mad to make any such agreement" (1999, p. 55).

Understood this way, the theory of the social contract takes us back to the Ring of Gyges (see Chapter 6), which is actually how Plato presents it. Those who could get away with acting immorally would have no need for morality. Indeed, as Glaucon says, they would be "mad" to follow the social contract if they can know they never will be caught. By this reading, the social contract looks more fragile and uncertain than many people want from an account of the basis of morality.

Even worse, Glaucon hints that the social contract is a device of oppression. Recall the character Raskolnikov from Dostoyevsky's novel *Crime and Punishment* (1866), discussed in Chapter 3. Raskolnikov, who disastrously acts as if he has the Ring of Gyges, comes very close to the view that morality is a type of conspiracy by the weak to hold the strong in check. And indeed this also seems to be Friedrich Nietzsche's account of Christian morality; as we have seen, he believes that it generalizes humility, meekness, and conformity and stifles those who have the potential to be truly great.

Other philosophers also thought that morality was a human device or an implicit contract, although not a device used by the weak to trap the strong. For example, the eighteenth-century Swiss French philosopher Jean-Jacques Rousseau (1712–78) saw things in exactly the opposite way. He was beguiled by the question of how human beings—who are broadly equal in strength, intelligence, and power—had fallen into a form of society in which the rich enslaved the mass. The mystery, when we think about it, is that the poor, who overwhelmingly outnumber the rich, are somehow held in check by the rich minority. In his *Discourse on the Origin of Inequality*, Rousseau concluded that the rich must have managed to conceive "the most cunning project that ever entered the human mind: this was to employ in his favor the very forces of those who attacked him, to make allies of his adversaries" (1754/1985, p. 121). Rules of law and morality favor the rich—think especially of laws protecting property and wealth—but the rules bind rich and poor alike and are enforced by recruits from the poor in their roles as police and soldiers. Here we are not far from a view often associated with Karl Marx (1818–83) that morality is a device by which the ruling class—the bourgeoisie—consolidates its power and controls the other classes.

Rousseau's critique has been extended by the contemporary British philosopher Carole Pateman (b. 1940) and Jamaican philosopher Charles Mills (b. 1951). As they convincingly point out, the "human being" of the social contract has always been a wealthy white male. The moral rules of the social contract devised by wealthy white men have been to the detriment not just of the poor, as Rousseau argued, but of women and those who are not white. Hence Pateman writes of a "sexual contract" and Mills of a "racial contract" in which different types of oppression have been reinforced and, to put it paradoxically, illegitimately legitimized.

Although the content of their views differs, Nietzsche, Rousseau, Marx, Pateman, and Mills all see conventional morality as a device used by one group or class to impose its will on everyone. And although Glaucon initially offered a "mutual advantage" theory, it soon was transformed into the view—very similar to Nietzsche's—that morality is a device for suppressing the strong. These views are in a sense critical of conventional morality; they suggest that ordinary people do not understand its real nature, and if they did, they might well be disgusted and rebel against it—at least if they were members of the group controlled by morality. Part of the philosopher's job, in this view, is to unmask conventional morality and reveal it as it truly is. This work is likely to be part of a deeper program in which a new morality, one that overcomes the defects in conventional morality, can be formulated.

THE SOCIAL CONTRACT

Those who defend the idea of the social contract may well complain that it has not been treated fairly in the argument thus far. They might claim that it is a much more inspiring idea than its critics have argued. True, its defenders will say, the social contract can be misused. And perhaps they will admit that it has been. But they also will say that the critics' accounts overlook another, much more compelling idea: a theory for constructing the "true" morality that does not oppress any particular group. In this view morality is indeed a social contract, but not one invented to trick one group into submission. Rather it is, or at least could be, made between all people as equals. We contract, implicitly at least, with each person to develop rules that are in everyone's interests—not just of the weak, or the rich, or men, or white people, but for the benefit of all. In fact Rousseau developed a much more positive account of what a social contract could be in his more famous text, *The Social Contract* (1762). Charles Mills shares this view. Once the racial contract has been identified, Mills thinks, it is possible to generate a new social contract that is fair to people of all races. (In Chapter 14, we will return to Mills's arguments.)

How, then, can the idea of an inclusive social contract between all people as equals be developed more fully? Recall the passage from Hobbes quoted earlier in the chapter; he wrote that in the state of nature there would be no industry, transport, international trade, architecture, science, art, culture, or society. Consequently the benefits of cooperation are immeasurable, and they enrich all of our lives whether we know and appreciate it or not. Hobbes argued that even if the social contract is a compromise, it is a compromise that leads to the conditions of peace and security in which all human life can flourish; and without it we will live in misery.

It is worth comparing the idea of the social contract with the theory of reciprocal altruism (see Chapter 6), which was presented as the idea of "You scratch my back, and I'll scratch your back." This theory, perhaps surprisingly, concludes that often the best way of advancing your own interests is to do things for others rather than for yourself. Now it is true that if this is all there is to social contract theory, it makes morality seem fragile, calculating, and limited in scope, and that is exactly what worries some critics. If you stop scratching my back, I'll stop scratching yours, and other people's backs are not even in the picture. If I wake up one morning to find that my back doesn't need to be scratched, then that day you'll have scratch your own itch if you can reach it. Can we provide something more substantial to ground the social contract?

The Prisoner's Dilemma

Luckily there are ways of deepening the social contract theory to make it much more appealing. One way of developing this idea is to use some ideas from a branch of social science in the overlapping area of economics, politics, and social psychology, known as **game theory**. As its name suggests, part of the point of game theory is to work out winning strategies in games. Its founders were particularly interested in poker. But it has a more serious purpose because many social situations can be modeled as being similar to games, and therefore we can use game theory to analyze those social situations.

The example most commonly used to explain the idea of the social contract is called the **prisoner's dilemma**, after an early example. The idea is that two people, let's call them Bonnie and Clyde, have been arrested. I've named them after the real-life gangster couple of Bonnie Parker (1910–34) and Clyde Barrow (1900–34) because their relationship helps bring out some interesting features of the example.

Suppose that the police have compelling evidence to convict both Bonnie and Clyde for a relatively minor crime, say stealing a car. But the police also believe the pair committed a violent robbery, something much more serious. They arrest Bonnie and Clyde and put them in separate cells. The police question each prisoner independently of the other, offering each of them the same deal. Here is what the interrogating officer says to Bonnie:

> We know you took that car, and we can prove it. You'd normally get a year in prison for that. But if you confess to the armed robbery and Clyde doesn't, we will let you off completely. On the other hand, if Clyde confesses and you don't, you'll go to prison for fifteen years. If you both confess, you'll both go to prison for seven years.

In other words the police are telling Bonnie that if she testifies against Clyde she will be let off, provided that Clyde doesn't testify against her. If they both testify against each other, they will both get a substantial sentence—though the worst thing for Bonnie would be to keep quiet and for Clyde to testify.

Some people can see this situation more clearly when the information is presented in the form of a two-by-two matrix. In the cells, the numbers represent possible prison sentences, Bonnie's first.

		CLYDE	
		Don't confess	Confess
BONNIE	Don't confess	1/1	15/0
	Confess	0/15	7/7

Suppose you are Bonnie, sitting in the cell. What would you do? You would realize that if you and Clyde both keep your mouths shut, you'll get a year in prison each. That isn't too bad, and collectively it is the best result. But you also see that if Clyde doesn't confess and you do, then you'll get off completely: no prison at all, which is much better than serving a year. So, Bonnie says to herself, if Clyde doesn't confess I'm actually better off confessing. What if Clyde does confess? In that case I'd better confess too, otherwise I'm going away for fifteen years. So it looks like whatever Clyde does, I'm better off confessing. Therefore, I'd better confess. But then if Clyde has any sense, which he does, he is going to reason the same way; so we will both confess. As a result we will both go to prison for seven years, when we could have got away with going to prison for only one year. How did that happen?

So Bonnie might start thinking again. Clyde loves me. He will never confess to put me away. Aha! Then I could confess and get away with it. That way I'll get away without going to prison at all! But of course exactly the same cunning option is open to Clyde. He might assume that because I love him, I won't confess. He could double-cross me and confess, just like I could betray him. How do I know he won't reason like this and turn me in? Maybe he doesn't love me as much as he loves his freedom. Once again, it seems rational for both of them to confess. Seven years in prison each, again.

Notice that even if Bonnie and Clyde had promised each other to stay loyal, once they are in the prison cell, they are still better off confessing. What can hold them to the promise? And if you believe the other person will keep their promise, you now have the chance of getting away free. But, once more, remember that the other person will reason in parallel terms.

Cooperation and Public Goods

Although of course it can happen, two people rarely face the situation of deciding whether to confess to a crime or keep quiet. So in that sense the prisoner's dilemma, while a fascinating example, is not a good model for thinking about morality. But the basic idea has wide application. In life you often face the choice of either cooperating and or not cooperating. For example, suppose there is a water shortage and the city government asks us all to follow a voluntary scheme to conserve reserves. I might reason like this: If everyone else is careful with water, then we will be fine; so I may as well have my usual deep bath and water my garden because in a city of millions, one person's wasteful use won't be enough to make a difference. On the other hand, if everyone else carries on as usual and the water runs out, my making a sacrifice won't solve the problem and my efforts are pointless. So whatever everyone else does, I may as well have my usual bath and water my flower beds. Of course if everyone reasons like this, the city will run out of water; but if we all are more careful, we may well be able to ride out the problem until the next rain increases the reservoir supply.

The intriguing thing about these examples is that in purely self-interested terms, the rational thing seems to be to act selfishly because that is better for you. But perversely, if everyone acts in their own self-interest, we all do worse than if everyone cooperates—even though, in a sense, it is irrational to cooperate. Once the example is explained in this way, we can see that many situations in life have this structure, although typically large numbers of people are involved rather than just two. This wider effect turns the game into what is called the multiperson prisoner's dilemma, which is broadly equivalent to an issue known as the **public goods problem**.

In economic theory, what are known as public goods can create problems. Consider, for example, the supply of streetlights. If I live on a dark street, I might very much want streetlights, as do my neighbors. If I decide to install and pay for the lights myself, all my neighbors will get the benefit too; this is why they are called public goods, because you cannot restrict their supply only to those who have paid for them. Equally, if my neighbor installs the lights, then I'll get the benefit free. So I might sit tight, waiting for someone else to put them up. But likely we will all do this, and so we will have to put up with the dark even if all of us would be happy to pay for the lights or at least make a contribution. The problem, then, is that public goods—things one person pays for but that benefit others—tend to be undersupplied relative to demand. Conversely, "public bads," such as pollution, tend to be "oversupplied" because they are ways for one person to dump his or her costs on the population as a whole.

The obvious solution to the problems of public goods and public bads, such as streetlights and pollution, is government action. The government should tax us to provide streetlights, and punish us if we pollute, thereby enforcing a level of cooperation that benefits us all. And indeed, this was Thomas Hobbes's argument calling for the Leviathan (as he named his book) to be an "absolute sovereign": in effect, a powerful dictator who would enforce cooperation and give us the safety and security we need to bring us out of the war of all against all in the state of nature. Now Hobbes is right that we will need some forms of structure to solve our coordination problems, though luckily it seems he was wrong to think that only an absolute dictator could do the job. Indeed a question arises, though: Do we need to appeal to political action at all to solve our basic problem of how to achieve beneficial cooperation? We might be able to do it by internalizing norms of behavior. These norms of behavior take the form of moral laws or principles and might work as well, or even better, than the force of law.

Accordingly, the idea of morality as a social contract reflects the idea that each of us, individually, will be better off if everyone is restrained and cooperative. For the point is that in many social situations, narrowly conceived, the rational thing for me to do is defect and pursue my own self-interest. But if we all do that, we find ourselves in the world of Colin Turnbull's Ik people (see Chapter 6) or Hobbes's state of nature. And who would want that?

In fact we can return to the case of Bonnie and Clyde to see the point. In the example described, Bonnie and Clyde are in a one-off situation. But suppose this sort of thing happens to them fairly often. They would soon learn that they are much better off cooperating rather than defecting, and so a practice of automatic cooperation may grow up: Never confess, never rat on anyone else. The idea of honor among thieves is exactly this. Giving evidence against others is bad for the group, and as a result they are likely to find ways of punishing you, somehow or other, if you do. Evolved conventions of not ratting are a form of social contract morality among criminals.

We can see now why the idea "You scratch my back, and I'll scratch yours" doesn't really capture the essence of the social contract. Rather, we need something like this: "I'll develop the habit of scratching other people's backs even if there is nothing in it for me, as long as other people develop the habit of scratching my back even if there is nothing in it for them." In other words, social contract morality works best when it doesn't look like a form of contract at all. If it looks too explicitly like a contract, people might start to ask whether it is in their interests to stop cooperating. And then the contract will unravel.

DEVELOPING THE CONTRACT ARGUMENT

So far, then, it seems that we can represent morality as a type of compromise agreement between self-interested people that works best if it doesn't look like a compromise. But does this argument really work?

Recall that we contrasted the idea of a social contract among equals with the one-sided social contracts introduced by Glaucon (a conspiracy of the weak against the strong) and Rousseau (a conspiracy of the rich against the poor), as well as with Pateman's sexual contract and Mills's racial contract. A social contract among equals would have to be equally appealing to all people, whatever their characteristics. But is it really possible to imagine the terms of a compromise agreement that would be equally acceptable to all?

Some philosophers have argued that if we accept social contract reasoning, we will end up with a very minimal moral code. Everyone will accept some basic rules of security: not to be killed for arbitrary reasons, for example. But what else? Would everyone agree that theft is wrong? What about those people who own nothing? To take even more troubling examples, a key part of our contemporary morality holds that sexual violence against women is a serious wrong, as is racial discrimination. But would every man sign up to a restriction on sexual violence against women? Disturbingly, as we know, some men would not wish to be bound by this restriction on what they are permitted to do. And would every member of the privileged races sign up to an agreement not to discriminate against other races? Remember that the argument is meant to be based on what would best advance each individual's own self-interest in the long run, rather than an independent appeal to moral intuitions. After all, the social contract theory is being offered as an account of the ultimate basis of our morality.

Therefore it pre-supposes that no "deeper" morality exists to constrain the social contract. So it is pretty unclear, given our wide and sometimes unsettling diversity of interests, whether we would get much if anything out of a social contract as an agreement among literally all people. We can call this the problem of opposed interests. If we have opposed interests, the scope for agreement shrinks. It might come close to vanishing altogether.

For this reason, the contemporary philosopher John Rawls (1921–2002) argued that we have to imagine the social contract taking place under very special and unusual conditions. Rawls, who was primarily a political philosopher, used the idea of the social contract to devise principles of political justice for society in terms of theories for the just distribution of liberty, opportunity, income, and wealth. He did not present the social contract as primarily a theory of individual morality. But nevertheless, his ideas are inspiring and will help us make progress in thinking through how to get beyond the problem of opposed interests.

As we saw, if we have opposed interests, then we are unlikely to be able to agree to very much beyond the most basic, limited security. And of course, we do have opposed or at least different interests. But in a brilliant move, Rawls suggested that in thinking about the contract you would make, you should suppose that you don't know what your interests are. Imagine you don't know whether you are rich or poor, male or female, black or white. Suppose you don't know how old you are, or what your religion is (if you even have one), or what skills or talents you have. Rawls uses the metaphor of the **veil of ignorance** to express this idea: In thinking about drawing up the social contract, you should imagine yourself being behind the veil, knowing nothing that differentiates you from other people. Using the device of the veil of ignorance allows the contract to reflect the idea of equality. Rawls also refers to this situation as the **original position**.

From behind the veil of ignorance, would you approve of sexual violence against women? Obviously not; because you have more or less a 50 percent chance of being a woman, you would not want to accept that amount of risk of being a victim of serious harm. Equally, you would not want to take the risk of living in a society that accepted racial discrimination, in case you ended up on the receiving end. And not knowing whether you were rich or poor probably means that you would not accept a morality that permitted theft (in case it turns out you are rich), but equally you would not accept a society in which the poor were left starving and homeless (in case it turns out you are poor). The advantage of this model is that it seems to be able to derive moral rules not by relying on our moral intuitions, but by combining concern for our own self-interest with ignorance about what our interests are. On this basis we have to come up with rules that are in the interests of everyone, and in that respect fair. Hence social contract theory can be a perfect tool for people thinking about gender and race equality as well as justice for other groups who have historically faced discrimination. Indeed it requires us to focus on the worst off, to see things from their point of view. And in this respect Rawls's position is reminiscent of a view expressed by Mahatma Gandhi (1869–1948), leader of the movement for Indian independence from British rule. Here is one of the last notes Gandhi wrote before he died:

> I will give you a talisman. Whenever you are in doubt, or when the self becomes too much with you, apply the following test. Recall the face of the poorest and the weakest man [woman] whom you may have seen, and ask yourself, if the step you contemplate is going to be of any use to him [her]. Will he [she] gain anything by it? Will it restore him [her] to a control over his [her] own life and destiny? In other words, will it lead to swaraj [freedom] for the hungry and spiritually starving millions?
>
> Then you will find your doubts and your self melt away. (Gandhi, 1948/1958, p. 65)

Here is an obvious question, though: Why should, say, a privileged, rich white man be interested in this argument? If I were behind the veil of ignorance, such a person might say, I might well choose rules that are fair to everyone; but from my position of knowledge, I prefer rules that favor me. This question shows that Rawls's methodology presupposes a type of human goodwill: that human beings do want to find fair terms of cooperation. Therefore, Rawls's contract methodology does not provide an answer to the moral skeptic. Its purpose is to offer a procedure for turning what he calls "a sense of justice" into an explicit moral code that is capable of taking everyone's interests into account.

Beyond Rules and Regulations

We have come quite a distance from the idea that the social contract provides simply a peace treaty or compromise between competing interests. Social contract theory opens up the possibly of thinking about morality in a much more positive way. In some respects, perhaps, morality has had relatively bad press: When we think about morality, we think about rules and regulations that hold us in check. When we use the term *ethics*, we often think about codes of professional conduct: medical ethics, business ethics, ethical investing, and so on, to keep us on the straight and narrow and stop us from falling into temptation or laziness. In this view morality is all about keeping us to the code, curbing our short-term selfish instincts for the sake of long-term mutual interest.

But as we have seen, there are other ways of thinking about ethical behavior. We admire people for their kindness, their friendliness, their openness, and their generosity. These people are good to be around, for they help create a spirit of collective enjoyment and enrich our lives. As David Hume (1711–76) puts it, they help bring about "at proper intervals play, frolic, and gaiety" (1751/1983, p. 79). Could morality exist not merely for mutual protection but also for mutual fulfillment? In this view, the point of morality is to help us add to the value of other people's lives both individually and collectively rather than to save us from each other.

Karl Marx criticized "bourgeois" politics and morality on the grounds that in giving us rights to protect us from each other, it encourages each of us to see others as a threat to our own freedom. Marx wanted us to think of a different form of society where we achieve fulfillment through our interaction with others. Admittedly this still represents morality as a device for mutual interest, but in a rather different way. It encourages us to see each other not so much as threats to our interests, but as encouragement to our own flourishing. And whether or not you believe, like Marx, that a radical transformation of society is possible, Marx surely has a good point, even about current society. How valuable and enjoyable would your life be without the existence of other people: not just your family and friends, but artists, actors, sportspeople, scientists, inventors, entrepreneurs, poets, writers; and, dare I say it, philosophers? Could it be that part of the nature of morality is to encourage us to take on roles and functions that enhance the lives of others and not just to save us from each other?

Social Contract Theory in Practice

It is plausible, then, to argue that behind the veil of ignorance we would agree to an extensive set of moral duties—both negatively, to ensure our safety and survival, and positively, to help us achieve flourishing lives of joy and well-being. At the same time, however, we can see some limitations. Let's consider two moral questions that a significant number of people face in their ordinary lives. First, when, if ever, should you decide that an elderly, very sick relative should not undergo further heroic surgery but should be allowed to pass in relative comfort? Second, under what circumstances, if any, should abortion be permitted? Can the social contract help us?

In many cases, putting yourself behind the veil of ignorance can help. Let's start with the case of the elderly relative. Suppose it is your great aunt, whom you love dearly, and you are her closest living relative. And suppose she is beyond the point where she can make decisions for herself, and she has never been very clear about what she would prefer in these situations. Here are some thoughts that might be going through your head:

1. Life is sacred and should be preserved at all costs.
2. I love my great-aunt very much and do not want her to die.
3. Her quality of life is very low, and she is in a great deal of pain.
4. Surgery might extend her life but will add to her pain, at least at first.
5. She might die during surgery or as a result of complications.
6. Visiting her in the hospital and arranging for her care are becoming a burden for me.
7. If she dies, I will probably inherit part of her estate.

How can you think clearly about this situation and make sure you do the right thing? The first thing you will try to do, most likely, is banish some thoughts from your head. The last one, that you will inherit something if she dies, seems "unworthy" in some sense; you would hope to be able to make a decision ignoring that factor. But what about the fact that you love her and don't want her to die, and that visiting her has become a burden? Are these reasons you should take into account, or are they "too selfish"? Perhaps, but perhaps not. Would your great-aunt be worried about becoming too much of a burden?

To use the veil of ignorance methodology, you need to work out what you would want in exactly this kind of case, where you don't know whether you were your great-aunt or yourself. This really comes down to three things. What do you want? What does your great-aunt want? And if you disagree, what are the most important considerations that should be decisive? The veil of ignorance allows you to come to a view about the relative importance of these reasons without considering the thought that the reasons may favor, or go against, your own interests.

Quite likely, therefore, the key factors will be not only the pain and distress that your great-aunt suffers and how that might become even worse if she has the operation but also how much she valued extending her life for its own sake. But the issue of the burden on others is a factor too, and how her death would affect people; although you are likely to think these are usually minor considerations when judged against life or death for another person. Cases will vary, leading to different outcomes, but the key idea behind veil of ignorance reasoning is that it seems a helpful way of focusing on the most serious issues. In effect it helps us to apply a very familiar idea about morality: the importance of seeing things from the other person's point of view. What would you want if you were the other person affected? In this case, what would you want if you were in your great-aunt's position? This is not to say that there will always be an easy answer, but it can move us forward in our deliberations.

The question of abortion, though, is much harder to approach based on contract methodology. As always we must ask which people are affected and therefore need to be part of the contract. Obviously, the woman considering having an abortion; and in most cases, her partner too. But what about the unborn fetus? Is a fetus a person who should be regarded as a party to the contract? If it is, then the social contract would presumably yield the outcome that abortion is almost always wrong. Why would you agree to an abortion if you were the fetus? You would be agreeing to your own death, and how could that be rational? On the other hand, if the fetus is not a person, at least at an early stage of pregnancy, then it cannot be a party to the contract. Although there may still be reasons against abortion, from a social contract point of view the question looks much less problematic. Social contract theory, then, defers the issue of the morality of abortion without solving it. We have to decide who or what is a party to the contract before we can even get started.

And we can make similar observations about human relations to animals. If animals are part of the social contract, then we should give up eating animals or experimenting on them because, for all you know, according to the methodology, you are an animal. And why, therefore, would you agree to be experimented on or eaten? But if animals are not part of the social contract, our current behavior looks much less problematic. In sum, although the veil of ignorance can be a helpful way of thinking about some moral problems, it cannot solve all of them. It needs to make a decision about who "counts"; and as Rousseau, Pateman, and Mills have argued, historically it has not been good at treating poor people, women, and people of color as equals. Nevertheless, as long as we avoid these traps, the veil of ignorance is an extremely valuable method to have available.

CHAPTER REVIEW
Summary

At the beginning of this chapter, Glaucon's speech presents the view that morality is a compromise. All people would ideally like to pursue their own self-interest, but, know that if everyone did the same thing, life would go very badly. Therefore we implicitly agree on a set of moral rules as a type of compromise or peace treaty. I then introduced various theories suggesting that the "real" social contract is one in which one group uses morality to consolidate its oppression of another. But we saw that this does not need to be so, and a contract of equals is also possible. The prisoner's dilemma was used to illustrate the reasoning involved. However, given that different people have opposed interests, social contract morality looks minimal: There is not all that much everyone would agree to.

One reply to this issue was to extend the idea of the social contract, using John Rawls's method of the veil of ignorance. If we tried to imagine what we would agree to without knowing which role we would play in the situation, then our decisions likely would converge much more, and we would devise rules that are fair to everyone. Indeed we might well devise rules that go beyond mutual protection to thinking about methods of advancing our interests in many positive ways. Still, we did notice some remaining problems. Who is a party to the social contract? Unborn children? Animals? In some of the most difficult cases, social contract methodology needs to be supplemented by other types of arguments. Even so, we did see that social contract reasoning can help us think our way through some thorny ethical issues. In particular, it helps us separate the genuinely important central issues from those that may seem important from one point of view but have less moral weight when compared to other reasons.

Discussion Questions

1. Is the idea of the social contract a way of advancing one group's interests over another?
2. How does the prisoner's dilemma help illustrate the idea of the social contract?
3. Explain Rawls's idea of the veil of ignorance.
4. What are the limitations of the social contract argument?

Key Terms

Sophist, p. 109

social contract, p. 109

instrumental value, p. 110

intrinsic value, p. 110

game theory, p. 112

prisoner's dilemma, p. 112

public goods problem, p. 114

veil of ignorance, p. 117

original position, p. 117

Key Thinkers

Plato (429?–347 BCE), pp. 108–110

Thomas Hobbes (1588–1679), pp. 109, 112, 115

Fyodor Dostoyevsky (1821–81), p. 110

Friedrich Nietzsche (1844–1900), pp. 110–111

Jean-Jacques Rousseau (1712–88), pp. 110–111, 121

Karl Marx (1818–83), pp. 111, 119

Carole Pateman (b. 1940), p. 111

Charles Mills (b. 1951), pp. 111–112

John Rawls (1921–2002), pp. 117–118, 122

Mahatma Gandhi (1869–1948), p. 118

David Hume (1711–76), p. 119

Further Reading

▪ Passages from Plato's *Republic* are quoted from the edition published by W. W. Norton (1999).

▪ The edition of Thomas Hobbes's *Leviathan* used here is from W. W. Norton (1996). (Original work published 1651)

▪ Fyodor Dostoyevsky's *Crime and Punishment* is available in a Penguin (2003) edition. (Original work published 1866)

▪ Friedrich Nietzsche's account of Christian morality is set out in his book *Beyond Good and Evil*, available in a Vintage (1989) edition. (Original work published 1886)

▪ Jean-Jacques Rousseau is quoted from *A Discourse on Inequality* (Penguin, 1985). (Original work published 1754)

▪ Jean-Jacques Rousseau's *The Social Contract* is available in a Penguin (1968) edition. (Original work published 1762)

▪ For a brief account of the thought of Karl Marx, see Jonathan Wolff, *Why Read Marx Today?* (Oxford University Press, 2002).

▪ The most accessible work by Marx is *The Communist Manifesto*, cowritten with Friedrich Engels. Many editions are available. It is reprinted in the *Marx-Engels Reader* (2nd ed.), published by W. W. Norton (1978), edited by Robert Tucker. (Original work published 1848)

- For a basic introduction to game theory, including the prisoner's dilemma, see William Spaniel, *Game Theory 101: The Complete Textbook* (CreateSpace Independent Publishing Platform, 2011).

- John Rawls's *A Theory of Justice* was first published in 1971, with a revised edition in 1999. It is published by Harvard University Press.

- Mahatma Gandhi's note on the "talisman" is hard to find, but can be viewed online at www.mkgandhi.org/gquots1.htm (retrieved January 17, 2017). It is from Pyarelal, *Mahatma Gandhi: The Last Phase, Volume II* (Navajivan Publishing House, 1958; out of print). (Original note written 1948)

- David Hume is quoted from *An Enquiry Concerning the Principles of Morals* (Hackett, 1983). (Original work published 1751)

- Relevant selections from Plato, Hobbes, Nietzsche, and Rawls are included in Jonathan Wolff (ed.), *Readings in Moral Philosophy* (W. W. Norton, 2018).

CHAPTER 8

Utilitarianism: Bentham and Mill

[The object of] the principle of utility .... is to rear the fabric of felicity by the hands of reason and of law. Systems which attempt to question it, deal in sounds instead of sense, in caprice instead of reason, in darkness instead of light.

But enough of metaphor and declamation: it is not by such means that moral science is to be improved.

JEREMY BENTHAM, INTRODUCTION TO
THE PRINCIPLES OF MORALS AND LEGISLATION

In the first few chapters of this book, we explored some ways that morality, and with it moral philosophy, has been under attack. Cultural relativism, skepticism, subjectivism, and determinism all threaten to disrupt our ordinary moral views, and therefore the merits of these challenges needed to be assessed. We then examined several approaches to morality that, in very different ways, attempt to produce positive moral theories. Theories of divine command, natural law, ethical egoism, and the social contract all propose accounts of what we ought to do, morally speaking, even though several of these views are related to positions that in many ways are critical of ordinary morality.

Beginning with Chapter 8 and continuing through Chapter 13, we will look in greater detail at the three theories currently dominating debate in moral philosophy: utilitarianism, Kantian deontology, and virtue ethics. In Chapter 14 we will focus on feminist ethics and also discuss the ethics of race. These newer approaches, which are growing in importance and influence, challenge mainstream ethical thinking and propose ways of recasting moral philosophy to overcome those critiques. Finally, in Chapter 15, we will explore how the theories explored here can help you develop your own moral outlook. But we start Chapter 8 by looking closely at the theory of utilitarianism, introduced by Jeremy Bentham and developed further by John Stuart Mill.

THE CONTEXT OF BENTHAM'S MORAL PHILOSOPHY

Jeremy Bentham (1748–1832) is normally regarded as the founder of utilitarianism, the theory that takes its inspiration from the creed known as the greatest happiness principle.

By the principle of utility is meant that principle which approves or disapproves of every action whatsoever, according to the tendency which it appears

125

to have to augment or diminish the happiness of the party whose interest is in question: or, what is the same thing in other words, to promote or to oppose that happiness. (Bentham, 1789/1970, chap. 1, sec. 2, p. 12)

Bentham's idea is that when we make a moral decision, the right action is the one that does most to maximize what he calls utility. **Utility** is understood first in terms of happiness and then as the balance of pleasure over pain. In each case these terms replace a more abstract idea with a more concrete one, thus ending up with concepts that are easy to understand and assess. Utility is a philosopher's abstraction, whereas pleasure and pain are real and can be felt. Happiness, as generally understood, is not quite the same thing as pleasure. Happiness or unhappiness seems to take place for an extended period, whereas pleasures and pains are often much shorter experiences. But generally happiness and pleasure are closely related, and Bentham finds that formulating the theory in terms of pleasure and pain makes it more precise and easier to apply.

And indeed applying the theory seems relatively straightforward. Where only one person is involved, utilitarianism approves of whatever maximizes the balance of pleasure over pain for that individual. When more than one person is involved, the calculation becomes a little more complex. We will have to compare and add together the different pleasures and pains of different people. Obviously this raises questions about how to measure and compare pains and pleasures. We will return to this issue, but for now we have the basic idea. Utilitarians have to consider the effects of an action on the pleasure and pain of everyone who is affected by it and then pursue the option that is expected to yield the greatest sum total of pleasure over pain. Doing so, they believe, will generate the greatest happiness for the greatest number.

This simple theory needs considerable unpacking; but before we look at the details, it is worth understanding the context in which Bentham produced his theory. Only then will we appreciate the importance and distinctive character of his approach. As with any thinker, it can be helpful to consider the intellectual climate in which he or she wrote, and in particular to consider who or what they opposed or felt compelled to dispute. Bentham gives us a powerful clue in an argument for the theory of utilitarianism early in his book *An Introduction to the Principles of Morals and Legislation*. Denying that it is possible to find a direct proof for utilitarianism, "for that which is used to prove every thing else cannot itself be proved" (Bentham, 1789/1970, p. 13), Bentham offers a type of indirect proof. He lays out what he considers to be all available moral positions, including utilitarianism, and presents arguments to defeat the alternative theories. This is an interesting argumentative strategy; if it succeeds, it leaves utilitarianism as the only theory left standing and therefore the victor. We can call this an **argument by elimination** because it attempts to eliminate all competitors.

In fact, though, Bentham considers only three moral positions, apparently regarding them as the only three possibilities. One, of course, is his own utilitarian view. A second is what he calls the principle of sympathy and antipathy, which approves or disapproves of actions purely on the basis of a person's attitudes. And a third is the principle of asceticism (using the term *asceticism* in a somewhat unconventional sense), which is the mirror image of utilitarianism. In considering this rather strange possibility, he supposes that we should maximize pain rather than pleasure. Bentham's arguments against these views will help us understand his position; on the surface it is curious that he chose to discuss these unusual positions rather than the writings of the great moral philosophers, such as Plato (429?–347 BCE) and Aristotle (384–322 BCE), which he virtually ignores. But Bentham's choice is highly revealing.

To see why, we need to look at the foundation for Bentham's utilitarianism. We can read Bentham as being driven by three fundamental convictions. First, he believed that morality requires everyone to be treated as an equal: "Everyone is to count for one, no-one for more than one." This view, which is implicit throughout his work, contrasts with elitist or discriminatory views that presupposed men were worth more than women, people of one race or religion more than another, or aristocrats worth more than commoners. In Bentham's time, forms of discrimination ran through much of ordinary life. For example, it was not until Bentham's old age that it became possible to obtain a university education in England for those who were not both male and prepared to assent to the articles of the Church of England. His fundamental premise of equality would have judged these restrictions as quite unjustified.

Second, Bentham believed that ultimately the only things in the world that matter are the pleasures and pains of sentient creatures—including humans, of course, but also animals. Although some readers will think it obvious that only pleasure and pain matter, in fact many common moral views have very different implications. For example, traditional religious moralities give value to suffering (paying penance) or rule some pleasures immoral (eating the wrong food, dancing in the wrong way, playing games on the Sabbath.)

Third, Bentham was convinced that morality, and good governance, has to be based on firm principles. The alternative to principled reasoning is, he thought, to let individual opinion dominate. Then we leave ourselves open to, at best, uncertainty and inconsistency; and at worst, prejudice and corruption, especially at the level of government. In his later work Bentham devised the concept of "sinister interests," by which he meant that those in power will often be tempted to advance their own interests rather than follow the common good. He argued that firm, reliable principles are needed to guard against this type of corrupt use of power.

Bentham's utilitarianism is an interpretation of the first conviction mentioned, that everyone is to count for one and no one for more than one. And in summary, Bentham's arguments against the principle of asceticism (the theory that we should maximize pain) rely on the second of these convictions, asserting the importance of pleasure and the avoidance of pain. And his arguments against the principle of sympathy and antipathy—what he also calls the principle of "caprice"—rely on the third conviction, asserting the importance of firm principles.

Elimination of Asceticism

Let's look at these alternative theories and the arguments against them in a little more detail. For Bentham the principle of asceticism, which demands maximizing pain over pleasure, is easily dismissed. Bentham points out, fairly enough, that probably no one has ever held such a view—which may make you wonder why he thinks it even worth considering. Those who seem to advocate it, so he suggests, are really defending another view: that mortifying your flesh on earth improves your chances of going to heaven and enjoying a blissful afterlife. The pain is worth the pleasure. But as Bentham points out, this is merely a form of the utilitarian view, albeit one held by those who believe in a religious doctrine about life after death and what they need to do on earth to enter heaven rather than hell. Bentham's real targets are the religious moralists, those who wish to suppress earthly pleasures based on what Bentham regards as a false and pernicious religious doctrine. In arguing against the principle of asceticism, he was attacking some version of severe religious puritanism.

In fact, as noted earlier, we should see utilitarianism as opposed not just to the principle of asceticism, which is an austere and implausible moral theory, but to a whole range of moral theories based on or influenced by religious views that see virtue in the practice of less-demanding kinds of self-denial. Customary and religious moralities contain rules that, in Bentham's view, lead to the denial of pleasure or the imposition of harm for no good reason. For example, we saw in an earlier chapter Bentham's response to the view that the only legitimate form of sex is that between husband and wife for the purposes of reproduction. This belief had led, in England during the 18th and 19th centuries, to the prohibition of contraception and the official suppression of sex in other forms. In practice this view caused people enormous anxiety and guilt, not to mention unwanted pregnancies, perilous illegal abortions, and the abandonment of newborn children. Indeed Bentham's follower John Stuart Mill (1806–73), who we will discuss shortly, spent a night in jail as a teenager for distributing a pamphlet explaining the principles of contraception. Mill took up that campaign after his shocking experience of finding a dead newborn baby in a London park (Reeves, 2008). Ignorance of contraception had led to great misery, especially for scared young women for whom pregnancy could mean ruin. And, Bentham and Mill would ask, what was the purpose of suppressing contraception? It was certainly not for the sake of human happiness. Bentham considered the principle of asceticism, and its milder forms in which customary or religious moral rules lead to great pain, not pleasure, to be wholly irrational.

And indeed Bentham points out that the principle of asceticism is really a personal code of conduct rather than a theory of morality:

> We read of saints who, for the good of their souls, and the mortification of their bodies, have voluntarily yielded themselves a prey to vermin: but though many persons of this class have wielded the reins of empire, we read of none who have set themselves to work, and made laws on purpose, with a view of stocking the body politic with the breed of highwaymen, housebreakers or incendiaries. (1789/1970, p. 20)

Elimination of the Principle of Sympathy and Antipathy

What, then, of the principle of sympathy and antipathy? What is this principle? Consider how you might ordinarily go about making a moral decision. Your friend has asked you to help him move some furniture over the weekend, but you are invited to a meal with a distant cousin who is on a rare visit to town, and it isn't possible to do both. Which should you do? Obviously a number of questions will go through your head. Does your friend have anyone else who could help? How critical is it for your friend to move the furniture this weekend? When could you next see your cousin? How much does it matter if you don't see her? And so on. In the end, if you are lucky, one of the options may seem clearly the correct thing to do. Alternatively the decision may continue to be difficult, and you just find yourself almost randomly choosing one over the other.

We are all familiar with situations like this one. When they arise, we consider the options carefully and try to work out what is most important. Although we might not think of our choice as explicitly a moral decision, it does involve a moral dilemma: the duties of friendship versus the duties of family. It may seem odd to describe friendship and family as involving "duties" because friendship and family involve much more than that, at least when they go well, but moral duty is at least part of the relationship. And so we try to discern the "plus" factors and the "minus" factors and weigh them up. But the problem is that we seem to be weighing without a scale. I can say that morally the right thing to do is to help my friend. But equally I could say that morally the right thing is to meet my cousin. If someone questions me, I can give my reasoning. But within certain limits I can twist what I say to fit my decision, whatever it is, and no one can confidently say that I have made a mistake. There is no formula that anyone else, or even me myself, can follow to check my reasoning.

This process, according to Bentham, is how we reason using the "principle of sympathy and antipathy" and why it is so problematic: It is liable to misuse, even corruption, because it has no principle or formula for decision making, no mechanism of accountability. It is hostage to the biases of the powerful. For example, Bentham worried that such reasoning would lead us to over-punish those who had broken the law. And this is why a formula, like the principle of utility, is so attractive. It provides a rigorous framework, unlike the methods used by some of Bentham's philosophical predecessors, who were known as **moral sense** thinkers. Bentham thought those philosophers wrapped up ordinary moral intuitions into a pretend moral theory, thereby giving us no insight into morality or assistance with moral reasoning. In contrast, utilitarianism offers a firm guide and principle.

CLARIFYING UTILITARIANISM

Bentham's formulation of utilitarianism seems clear and succinct, but it is worth spending the time to come to a fuller understanding. Later theorists have helpfully split the theory into two parts, what they call a **theory of the good** and a **theory of the right**. A theory of the good tells us what sort of things in the world are good (and bad); a theory of the right focuses on our actions, telling us which actions are right and wrong. Utilitarianism is the theory that the *right* thing to do is always to bring about as much *good* as possible. This may seem to be obviously true, to the point of triviality. After all, what else should we do? Bring about less good than we could? But we will see, especially in the following chapters, that this apparent obviousness is deceptive: Oddly, sometimes the right thing to do might be to bring about less good than we could have done, at least when we understand the term *good* as Bentham defines it. Therefore let's look first at Bentham's theory of the good in order to understand what is at stake in this debate.

Bentham's Theory of the Good

To start, we need to investigate what sorts of things Bentham considers good and bad. Quite clearly he regards happiness, which as we saw he understands in terms of pleasure, as good; and he views unhappiness, or pain, as bad. Few would disagree with Bentham that happiness or pleasure is generally good or that unhappiness or pain is bad—although as we have already seen, Bentham did think he had opponents even on these points.

But there are at least two points of potential controversy. First, Bentham has a wide concept of pleasure, and he divides it into many subcategories. His philosophical habit was to be as systematic as possible, racking his brains to find every variety of the phenomenon he was discussing. He distinguished many varieties of pleasure: from the relatively innocent, including the pleasures of sense (such as enjoying the fragrance of a rose) to the much more questionable, such as the pleasures of being malevolent. Would we agree that the world is a better place if people take pleasure in the misfortune of others, for example, cheering up when hearing that someone they dislike has been injured in a car crash?

Bentham also makes the important claim that pleasure or happiness is the *only thing* that is good, and pain or displeasure the *only thing* that is bad. Can this be right? John Stuart Mill made the same claim. We will postpone discussion of this important topic until Chapter 9, where we will also look at criticisms of the theory.

Measuring Happiness

In the meantime, let's consider one serious question about utilitarianism. Remember that the theory requires us to maximize the sum total of pleasure over pain. But can we even make sense of the idea of maximizing pleasure? If we are to maximize the totality of pleasures over pain, first we have to be able to measure them and put them on the same scale. How can we even compare pains and pleasures against each other?

Bentham was keenly aware of this problem. In his book *Introduction to the Principles of Morals and Legislation* (1789/1970), he wrote a short chapter attempting to explain how to measure pleasure and pain; in a footnote added later, he includes a short verse as a type of aide-mémoire for the theory. The verse begins:

> *Intense, long, certain, speedy, fruitful, pure—*
> Such marks in *pleasures* and in *pains* endure.

The first line picks out the six features by which, according to Bentham, we can measure individual pleasures and pain: (1) intensity; (2) duration;

(3) certainty or uncertainty; (4) propinquity or remoteness, meaning distance in time; (5) fecundity, explained as its likelihood of being followed by other pleasures; and (6) purity, or its chances of not being followed by the opposite (i.e., that a pleasure will not be followed by a pain).

Some of these ideas seem straightforward, such as that we should take duration into account. Others, such as remoteness, are controversial. Should we discount future pleasures and pains in the sense of giving them less weight in our calculations? True, future anticipated pleasures or pains are less certain to happen. But this thought should be accommodated already under the category of certainty. This somewhat technical sounding issue is a matter of enormous practical importance in the contemporary world. If, for example, we do discount future pleasures and pains, then the issue of climate change, which will affect people in the distant future, will be less morally important. Arguably, including remoteness violates the idea that everyone—including future people—is to count as one.

But the main question is whether Bentham has given us enough information about measurement to be able to apply the theory. Now, some types of comparison of pleasure and pain are easy. A pain that lasts two days must surely be worse than one of the same intensity that lasts two minutes. Accordingly, we can rank one as worse than the other. This is known as an ordinal scale: putting different items into an *order* of better or worse, in the same way we can say that today was warmer than yesterday. But this is not enough to allow us to make the necessary utilitarian calculation. First, it seems, we need to make what are known as cardinal measurements: being able to put *numbers* on different pleasures and pains, just as a thermometer allows us to do for temperature or scales for weight. For maximizing to make sense, we need numbers. And not only that, but we need to be able to compare one person's pleasure or pain with another; this is known as the problem of **interpersonal comparisons of utility**. The difficult question is how to measure intensity. Bentham is clear that intensity matters: after all, it is the first thing on his list. But he passes over the issue of intensity very quickly and gives us no real help in working out how to measure it.

And so we can see that the information we need in order to be a utilitarian is demanding, but also worrying, lacking. We need a "pleasure measure"—but even with recent advances in neuroscience, we don't have a device like a thermometer that can measure our happiness.

But perhaps we should not exaggerate the problem. Maybe it is possible to make intuitive judgments that are close enough. After all, a thriving body of research is now asking what makes us happy. It also asks whether we are happier now than people used to be in less technologically advanced times (apparently not) and whether the people of one nation are happier than another. In 2014, for example, a study called "The World Happiness Report" named Denmark as the happiest country on earth, while the OECD Better Life 2012 Index (which looks only at wealthier countries that are members of the Organisation for Economic Co-operation and Development) put Switzerland on top for life satisfaction, Norway in second place, and Denmark in third.

And what innovative scientific methodology was used to derive this ranking? Brain scans? Advanced computer modeling? In fact two simple methods were used. In one, people from each country were asked to rank their satisfaction with life on a scale from 0 to 10. Switzerland topped the scale with an average of 7.7. Greece, in severe economic recession, was at the other end of the scale, and the United States fell somewhere in the middle. The other method measured happiness through positive experiences and feelings such as enjoyment, feeling well-rested, smiling or laughing, together with the absence of negative experiences and feelings such as pain, worry, or sadness. Iceland, Japan, and New Zealand do well on this measure, with troubled Greece again near the bottom.

In other words, it seems we can do some sort of measurement of happiness just by talking to people and asking questions about how they feel. Perhaps measuring happiness is not so hard after all. Remember that Bentham replaced the notion of happiness and unhappiness with pleasure and pain at least partly on the grounds that these are more precise, observable, and scientific notions. The first of these measures, asking about life satisfaction, seems to be concerned with happiness. The second one, in asking about positive and negative experiences, seems closer to measuring pleasure and pain.

Now, many questions could be raised. If I say that my satisfaction is 7 out of 10, and you also say the same thing, does that really mean we are equally happy? Perhaps I am fairly miserable but have low expectations of what is possible, while you are ecstatically happy but feel that you have not yet reached your full potential. We must concede that, at best, these types of methods are imprecise or rough and ready. Yet there does seem to be something to them.

We might be able to measure pleasure and pain precisely enough to apply utilitarian theory and then choose to act in a way that maximizes the balance of pleasure over pain. Bentham certainly assumed so. We can be at least moderately confident that the theory can be applied, but it does seem to require a degree of intuitive judgment that Bentham would have regarded as less than ideal.

UTILITARIANISM AND EQUALITY FOR WOMEN

Jeremy Bentham's utilitarianism became very well known in the early part of the 19th century, attracting both devoted followers and severe critics. In 1861, more than 70 years after Bentham first published *An Introduction to the Principles of Morals and Legislation*, John Stuart Mill published *Utilitarianism* (1861/2001) to provide further support for the theory and ward off what had become, in Mill's view, serious misunderstandings that had made many people regard the theory as narrow and uninspiring.

One such mistake, heard even today, concerns the word *utilitarian*, which seems to have the connotation of dull efficiency. For example, long after Mill's death, during the Second World War, furniture produced in the United Kingdom was stamped with something called a utility mark. This mark showed that the furniture met a standard of making the best use of scarce resources with no unnecessary frills, details, or ornamentation. A utilitarian, based on this understanding, is one who is well organized and sets out to achieve a goal but lacks style or flair. Calling someone utilitarian is often intended as a slight or insult, suggesting perhaps that they are focused only on short-term financial, bureaucratic, or narrowly practical issues and are ignoring what really matters. But for Mill a greater misinterpretation of the theory could hardly exist. The theory of utilitarianism of course seeks to achieve efficiency, but aims for efficiency in creating happiness or joy—the greatest happiness of the greatest number. In this sense there is nothing "utilitarian" about utilitarianism, as Mill understands it.

It may have been Mill's destiny to defend Bentham's theory. Mill was brought up to be a philosophical disciple of Jeremy Bentham, whom he regarded as his godfather. (In turn, Mill would later be godfather to one of the 20th century's most important philosophers, Bertrand Russell [1872–1970]—an odd chain of connection for three generations of antireligious philosophers.) Mill had an astonishingly rigorous education. He was taught Latin and Greek at a very early age, utterly devoting himself to his studies and to radical politics. He did not mix with other children, or do ordinary childhood activities such a riding a bike. Perhaps not surprisingly, he suffered something like a nervous breakdown in his twenties, after which he began to develop views that were distinct from Bentham's. Yet he continued to be greatly influenced by Bentham's thought. We will look at some of those differences later. But first, let's look at Mill's reasons for being so attracted to the utilitarian approach to ethics.

The Subjection of Women

Although Mill's text *Utilitarianism* is written to defend the theory, it gives surprisingly few examples of the advantages of utilitarianism compared to other systems of morality. In many of his other writings, however, Mill applied Bentham's ideas on the moral importance of individual happiness in order to propose liberating social reform.

For example, in his important and influential work on women's equality, *The Subjection of Women* (1869), Mill catalogues the pervasiveness of male domination, especially within conventional marriage, and examines its detrimental effects on human happiness. He likens the tyranny of marriage to slavery: the absolute and deeply unjust power of husband over wife. Mill comments that with the ending of legal slavery in the United States, "Marriage is the only actual bondage known to our law. There remain no legal slaves, except the mistress of every house" (1869/1996, p. 197). Mill was deeply influenced by his wife, Harriet Taylor, who had written on feminist topics. Indeed it is sometimes argued that Mill and Taylor effectively cowrote *The Subjection of Women*, even though it was published under Mill's name only. If so, this is a peculiar outcome for a book on this topic, although that would, perhaps, be a sign of the times in which it was written.

Mill offered many arguments for ending the tyranny and domination of men over women. He insisted that women had a right to equality. But he also appealed to utilitarian arguments, and here we can pick out four. These arguments all hold that utilitarianism demands the liberation of women because their subjection is detrimental to human happiness. First, Mill argues that it is bad for men to grow up falsely believing in their superiority over women, for this "arrogance and overbearingness" (1869/1996, p. 199) and expectation of service is likely to lead to their own misery over time. Second, by excluding women from employment in professions such as law and medicine, society is shunning half the potential talent pool. Therefore emancipation would have the effect of "doubling the mass of mental faculties available for the higher service of humanity" (p. 199). Third, the utter economic dependence of wives on their husbands gave husbands a duty to adopt safe, conventional lifestyles. In Mill's time married women could not own property, and from the moment of marriage a wife had to rely on her husband. According to Mill, having such responsibility for their wives and children led many men into quite conventional occupations. Mill claims that men became focused on accumulating resources to support their wife and provide an "advantageous match" (p. 207) for their daughters, rather than taking the risk of doing work that was more personally fulfilling or

advocating unpopular causes. Mill worries that a man known for unconventional opinions would be shunned by polite society; this would then
damage his daughters' marriage prospects. Finally, and perhaps most obviously, women in subjection lose, so argued Mill, "the most inspiriting and
elevating kind of personal enjoyment," as well as suffering "the weariness,
disappointment, and profound dissatisfaction with life" which "dries up ...
the principal fountain of human happiness" (p. 215).

Interestingly, there is a mix of arguments here. Arguments one and three
claim that men are worse off if women are subjugated, for they will become
arrogant and make conservative choices. Argument two claims that society
as a whole suffers if half its talent goes unused. And lastly, argument four—
finally, an argument that concentrates on women's interests—suggests that
women will be much happier if they have a full range of opportunities and
greater freedom. And, of course, female happiness is part of the general happiness. The utilitarian theory therefore encourages, even demands, liberation
from oppression. And this last point is the general theme of Mill's important
book *On Liberty* (1869), which again argues that creating the conditions to
encourage and enhance individual liberty advances collective happiness.

Seeing how Mill applies the theory of utilitarianism, it is easy to understand his irritation with critics who accuse utilitarianism of being a rather
dull and petty theory. For Mill, utilitarianism inspired his life's work of
arguing for the radical reform of Victorian institutions that had narrowed
and constrained human lives into conventional and frustrating patterns.
Utilitarianism, for Mill, unlocks human potential. It creates a world in
which each person can achieve happiness in his or her own way, free from
the crushing conformity that results from uncritical adherence to what has
become traditional morality.

JUSTIFYING UTILITARIANISM

Let's now take up Mill's main task in the book *Utilitarianism*: to provide
philosophical foundations for the theory, which Mill explains in terms very
similar to those of Bentham:

> The creed which accepts as the foundation of morals, "utility", or the "greatest
> happiness principle" holds that actions are right in proportion as they tend to
> promote happiness; wrong as they tend to produce the reverse of happiness.
> By happiness is intended pleasure, and the absence of pain; by unhappiness,
> pain, and the privation of pleasure. ... [P]leasure and freedom from pain,
> are the only things desirable as ends; ... all desirable things ... are desirable
> either for the pleasure inherent in themselves, or as means to the promotion
> of pleasure and the prevention of pain. (Mill, 1861/2001, p. 7)

But how, after all, is utilitarianism to be justified? Mill, like Bentham before him, recognizes the difficulty of this question. The same methodological problem seems to affect any theorist putting forward what they believe to be the most fundamental principle in any area. Normally, we show that a theory or principle is true by deriving it from a more fundamental principle. This is common practice in branches of mathematics or logic, where proofs are sometimes called derivations because they are derived from more fundamental axioms or principles. But as we go deeper and deeper, the problem becomes stark. From what can we derive the most fundamental axioms? In his memoirs, the philosopher and mathematician Bertrand Russell (mentioned above as Mill's godson) expresses his disappointment as a child on finding that in the Euclidian geometry his older brother tries to teach him, the most fundamental axioms had no proofs. They simply had to be taken on trust if any progress was to be made. But the young Russell wanted proof, not trust.

We can feel sympathy for the predicament of the utilitarian. If the principle of utility is the most fundamental axiom, how can it be proven? Yet at the same time, the attitude of not offering a proof leaves the defender of utilitarianism vulnerable. Suppose another theorist proposes another fundamental axiom that differs from utilitarianism. How are we supposed to decide between them if no form of proof is possible?

In fact we have already seen Jeremy Bentham's ingenious approach to this issue, using what we called an argument from elimination. Although he says explicitly that it is not possible to find a "direct" proof of utilitarianism, he does seem to offer an indirect attempt at proof. Recall that he argued against two other moral theories, the principle of asceticism and the principle of sympathy and antipathy. In effect he is presenting an argument for utilitarianism in two stages. In the first stage he invites us to accept that there are only three moral theories, or, at least, types of moral theories. In the second stage he argues that two of these are faulty and need to be rejected. From this it seems to follow that only one moral theory is acceptable: utilitarianism. The case is made.

How good is this argument? Well, it is not difficult to find some holes. First off, is it really true that there are only three types of moral theories? Bentham does not explain why there are only three types; and, as we noted, he has left out many other approaches to morality. But even putting that question aside, there is another weakness. Let's think about Bentham's arguments.

He rejected the principle of asceticism on the grounds that no one could really accept it. We also noted that weaker versions advocating some, though not all, self-denial seem irrational because they obstruct human happiness for no apparent good reason. Let's accept Bentham's criticism against the principle of asceticism just to see where the argument leads us. Next, he rejected the principle of sympathy and antipathy on the grounds that its approach to morality was not rigorous. In effect, this principle lacks a formula for making moral decisions. Later on we will ask whether it is too much to expect a formula. But again, for the sake of the argument let's accept that this objection points to a genuine weakness. So where are we left? Only with the conclusion that we need a formula to help us make moral decisions, and it needs to be an approach that does not suppress pleasure for no good reason.

Certainly utilitarianism is a candidate theory that meets these criteria. But—and here is the critical question—is it the only theory that does this? Do other theories provide a formula and refuse to deny happiness for no good reason? Well, yes. One simple theory says that what matters is not maximizing happiness, but equalizing it. In other words, we should strive to make sure that everyone in the world is equally happy; and so we need to pay special attention to the people who are unhappiest, even if it results in less total happiness for society. If we believe that everyone should be equally happy, we have a formula to solve our moral problems. And with a bit of ingenuity, we could devise many other formulas. Bentham has not shown that utilitarianism is our only alternative, after all.

Mill's "Proof"

Can Mill do better? He also attempted a form of proof, and it has become one of the most discussed passages in moral philosophy. Here is what he says:

> The only proof capable of being given that an object is visible, is that people actually see it. The only proof that a sound is audible, is that people hear it: and so of the other sources of our experience. In like manner, I apprehend, the sole evidence it is possible to produce that anything is desirable, is that people do actually desire it. If the end which the utilitarian doctrine proposes to itself were not, in theory and in practice, acknowledged to be an end, nothing could ever convince any person that it was so. No reason can be given why the general happiness is desirable, except that each person, so far as he believes it to be attainable, desires his own happiness. This, however, being a fact, we have not only all the proof which the case admits of, but all which it is possible to require, that happiness is a good: that each person's happiness is a good to that person, and the general happiness, therefore, a good to the aggregate of all persons. Happiness has made out its title as one of the ends of conduct, and consequently one of the criteria of morality. (Mill, 1861/2001, pp. 35–36)

Perhaps it is a little puzzling that Mill does try to prove his position even though earlier he said that questions of "ultimate ends" were not capable of direct proof. Presumably this argument is considered to be some sort of indirect proof. But in any case, how is it to be understood?

The first thing to say is that the proof seems to fall into two halves. The first half is meant to show that happiness is desirable. The second, Mill said, attempts to show that "general happiness ... [is] a good to the aggregate of all persons," a comment he seemingly intended to be another way of stating the utilitarian principle.

Let's now look more closely at the two arguments Mill makes in his "proof." The first argument begins by looking at some other questions of proof. How do we prove something is visible? How we do prove something is audible? As Mill suggests, the only way is from the fact that people see it, in the case of visibility, or hear it, in the case of audibility. Now, we could raise some questions; but for the sake of argument, let's accept Mill's claim that the only proof that something is visible is that people see it.

The argument then proceeds to the next stage. Just as the only proof that something is visible is that people see it, the only proof that something is desirable is that people desire it. This is what we saw is called an argument by **analogy** (see Chapter 1). Mill has just set out what we could call the logic of visibility. He is suggesting that the logic of the terms *visible* and *desirable* are similar enough that what we say about *visible* should, by analogy and with suitable adjustments, apply equally to *desirable*. If so, then he must next show that people actually desire happiness. But this step he takes to be so obvious that it barely needs further elaboration. And so it would follow that happiness is desirable, and the first stage of the argument is complete.

But does it all work out so neatly? Not according to the moral philosopher G. E. Moore (1873–1958):

> Well, the fallacy in this step is so obvious, that it is quite wonderful how Mill failed to see it. The fact is that "desirable" does not mean "able to be desired" as "visible" means "able to be seen." The desirable means simply what *ought* to be desired or *deserves* to be desired; just as the detestable means not what can be but what ought to be detested and the damnable what deserves to be damned. (Moore, 1903/1993, pp. 118–119)

This stinging criticism is that the terms *visible* and *desirable* simply are not analogous. *Visible* means "capable of being seen." If the analogy is to hold, then *desirable* should mean "capable of being desired." But it doesn't. Normally when we use the term *desirable*, we mean "ought to be desired." At best, when people desire something, it shows that the thing is *capable of being* desired. But it does not show that it *ought to be* desired. For example, a recovering alcoholic might say, "I really desire a drink of whiskey, but having one is not at all desirable." This is enough to show that just because someone desires something, this does not prove that it is desirable. Therefore the analogy between visible and desirable does not hold and the argument falls apart, or so say the critics such as G. E. Moore.

Certainly it is possible that Mill could have made this mistake. And if he had explained himself more clearly, that would have helped. But often in the works of the great philosophers, more is going on than appears on the surface. It is generally worth taking a bit of time to search for another way of understanding their texts before concluding that they have committed an obvious fallacy. So let's consider the distinction between *desired* and *desirable* a little further.

Essentially, as Mill's critics have claimed, simply desiring something is not enough to show that it is desirable. The alcoholic desires a drink, but having one is not desirable. Now, Mill could ask, why is it undesirable for the alcoholic to have a drink? Well, one drink could lead to another, and another, and to disastrous consequences. It turns out that what the alcoholic desires is undesirable because it is likely to defeat more substantial or important desires: to stay sober and healthy. This example, then, shows only that desires can conflict. Something desired turns out to be undesirable only because it conflicts with a more substantial desire. By this reading, we can understand Mill's position in this way: Something that is desired is desirable, unless its satisfaction would conflict with a weightier desire. He would have to admit that for the alcoholic, merely desiring a drink does not show that the drink is desirable. But he would claim that the only way we have of assessing whether something is desirable is by looking at whether, on balance, it satisfies more, or greater, desires than it frustrates. In conclusion, then, Mill would argue that the distinction between *desired* and *desirable* is not as important as G. E. Moore and other critics allege.

On this account *desirable*, for Mill, would mean something like "desired when taking everything, including future consequences, into account." Does this save the argument? Well, there are some complexities here. The view that actions can be undesirable only if they are in some way harmful is at the center of the utilitarian doctrine. So possibly Mill could be accused of using the utilitarian theory itself in his argument for the utilitarian theory. This, we saw, is known in philosophy as **begging the question**: an odd phrase that really means you are assuming what you are setting out to prove. If an argument does beg the question, then it proves nothing. Another similar way of putting the criticism is to say that Mill has used a **circular argument** (introduced in Chapter 1). An opponent of Mill could argue that an action can be desirable in ways other than by being desired. For example, an act that no one desires could still be judged as desirable for being in accordance with the will of God or the ancient traditions of our society. So it seems you do need to agree with Mill about quite a lot to find the analogy between *desirable* and *visible* plausible. Mill's "proof" is perhaps more of an *illustration of* the utilitarian view rather than an *argument for* it.

Aggregating Happiness

Perhaps I have been too hard on Mill. Perhaps he has shown that something is desirable if and only if people actually desire it (all things considered). Even so, that was only the first step in a two-stage argument. The first tries to show that happiness is desirable, and so if this stage of the argument does anything at all, it establishes what we referred to earlier in the chapter as the utilitarian *theory of the good*: that happiness and only happiness is good. It is another thing to show that the correct moral theory is the one that maximizes total or aggregate happiness, which also incorporates the utilitarian *theory of the right*. This is what the second step attempts.

Mill suggests that once it is established that each person's happiness is a good to that person, then it follows that the general happiness is to the good of the aggregate of all persons. But it is not completely clear what this means. Does it mean that the general happiness is to the good of each and every person? That could possibly follow if exactly the same things made us all equally happy. But that is not how the world works. When your team plays mine and yours wins, our happiness will go in opposite directions. Utilitarianism has to cope with the facts of life: that sometimes to make one group happy, others will have to suffer. Writing in 1788, almost 100 years before Mill published *Utilitarianism*, the great German philosopher Immanuel Kant (who we will discuss in detail in later chapters) pointed out that if each one of us pursues our own happiness, the result is much more likely to be the annihilation of society than harmony because our wills are likely to conflict. Remember from earlier chapters the Ik people, Hobbes's state of nature, and the prisoner's dilemma.

It may be tempting to say that the best defense of utilitarianism is that it just seems right. But to say this would be highly problematic. It would be approving of utilitarianism merely on the grounds that we like it. Yet this was exactly what Bentham found wrong with the principle of sympathy and antipathy. What do we say to someone who says that they don't like utilitarianism? This is why the proof of utilitarianism is so important, and why utilitarians are frustrated that it is so problematic.

CHAPTER REVIEW

Summary

This chapter began with an explanation of the theory of utilitarianism as presented by Jeremy Bentham, setting the context in which he wrote and showing his arguments against the views he opposed. I then clarified Bentham's theory by looking at his concepts of pleasure and pain, and we explored the thorny issue of the measurement of happiness. We then looked at how John Stuart Mill used the theory of utilitarianism to argue against the subjection of women. We also explored the question of how it is possible to argue for utilitarianism, looking at Bentham's argument from elimination, Mill's notorious "proof," and G. E. Moore's equally notorious reply. Utilitarianism probably remains unproven. But Bentham and Mill have shown us the significant potential of the theory for dissolving the prejudices of ages and liberating human happiness.

Discussion Questions

1. How does Bentham argue for the truth of utilitarianism?
2. How serious is the problem of interpersonal comparisons of utility?
3. Why would utilitarianism lead to the end of the subjection of women?
4. How convincing is Mill's "proof" of the principle of utility?

Key Terms

utility, p. 126

argument by elimination, p. 127

moral sense, p. 130

theory of the good, p. 130

theory of the right, p. 130

interpersonal comparisons of utility, p. 132

analogy, p. 139

begging the question, p. 140

circular argument, p. 140

Key Thinkers

Jeremy Bentham (1748–1832), pp. 125–138

Plato (429?–347 BCE), p. 127

Aristotle (384–322 BCE), p. 127

Bertrand Russell (1872–1970), pp. 134, 137

G. E. Moore (1873–1958), pp. 139–140

Immanuel Kant (1724–1804), p. 141

Further Reading

- Jeremy Bentham's *Introduction to the Principles of Morals and Legislation* was published by Athlone Press (1970; original work published 1789). Selections from this work appear in Jonathan Wolff (ed.), *Readings in Moral Philosophy* (W. W. Norton, 2018).

- The story of John Stuart Mill finding a dead baby in a London park is taken from Richard Reeves, *John Stuart Mill: Victorian Firebrand* (Atlantic Books, 2008).

- Measurements of happiness can be found online at The World Happiness Report 2016 (worldhappiness.report) and the OECD Better Life Index (oecd-betterlifeindex.org/topics/life-satisfaction/). Retrieved January 25, 2017.

- Many editions of Mill's *Utilitarianism* are available, including one published by Hackett, edited by George Sher (2001; original work published 1861), from which the quotations used here are taken. A selection is included in Jonathan Wolff (ed.), *Readings in Moral Philosophy* (W. W. Norton, 2018).

- Quotations from Mill's *The Subjection of Women* (original work published 1869) are from *Mill: The Spirit of the Age, On Liberty, The Subjection of Women* (W. W. Norton, 1996).

- Bertrand Russell's remarks about proof are taken from his *Autobiography* (Routledge, 2009), p. 25. (Original work published 1951)

- G. E. Moore's argument is taken from his *Principia Ethica*, revised edition, edited by Thomas Baldwin (1993). (Original work published 1903)

- Immanuel Kant's argument about self-interest and chaos is taken from his *Critique of Practical Reason* (Bobbs-Merrill, 1956), p. 27. (Original work published 1788)

CHAPTER 9

Challenges for Utilitarianism

It is better to be a human being dissatisfied than a pig satisfied; better to be Socrates dissatisfied than a fool satisfied. And if the fool, or the pig, are of a different opinion, it is because they only know their own side of the question. The other party to the comparison knows both sides.

JOHN STUART MILL, UTILITARIANISM

IS HAPPINESS THE SOLE ULTIMATE GOOD?

In Chapter 8 we looked at the origins of utilitarianism, how John Stuart Mill (1806–73) applied the theory to argue for the end of the subjection of women, and how Jeremy Bentham (1748–1832) and Mill attempted to prove it. Giving a proof was difficult, but that does not mean no proof is possible. The many positive aspects of the theory make it worth looking at it in more detail, to see what advantages or disadvantages it may have.

We saw earlier that utilitarianism can be divided into two sub-theories: a **theory of the good**, which tells us the sole ultimate good is happiness (or pleasure and the avoidance of pain); and a **theory of the right**, which says the right thing to do is always to maximize the good—happiness. By observing that ultimately happiness is the only thing human beings seek, either directly or indirectly, Mill thinks he has shown that happiness is the sole good. Now let's explore this question and see whether Mill is correct. In particular we will look at a range of objections raised by other philosophers aiming to show that Mill is wrong. Happiness, according to these critics, is not the sole ultimate good; therefore, the utilitarian theory of the good is incorrect.

The Narrowness Objection

Most obviously, one challenge to Mill's theory is what we could call the narrowness objection: that the utilitarian theory of the good is too narrow because happiness is only one type of good. Knowledge, for example, and great works of art can be claimed to be good independently of their effect on happiness. Mill, however, regards this as a superficial objection. Why are such things valued? Only, Mill thinks, because of the happiness they bring. It is worth struggling for your art because of the pleasure it will eventually bring, if not to you then to others—or rather, the pleasure you hope it will bring; but you must judge the gamble worth it.

How plausible is this argument? It is hard to know how to assess it. Certainly people can say that their actions are not aimed at pleasure. Great artists or writers may be obsessed with their work and spend all their time and energy on it, sometimes becoming ill or deeply miserable; but they feel driven to produce the best work they can, even if it is never finished, even if no one ever sees it. What should we say about such people? Suppose you devote a great deal of time and energy to sports or even philosophy. Are you doing this to seek happiness? If so, surely you can find easier ways to get there, such as watching TV and eating pizza. Rather, it may seem, you are making the effort simply to become as good as you can at sports or philosophy. Or, in the words of the 19th-century utilitarian philosopher Henry Sidgwick (1838–1900), in his book *The Methods of Ethics*, you seek excellence for its own sake. You might want to be great at sports just because you want to be great at sports. If we accept this point, then we have to accept that some people desire to create art, or pursue sports or philosophy, simply for the sake of achieving excellence in these areas, rather than for the happiness it may or may not bring. And if Mill argues, as we have seen, that the only proof that something is desirable is that people desire it, then he would have to concede that the creation of art and so on is desirable, and hence that the creation of art is good. No doubt we could include many other goals as well.

Of course, for Mill this is not a decisive objection. He could continue to insist that basically all human activity is subconsciously aimed at feeling pleasure and avoiding pain. Nevertheless, as we saw with the defense of psychological egoism in Chapter 6, an appeal to subconscious motivations looks increasingly desperate and dogmatic.

Sidgwick, though, may have a better answer. Having made the point that we seek excellence as well as happiness, he asked why we do so. Not, so it seems, always for our own pleasure. But, he thought, ultimately—and consciously or unconsciously—we try to achieve works of excellence for the happiness of others. Consider great artists or musicians who suffer for their art. Would they do this if they thought their paintings would never be seen, or their music never heard? There are, of course, romantic stories of artists who create works and then destroy them, but we regard those people as teetering on the edge of madness. This may be why Sidgwick presents the idea that excellence is pursued as a means to the happiness of others as a theory of rationality rather than one of necessity. That is, although it is possible to seek excellence entirely for its own sake, Sidgwick regards doing so as irrational (1874/1981, p. 406). Is he right? It is hard to know how to answer; but it is not obviously irrational to want to produce something just to see what you are capable of doing without caring whether others appreciate it. Maybe people who obsessively bench-press are like this.

The Agency Objection

I called the challenge we just discussed the narrowness objection because it argues that the utilitarian identification of the good with happiness is too narrow. A second objection is an important variant of the first: that what matters is not just the subjective feelings of pleasure and pain we have, but also how we act. We can call this the agency objection, which was made strikingly in the following passage from *Anarchy, State, and Utopia*, written by the American philosopher Robert Nozick (1938–2002):

> Suppose that there were an experience machine that would give you any experience you desired. Superduper neuropsychologists could stimulate your brain so that you would think and feel you were writing a great novel, or making a friend, or reading an interesting book. All the time you would be floating in a tank, with electrodes attached to your brain. Should you plug into this machine for life, pre-programming your life's experiences? If you are worried about missing out on desirable experiences, we can suppose that business enterprises have researched thoroughly the lives of many others. You can pick and choose from their large library or smorgasbord of such experiences, selecting your life's experiences for, say, the next two years. After two years have passed you will have ten minutes or ten hours out of the tank, to select the experiences of your *next* two years. Of course, while in the tank you won't know that you're there; you'll think it's all actually happening. Others can also plug in to have the experiences they want, so there's no need to stay unplugged to serve them. (Ignore problems such as who will service the machines if everyone plugs in.) Would you plug in? *What else can matter to us, other than how our lives feel from the inside?* (Nozick, 1974, pp. 42–43)

Nozick's fascinating thought experiment makes us focus on the question of what matters to us most. His suggestion, of course, is that what matters is not so much how things feel to us, but whether we really have accomplished the things we set out to accomplish in our lives. A life of mundane small achievements seems preferable to a life with the intense joy of believing that you have lived a life of great excitement, pleasure, and accomplishment if all of that is built on an illusion. Less dramatic, but much more important versions of this problem arise occasionally in real life, such as in medical ethics. In earlier decades it was common not to let people know they were suffering from a fatal disease, based on the assumption that it was better for them to live their last few years or months in happy ignorance. These days, deliberately withholding such important medical information—however unhappy it would make the person—would be actionable in a court of law. We must, I think, concede that these examples weaken the claim that pleasure is the sole good.

The Evil Pleasures Objection

A third challenge for utilitarianism is the argument that not all pleasures are good: We can call this the evil pleasures objection. Does the pleasure of a sadistic torturer deserve to be called good, and weighed against the pains of the victim? We can find many other examples: the pleasures of the rapist, the pedophile, or the terrorist. In Chapter 8 we considered the example of someone who is cheered up on finding that someone they dislike has been injured in a car crash. Knowing that some individuals take pleasure in evil acts or other people's misfortunes seems to make the situation worse rather than a little bit better. It seems hard to find a plausible response to this objection. The only thing that can be said, I think, is that the pleasure of the torturer is good, but it is completely overwhelmed by the pain the torture causes. Yet this idea seems quite implausible. Surely it would be a morally better world if torturers were unhappy in their work.

The Quality Objection

Mill himself worried about a fourth challenge to utilitarianism: that in Bentham's view, all pleasures are on the same level and are to be evaluated purely according to their intensity and length. Bentham was adamant on this point: What matters is the pleasure, not its source. Notoriously, and provocatively, Bentham asserted that "pushpin is as good as poetry," or at least this is how Mill, slightly inaccurately, quotes him. (Pushpin is a game similar to solitaire.) Mill found this view hard to accept and argued that in addition to the quantity of pleasure, quality matters too.

For that reason, we can call this argument the quality objection. It is, Mill says, "quite compatible with the principle of utility to recognize the fact that some kinds of pleasure are more desirable and more valuable than others" (1861/2001, p. 8). In one sense, of course, Bentham would immediately agree. One pleasure is better than another if it is more intense or it lasts longer. But Mill has something else in mind—that the *quality* of pleasure differs. One pleasure is "higher" than another if those who have experienced both would not give up the higher for any amount of the "lower." To use Bentham's example against him, we might reasonably suppose that those who have fully and richly experienced both poetry and pushpin would not give up poetry for any amount of pushpin. As Mill says (in the quotation at the start of this chapter):

> It is better to be a human being dissatisfied than a pig satisfied; better to be Socrates dissatisfied than a fool satisfied. And if the fool, or the pig, are of a different opinion, it is because they only know their own side of the question. The other party to the comparison knows both sides. (Mill, 1861/2001, p. 10)

It is often thought that Mill split all pleasures into just two categories, higher and lower pleasures, and that may have been his intention. But strictly interpreted, his argument would allow several different levels of the quality of pleasure. I might not give up poetry for any amount of pushpin; but equally I might not give up my ambition to complete my college degree for any amount of time spent reading poetry, even if I do find poetry highly pleasurable.

Once again, though, we can raise questions about Mill's argument. First of all, is there really such a consensus among the experienced on the view that poetry is so much superior to pushpin? Virtually all of us studied poetry in school, and some of us in real depth and with interest and commitment. And yet most of us have barely opened a book of poetry since. Meanwhile, many people spend thousands of hours of their lives on the modern equivalent of pushpin: playing the latest video or smartphone game. Furthermore, even those who would not give up poetry for pushpin might not give up pushpin for poetry, either. Mill could be accused of confusing differences in quality with the point that we all seek variety in our lives. Most pleasures fade, the more often they are done. In economics this is known as the theory of **diminishing marginal utility**: The first chocolate from the box gives more pleasure than the second, and the second more than the third. Hence we would not normally want to concentrate on just one type of pleasure, whatever it is.

In passing it is worth noting how important the theory of diminishing marginal utility has been to utilitarian theory. On this basis, for example, the contemporary utilitarian philosopher Peter Singer (b. 1946) argues for radical redistribution of income (Singer, 1972). A dollar in the hand of a rich person gives him or her far less utility than a dollar in the hand of a poor person, and therefore it would maximize total happiness to redistribute from the rich to the poor. Therefore this is what utilitarianism generally recommends, provided it is done in a calm and controlled way and the process of redistribution does not itself cause great unhappiness.

To return to the main argument, we might accuse Mill of a certain type of pro-human arrogance. He tells us that it is better to be Socrates unsatisfied than a pig satisfied; and if the pig disagrees, that is only because it knows only its side of the comparison. This may be a nice joke, but we could equally ask how much Socrates knows about the life of a pig—rolling around in the mud with a full stomach and not a care in the world. Perhaps, though, it isn't so hard to imagine. At times of stress, a pig's life may even seem rather attractive.

Perhaps the greater problem for Mill arises if we do accept his distinction between levels of happiness. The beauty of Bentham's simpler utilitarianism was that we know, in principle at least, how to apply it. All pleasures and pains are to be put on a single scale and weighed and balanced against each other. But once we have accepted Mill's distinction between higher and lower pleasures (and higher and lower pains?), the theory is enormously complicated. Does he suggest that society must never give up a higher pleasure for any amount of a lower one? Should we give up everything else for poetry? Mill certainly would not argue for that. Some lower pleasures are needed to make higher pleasures possible. We need to eat before we can create poetic masterpieces. So is Mill proposing that we ought to pursue lower pleasures only to the extent that they enable our enjoyment of the higher pleasures?

This theory is beginning to look much less like Bentham's democratic utilitarianism (everyone is to count for one and nobody for more than one) and more like a highly elitist view, such as that of Friedrich Nietzsche (see Chapter 3). If some, like Socrates, are capable of higher pleasures than the fool, then should they be given extra weight in the utilitarian calculus? Mill did not explain how to modify utilitarianism to accommodate differences in quality of pleasures.

The Irrelevance Objection

Finally, we should at least touch on the possible objection that happiness is not a good at all. Let's call this the irrelevance objection. Bentham considered the theory, as we saw, that he called asceticism, which inverts utilitarianism by suggesting that pleasure is bad and pain good. But there is another view: that happiness has nothing to do with morality and in itself is neither good nor bad. In *Twilight of the Idols*, Friedrich Nietzsche (1844–1900) contemptuously remarked that "Man does *not* strive for pleasure; only the Englishman does." (1888/1954, p. 468). Quite likely he had the utilitarians in mind when he wrote this, perhaps not knowing that John Stuart Mill was a Scotsman, at least by ancestry. In fact, an important tradition in ethics suggests that it is quite wrong to base moral reasoning on ideas of happiness: I will discuss it in Chapter 10, so we can postpone the issue for now.

To summarize this section, I raised the question of whether Mill is right to view happiness as the only good, and we reviewed what I called the narrowness, agency, evil pleasures, quality, and irrelevance objections. None of these are knockdown refutations of the theory, and therefore a dedicated advocate of utilitarianism could insist that the objections can be defeated. Nevertheless, these challenges do make things uncomfortable. Still, only the last objection suggests that Mill is wrong in thinking that happiness is a central component of the human good. And many people will find that objection hard to take seriously.

MAXIMIZING HAPPINESS

What if, after all, Mill is right that happiness is the sole ultimate good? Does it follow that it is right to try to create as much happiness as possible? In the attempted proof of the principle of utility that we looked at in Chapter 8, Mill said, "Each person's happiness is a good to that person, and the general happiness, therefore, a good to the aggregate of all persons" (Mill, 1861/2001, pp. 35–36). The difficulty, as we saw, is that what makes some people happy sometimes makes other people unhappy. Utilitarianism tells us to pursue the course of action that creates the greatest total of happiness over unhappiness. The question for Mill (and Bentham) is whether this really is always morally the right thing to do.

To broaden the discussion, though, we should note that the same issue would arise for many other theories too. Take, for instance, a theory that accepts some of the criticisms set out in the last section—so that, for example, malicious pleasures such as those of the torturer no longer count as good, while art and culture are included as good independently of their effect on happiness. This modified view is not strictly speaking utilitarian, because it no longer claims that happiness is the sole ultimate good. Suppose, though, the theory states that we should maximize non-malicious happiness, as well as art and culture. Thus it still defines right action in terms of the good. As such, this view is a form of **consequentialist** theory; it judges the rightness or wrongness of actions based on their consequences. Utilitarianism is just one example of consequentialism.

Alternatives to consequentialism include **deontological** or duty-based theories such as Kant's theory, which we will examine in detail in Chapters 10 and 11. Deontological theories typically define right action not in terms of maximizing the good, but rather in following a set of moral rules that set limits to what we may do. Consider, for example, two possible justifications for the moral prohibition of murder. A deontological theorist might say murder is always wrong because we have a basic moral duty to respect other people, and murder is a form of gross disrespect. A consequentialist would have to locate the wrong of murder, ultimately, by determining that murder leads to greater unhappiness than happiness. This example illustrates the main distinction between the theories: Consequentialism diagnoses wrongful actions as those that lead to detrimental consequences, whereas deontological or duty-based theories state that actions are wrong if they break a particular moral rule.

There is something greatly appealing about consequentialism. In evaluating the morality of actions, it looks primarily to the future rather than the past, and thus it seems quite practically oriented. Yet a critical problem for utilitarianism is that focusing only on the consequences can lead a utilitarian to make what appears to be the wrong judgment. This is how utilitarianism can arrive at counterintuitive consequences, which, as we saw, means consequences that intuitively we find hard to accept, for they seem to run against a type of moral common sense. Another related problem is that in some cases, its critics claim even if utilitarianism gets to the right answer, sometimes it does so for the wrong reason. It is an accident, or a contingent fact (it could have been otherwise) that this theory gets it right. We can call this the problem of **contingency**. After further exploring the problem of counterintuitive consequences, we will look in the next section at how utilitarianism could respond. In the final section of this chapter, we will turn to the problem of contingency.

Counterintuitive Consequences

One famous example of counterintuitive consequences focuses on how utilitarian theory might treat the issue of punishment. An early version of the criticism was set out by the philosopher E. F. Carritt (1876–1964) in his book *Ethical and Political Thinking* (1947), many years after Mill's death:

> The utilitarian must hold that we are justified in inflicting pain always and only to prevent worse pain or bring about greater happiness. This, then, is all we need to consider in so-called punishment, which must be purely preventive. But if some kind of very cruel crime becomes common, and none of the criminals can be caught, it might be highly expedient, as an example, to hang an innocent man, if a charge against him could be so framed that he were universally thought guilty . . . it would be perfectly deterrent and therefore felicific. (Carritt, 1947, p. 65)

(*Felicific* is a semi-technical term meaning "likely to lead to happiness.")

Philippa Foot (1920–2010) used a similar example, the "trolley problem," involving the sacrifice of one innocent person to save others (see Chapter 1).

A further, much-discussed example concerns deathbed promises. Here is one version: Suppose your grandfather always wanted you to study the great works of philosophy. On his deathbed he asks you to promise to take at least one philosophy course in college. Your ambition, though, is to become a marine biologist, so taking a philosophy course would be an irrelevant nuisance. You find philosophy hard and annoying. But to avoid upsetting your grandfather in his dying moments, you promise—sincerely believing, at that moment—that you will take the course and make the best of it. Soon after, sadly, he dies. Nobody knows that you made this promise. Do you have a moral obligation to take the course? You know that it will bring you, and perhaps your instructor, unhappiness. Happiness, it appears, will be maximized by breaking the promise. From this it seems to follow that utilitarianism is instructing you that you have a moral duty to break the promise. Is that right?

These examples rest on the idea that all utilitarianism seems to care about is maximizing utility or happiness. It says nothing about how we are to do this. In Carritt's example the government could maximize utility by punishing an innocent person, for that would deter others and reduce crime to overall beneficial effect. This approach may be particularly beneficial, from a utilitarian point of view, if anxiety is riding high—perhaps to the point of civil unrest, which threatens violence and destruction. Under these conditions, framing an innocent person could calm everyone down again. In an emergency situation, desperate measures might be thought needed. However, taking this step would be terribly unjust. The innocent man in Carritt's example could surely complain that no innocent individual should be sacrificed to the common good in that way. It seems that utilitarianism permits, maybe even requires, injustice.

The utilitarian philosopher has much to say in response. First, the uncertainties of the situation mean that framing an innocent person might do no good. After all, the crimes may well continue just as before. The real criminals are still out there; and if we think they are not, we might let our guard down. Second, if word gets out that an innocent man has been framed, then even bigger problems could crop up later. The legal system will be seriously discredited, and who knows what would follow next? It seems implausible that by framing this unfortunate person, we can maximize utility.

But nevertheless, something has been exposed here. The critic claims to have found an example where utilitarianism requires an injustice. The utilitarian replies that when we look at the example more carefully, it probably doesn't work. But that response is not enough to show that better examples could not be devised. The point has been made: In principle utilitarianism could permit gross injustice if it advances the general good. The critic could allege that no sound theory can permit injustice, even in principle. This criticism has been regarded as probably the most serious one faced by the utilitarian. Accordingly, utilitarian thinkers have devised a series of more sophisticated versions of the theory to deal with the objection. Let's now consider these more sophisticated forms of utilitarianism.

MODIFYING UTILITARIANISM

The most obvious response to Carritt's "scapegoating" objection is yes, framing an innocent person might act as a deterrent and calm things down for a while. But if word gets out that innocent people could be punished for crimes that they truly did not commit, the consequences will be disastrous for happiness. Many people will be outraged at the injustice and become highly anxious about what the future might bring for any of us—who will be the next scapegoat? The apparent paradox is that trying to maximize utility in the short term could create serious problems in the longer term. This thought has led to a number of attempts to modify utilitarianism and separate the immediate consequences of an act from the much broader context.

Act and Rule Utilitarianism

Perhaps the best-known attempted modification of utilitarianism makes a distinction between two varieties: **act utilitarianism** and **rule utilitarianism**. So far we have been discussing act utilitarianism, which is the view that the morality of an action is to be determined by its anticipated consequences. Rule utilitarianism, however, concentrates in the first instance not on actions but on rules.

Rule utilitarianism is implicit in both Bentham and Mill, but it was probably first explicitly stated by the economist Roy Harrod (1900–78). He used the example of the utilitarian approach to truth-telling (Harrod, 1936). Suppose I am considering whether or not to tell a lie. On the one hand, a lie could have some positive effects: I might be sparing someone's feelings or getting myself out of a difficult situation. A single lie, told on a single occasion, is unlikely to have much negative effect unless it is found out. But imagine a world where people are permitted to lie whenever the utilitarian calculation is favorable. Every statement uttered by every individual would immediately come under suspicion. How can I take your word for anything when I know you are willing to lie if lying will advance utility? The very practice of truth-telling would collapse, and the result would be disastrous even in utilitarian terms.

Accordingly, Harrod proposes that utilitarianism should instead be a morality of laws or rules. He concedes that of course the utilitarian needs to set up a morality that maximizes utility. But, he argues, the morality that really does maximize utility is likely to contain a number of rules that should not be broken except, perhaps, under the most unusual circumstances. The rule of "never lie," almost paradoxically, will do more to advance utility than the rule of "lie whenever doing so would advance utility."

In a similar way, rule utilitarianism also provides a reply to the scapegoat example we considered above. Even if act utilitarianism would justify punishing an innocent person, the rule of "punish someone, guilty or not, whenever it would maximize utility to do so" would frighten everyone, causing extreme anxiety. None of us would know whether we might be the next scapegoat. This loss of confidence in the rule of law and the right to fair trial would again lead to a collapse of overall utility. We need a better rule; and the rule that appears to maximize utility is "never punish the innocent."

Nevertheless, some critics have said rule utilitarianism is irrational. Suppose we had the rule of "never punish the innocent," yet on a particular occasion a significant utilitarian gain can be made. Suppose, to modify Carritt's example, the president has been assassinated, there are riots on the street, and the country is on the verge of a civil war unless the murderer is found. If we arrest an innocent person and keep him behind bars for a few weeks before letting him out, we might quell the rioting and buy enough time to catch the true culprit. There is a miscarriage of justice, but it seems small in comparison to the good it might do. It seems, then, we should replace the rule we had with a new rule: "Never punish the innocent unless it results in a significant utilitarian gain." But with this rule we have to start considering acts one by one again, and so rule utilitarianism collapses into act utilitarianism. Hence, eventually, we are back where we started.

The rule utilitarian has to resist the temptation to modify the rules. Or perhaps simply make sure that ordinary citizens never know the rules have been modified. After all, the case of mild scapegoating just discussed—where someone is imprisoned for a few weeks rather than executed—may seem to be justified on occasion. But as soon as the public finds out what has happened, things may well get even worse. What sort of theory can justify misleading the public in this way?

One way of doing this revives an older argument made by Henry Sidgwick in his book *Methods of Ethics* (1874/1981). Sidgwick points out that calculating in utilitarian terms is a hazardous business. Consider what it would take. First I would need to consider all the possible alternatives in front of me. In the simple case of deciding whether to lie, the alternatives would be either to lie or tell the truth, although cases are rarely that simple.

But even in this simple case, I would then need to reflect on the possible further outcomes. Will I be found out or not? If I am found out, will gossip spread that I am a liar? If it does spread, will other people laugh or be shocked? How damaging might this be to me, to my friends, or even to the institution of truth-telling? Even a simple action can produce a whole tree of branching possible futures. A utilitarian would need to estimate how likely each outcome is, and what its consequences would be.

Several problems arise here. First, can I really imagine all the possible futures? Second, even if I can, will I estimate their probabilities and consequences properly? Third, when I do estimate the probabilities and consequences, if I make any errors they very likely will favor my own interests. My own problems will weigh more heavily in my calculations than the problems of others. For all these reasons, our limited natures as human beings make utilitarian calculations difficult and, in fact, unlikely to be right.

Two-Level Utilitarianism

What is the solution? Sidgwick considers the extraordinary and ingenious idea that for utilitarian reasons, ordinary people have to be taught that utilitarianism is false. Instead of reasoning in utilitarian terms, people should be taught some simple rules: Do not lie, be kind to others, and so on. Only the moral elite—presumably professors of moral philosophy and people of similar standing—can be trusted with the moral truth. These people have the job of devising and teaching others the simple rules and of teaching them the falsity of the true view, utilitarianism.

> Thus, on Utilitarian principles, it may be right to do and privately recommend, under certain circumstances, what it would not be right to advocate openly; it may be right to teach openly to one set of persons what it would be wrong to teach to others; it may be conceivably right to do, if it can be done with comparative secrecy, what it would be wrong to do in the face of the world. (Sidgwick, 1874/1981, p. 489)

For good reason, this theory has been called **government house utilitarianism** because it treats ordinary citizens in the condescending way that colonial rulers, living in the government house, treated colonial subjects in the days of British rule. It builds on Sidgwick's insight that utilitarianism is a theory to judge which outcomes are better or worse, but it is not the same as giving individuals a motive to act. Being motivated to be honest, kind, and obey the rules of commonsense morality may well bring about a better utilitarian outcome than being motivated to bring about the best outcome. And Sidgwick floats the idea that these simple rules are all that ordinary people should be taught.

I have to admire the intellectual audacity of this view. But politically it is hard to take. Can we really accept that the correct moral position splits society into two groups: the tiny, intellectually privileged minority, who can be trusted with the moral truth, and the great majority, who are in effect taught a series of lies about morality in order to bring about the greatest happiness without having to go through the pain and risks of elaborate calculation?

The moral philosopher Richard Hare (1919–2002) came up with a different way of defending a form of two-level utilitarianism in his book *Moral Thinking: Its Levels, Method, and Point* (1981). Hare suggests that rather than having two different social groups, one permitted to think in higher utilitarian terms and the other following basic rules of morality, the two levels exist in each one of us. Hare made a distinction between critical moral thinking and ordinary, intuitive moral thinking. The intuitive moral contexts are those of everyday life. In these situations, people should follow simple moral rules. But there will be times when we face situations where the simple moral rules don't apply, or they come into conflict with each other. What should we do in a situation that almost none of us will ever face—at least outside conditions of war, where, for example, many lives can be saved by killing an innocent person? In Hare's view the simple moral rules of intuitive morality will leave us floundering, and so we will need to turn to critical thinking and reason in utilitarian terms. Utilitarianism tells us to kill the innocent person. If we are well schooled in intuitive morality, we will find it almost—or actually—impossible to kill an innocent person. But Hare argues that from the utilitarian, critical point of view it is obviously the right thing to do. Nevertheless, even though the decision is obvious, carrying it out will not be at all easy.

Hare's two-level theory is a sophisticated version of utilitarianism. It combines act and rule utilitarianism, and it avoids the collapse of rule utilitarianism into act utilitarianism by permitting act-utilitarian reasoning only in the most extreme or difficult circumstances. Like every theory in philosophy, this one has its critics. Some we have already encountered. As we have seen, Hare's utilitarianism will sometimes allow the sacrifice of the innocent. Another objection is specific to Hare's theory. Can we really split ourselves into two in the way Hare suggests? Is it psychologically possible to spend our lives primarily in intuitive mode, but switch to critical thinking when things get awkward or difficult? Perhaps that is possible; but once in critical mode, can we switch back to more comfortable, automatic intuitive thinking? Or will we feel it is morally irresponsible to make decisions in such an apparently unthinking way?

THE PROBLEM OF CONTINGENCY: GENDER AND RACE

Let's recall one of the underlying concerns with the scapegoat objection. Suppose it turns out that, through a sophisticated utilitarian calculation, scapegoating is not accepted by utilitarianism. There is still a worry that even if the resulting judgment is correct, the utilitarian is right for the wrong reason. The problem with scapegoating is not that it might lead to diminished aggregate happiness but, some would argue, that it is simply wrong in itself. In this view, the calculation is irrelevant.

For another example, consider again the arguments from John Stuart Mill that we considered earlier (see Chapter 8) in defense of women's emancipation—although in fairness to Mill, he had other arguments that I haven't mentioned. In that discussion, I picked out four utilitarian arguments: (a) Keeping women in subjection led to male arrogance, which was problematic for the men; (b) by excluding women from the workplace, we lose half the talent in the world; (c) having to take care of a wife and daughter pushed men into conventional lifestyles; and (d) being emancipated would bring women greater happiness.

What I have called the problem of contingency suggests that women's emancipation should not be contingent on showing that it has these beneficial outcomes. Someone making this objection would say that it is simply unjust for women to remain in subjugation even if, amazingly, it turned out that subjection maximized their happiness. Suppose, for example, detailed research showed that men's arrogance was actually a great source of pleasure; that we already have, just among men, all the talent we need; that most people are much happier living conventional lives; and that women are happier looking after the household than entering the world of work. I agree that research is unlikely to yield these conclusions; but as a thought experiment, let's suppose that it does. Would we then conclude that women should not be emancipated after all? It seems that a utilitarian would be committed to that (hypothetical) conclusion. If you think this is the correct result, then you are likely to be someone with strong utilitarian or consequentialist sympathies. But if you think women should be emancipated, whatever the consequences (at least within reason), then your intuitions tend much more in an anti-utilitarian direction, at least about this issue. Mill himself probably thought that all available rational arguments supported emancipation, so he did not have to form a view on this question. But the critics have made their point: Even when utilitarianism gets to the right result, we have to ask whether it gets there for the right reason.

As it turns out, this is much more than a thought experiment. We have seen that Mill was a passionate defender of sexual equality. But what did he think about racial equality? He did write that in the future all races would secure equality, and he clearly thought this would benefit everyone: Europeans would be learning from other races just as other races learned from Europeans. But the story has another side. Mill, although perhaps the greatest philosopher writing in the English language in the 19th century, never held a university post. Instead he worked as an official for the East India Company, a private firm administering British colonial affairs in India. His father, James Mill (1773–1836), was a historian of "British India," though neither father nor son ever visited the country.

Mill, like the vast majority of 19th-century European writers, assumed that white Europeans were more able, industrious, and civilized than Indian, African, and Eastern people. The great debate at that time was whether this presumed difference was one of intrinsic nature or a consequence of social factors. Of course this issue was of the greatest importance: If inferiority was "natural," then nothing could be done about it, and a type of racial hierarchy was a permanent fact of life. Alternatively, if the difference was one of "nurture" rather than nature, then changing the circumstances in which non-European peoples lived could eventually bring them to the same high level of civilization that Europeans occupied. This was Mill's view, which at the time was considered highly radical. For example, typically people who opposed Mill's position assumed that God had permanently placed different races at different levels of superiority and inferiority. Mill did not doubt European superiority, but he felt it was the duty, and destiny, of Europeans to "civilize" barbarian nations to bring them up to equality. This is one reason why he supported the colonial enterprise.

To see how this played out in Mill's thinking, let's look at another of his famous texts, *On Liberty* (1859). In this book he argues that the government may not legitimately interfere with your liberty unless it is to prevent you from harming others. According to Mill, then, the government may not intervene based on what are now known as **paternalist** grounds: to require you to perform, or refrain from, actions for your own good. Notoriously, Mill makes an exception for children and what he calls "barbarians":

> Despotism is a legitimate mode of government in dealing with barbarians, provided the end be their improvement, and the means justified by actually effecting that end. (1859/1996, pp. 48–49)

Mill justifies this exception by saying that until people have reached a certain level of civilization, they are not capable of what he calls "improvement" through freedom of speech and thought, nor of conducting "experiments in living" and learning from each other's experience. At "lower" levels of civilization, freedom would lead to chaos and deterioration rather than improvement. Therefore despotism—strict government of the sort the colonial powers imposed—is justified to bring barbarians to the level of civilization at which they can enjoy their freedom. Despotism becomes a form of paternalism, imposed for the good of the people. In other words, although utilitarianism decrees freedom for the civilized, it recommends severe restrictions for the uncivilized to bring them up to the necessary level where they can profitably use their freedom. Hence Mill was comfortable with his position as a colonial administrator despite being one of the great champions of freedom and equality. Here, then, we see the contingency of utilitarianism in practice. Whether it recommends equality depends on the contingency of many surrounding circumstances.

Among the many possible responses to Mill, here are four that probably have crossed your mind already. First, India was much more "civilized" than Mill supposed. For example, its philosophical traditions go back almost 3,000 years—even before Ancient Greek philosophy. Before the British arrived, India was the center of world trade. If anything colonialism sent India sharply backward, not forward. Second, it could be argued that even the "uncivilized" will be happier with freedom than with despotism. Third, the former Kenyan President Jomo Kenyatta (see Chapter 2) argued that limiting individual rights is more likely to lead away from civilization than toward it. Finally, it doesn't matter if "barbarians" would use their freedom in good or bad ways; they still have the same rights as everyone else.

Note that of these replies, the first three broadly accept the utilitarian framework and suggest that Mill has done his calculations incorrectly. Utilitarianism, it is argued, favors freedom—at least in the conditions of India. The last response, however, is quite different. It says the calculations are irrelevant, and all human beings have a right to freedom. This type of unconditional right is something that, it seems, utilitarianism simply cannot accommodate. And this is the reason many people think that despite its many appeals and its underlying humanity, utilitarianism is fundamentally flawed as a moral theory.

CHAPTER REVIEW

Summary

We began Chapter 9 by looking at a battery of objections to the utilitarian theory that happiness is the sole good. I called them the narrowness, agency, evil pleasures, quality, and irrelevance objections. We then looked at some problems involved with the idea of maximizing the good: essentially that doing so could lead to counterintuitive consequences. We next explored some more sophisticated versions of utilitarianism—rule utilitarianism, government house utilitarianism, and two-level utilitarianism—to see if they could avoid these consequences. Although these theories at least superficially succeeded in showing how to get to the right answer, they faced the more subtle objection that they got to the right answer for the wrong reason. We saw this difficulty demonstrated by looking at Mill's different approaches to questions of gender and race. He seemingly was content to defend aspects of colonialism in utilitarian terms, at least as a means of preparing subjugated peoples for their future freedom. And this position, despite the humane appeal of utilitarianism, shows that it is also vulnerable to criticism.

Discussion Questions

1. What, in your view, are the strongest objections to the utilitarian view that happiness is the sole good?
2. Explain the scapegoating objection to utilitarianism.
3. What is the distinction between act and rule utilitarianism?
4. What is the problem of contingency? Answer in reference to Mill's ideas on gender and race.

Key Terms

theory of the good, p. 144

theory of the right, p. 144

diminishing marginal utility, p. 148

consequentialism, p. 150

deontology, p. 150

contingency, p. 151

act utilitarianism, p. 153

rule utilitarianism, p. 153

government house utilitarianism, p. 155

paternalism, p. 158

Key Thinkers

John Stuart Mill (1806–73), pp. 144–145, 147–159

Henry Sidgwick (1838–1900), pp. 145, 154–155

Robert Nozick (1938–2002), p. 146

Jeremy Bentham (1748–1832), pp. 147–149

Peter Singer (b. 1946), p. 148

Friedrich Nietzsche (1844–1900), p. 149

E. F. Carritt (1876–1964), pp. 151–154

Philippa Foot (1920–2010), p. 151

Roy Harrod (1900–78), p. 153

Richard Hare (1919–2002), p. 156

Jomo Kenyatta (c. 1891–1978), p. 159

Further Reading

- Many editions of John Stuart Mill's *Utilitarianism* are available, including one from Hackett (1982; original work published 1861).

- Quotations from *The Subjection of Women* (original work published 1869) are from *Mill: The Spirit of the Age, On Liberty, The Subjection of Women* (W. W. Norton, 1996).

- Henry Sidgwick's *Methods of Ethics* is available from Hackett (1981; original work published 1874).

- Robert Nozick's *Anarchy, State, and Utopia* was published by Basic Books (1974).

- Peter Singer's paper "Famine, Affluence, and Morality" was first published in *Philosophy & Public Affairs*, 1, 3(1972): 229–243.

- The quotation from Nietzsche's *Twilight of the Idols* (1888) can be found in *The Portable Nietzsche* (Penguin, 1954), edited by Walter Kaufmann.

- E. F. Carritt's criticism of utilitarianism can be found in his book *Ethical and Political Thinking* (Oxford University Press, 1947).

- For an important debate on utilitarianism, see J. J. C. Smart and Bernard Williams, *Utilitarianism: For and Against* (Cambridge University Press, 1973).

- Roy Harrod's discussion of rule utilitarianism appears in his paper "Utilitarianism Revised," *Mind*, 45, 1936: 137–156.

- An extended discussion of different forms of utilitarianism appears in David Lyons, *Forms and Limits of Utilitarianism* (Oxford University Press, 1970).

- The term *government house utilitarianism* comes from Amartya Sen and Bernard Williams, "Introduction: Utilitarianism and Beyond" in the collection they co-edited *Utilitarianism and Beyond* (Cambridge University Press, 1982).

- Richard Hare's defense of two-level utilitarianism can be found in his book *Moral Thinking: Its Levels, Method, and Point* (Oxford University Press, 1981).

- The version of Mill's *On Liberty* (1859) used here is from *Mill: The Spirit of the Age, On Liberty, The Subjection of Women* (W. W. Norton, 1996).

- Selections from Mill's *Utilitarianism* and *On Liberty*, as well as the relevant texts from Nozick and Singer, appear in Jonathan Wolff (ed.), *Readings in Moral Philosophy* (W. W. Norton, 2018).

CHAPTER 10

Deontology: Kant

[Aiming at popularity in moral thinking leads to] a disgusting hotch-potch of patchwork observations and half-rationalized principles, in which shallow pates [i.e., heads] revel because it is useful in everyday chit-chat.

IMMANUEL KANT, GROUNDWORK OF THE METAPHYSICS OF MORALS

THE SUPREME MORAL PRINCIPLE

One powerful criticism of the utilitarian position that we discussed in the last two chapters is that maximizing total happiness could mean inflicting great unhappiness, or worse, on a small minority. Punishing an innocent person to deter others was one example. Although it causes undeserved suffering to one person, the suffering could, according to utilitarianism, be outweighed by its total beneficial effects. If it is successful in deterring crime, it will protect those who would otherwise be victims and reduce everyone's anxiety.

It is not hard to think of other cases where maximizing the sum total of pleasures over pains could lead to results most people would regard as abhorrent. Consider, for example, the alleged Roman spectacle of throwing Christians to the lions. The barbaric pleasures of the large, frenzied audience when added together could outweigh the terror and intense pain of the small number of victims. Most of us will regard such a situation as deeply immoral, perhaps just about as bad as things could be, and therefore certainly not as something a moral theory can approve of, let alone promote. Many utilitarians agree with this criticism and try to avoid it by proposing forms of rule utilitarianism; but, as we noted in Chapter 9, their success is controversial.

As introduced by economist Roy Harrod (1900–78), rule utilitarianism was in fact claimed to be inspired by an idea from a very different type of philosopher—Immanuel Kant (1724–1804). The leading idea is that we need to look at actions not in isolation but as following from rules of conduct. In this approach morality is rule governed, or better yet, law governed (though not in the sense of laws of nature or of the legal system), and this is certainly a key theme of Kant's moral philosophy. It is important, though, to look at Kant's theory in detail, for he would have regarded all forms of utilitarian thinking, including rule utilitarian thinking, as deeply mistaken and probably immoral. In Kant's *Critique of Practical Reason*, he writes, "Morals is not really the doctrine of how to make ourselves happy but of how we are to be worthy of happiness" (1788/1956, p. 134).

Kant's defense of strict rules of morality, and his rejection of the type of **consequentialist** thinking that is at the heart of utilitarianism, allows us to present him as a trenchant critique of Jeremy Bentham and John Stuart Mill's utilitarianism. This is so even though the work we will focus on— *Groundwork of the Metaphysics of Morals* (here referred to as the *Groundwork*)—was published in 1785, before the first publication of Bentham's *Introduction to the Principles of Morals and Legislation* in 1789. Mill published *Utilitarianism* many years later (in 1861 as a series of articles and in 1863 as a book). Mill was keenly aware of Kant's work; although as we shall see later, he dismissed Kant's contribution as at best ultimately little more than utilitarianism in disguise. Kant would have viewed this criticism with contempt, regarding it as displaying an utter lack of comprehension of his views.

Kant's writing is in stark contrast to Mill's. While many of Mill's works were aimed at a general educated audience, Kant was an academic through and through. He earned a doctorate at the University of Königsberg, in the town where he was born and that he never left, and he spent his working life as a highly respected professor at the university. Kant wrote in a far more academic style than Mill, and his works are typically much harder to understand than Mill's, even though he did also sometimes claim to write for a "popular" audience.

Kant was a prolific writer on philosophical topics, addressing the entire scope of metaphysics, aesthetics, politics, and ethics as well as geography, anthropology, and astronomy. His most important books were written in the last 25 years of his long life (he died at age 79); they include our focus here, *Groundwork of the Metaphysics of Morals*. As the elaborate title suggests, it is a philosophically rigorous work, and its real interpretation is still contested today. In this book, Kant raises some fundamental **metaphysical** questions that relate to his entire philosophical system: questions about what exists in the universe and about the limits of human knowledge. At its heart is a fascinating moral theory, however, and in this chapter we will concentrate primarily on that theory. I will also touch on some of its connections with his deeper theories in the next chapter.

Summary of Kant's Ethics

Every moral theory starts somewhere. We saw in previous chapters that utilitarianism starts with a theory of the good: that happiness or pleasure is the sole good, and unhappiness or pain the sole bad. This theory is

Nevertheless, Kant believes that a philosophically profound and rigorous approach to morality is necessary. If we remain at the level of popular thought about morality, we will be left with, to revisit the quotation from the *Groundwork* at the start of this chapter, "a disgusting hotch-potch of patchwork observations and half-rationalized principles, in which the shallow pates revel because it is useful in everyday chit-chat" (1785/1997, 4:409, p. 22). Like Bentham, Kant wants to impose rigor and method on morality, and he refuses to tolerate the disorder of ordinary moral thought.

THE CATEGORICAL IMPERATIVE

How, though, do we get from the idea of the good will, which acts for the sake of duty, to that of the supreme moral principle as introduced in the first section of this chapter? One formulation of that principle in Kant's *Groundwork* is "I ought never to act except in such a way that I could also will that my maxim should become a universal law" (1785/1997, 4:402, p. 15). As we have already seen, Kant emphasizes that morality cannot be based on desire, sympathy, or inclination because they are not unconditionally good. He makes the point more generally by saying that morality cannot be based on anything empirical, by which he means that morality, surprisingly enough, cannot be based on ordinary facts about human beings. In philosophy the term **empirical** generally is used to refer to what we can observe in experience. Science, for example, is an empirical discipline insofar as it generates knowledge built on experimental data accumulated by observation. *Empirical*, for which the Latin term **a posteriori** is also used, is generally contrasted with the term **a priori**. The literal meanings of these terms are not much help: *a posteriori* means "from the later" and *a priori* means "from the earlier." Perhaps the best way of understanding *a priori* is simply in contrast to *empirical*; therefore, a priori knowledge is knowledge that is acquired not through a process of experience or observation.

It is puzzling—and a real philosophical question—to understand the concept of a priori knowledge, for it implies that we can know things without having to experience them. But a priori knowledge does seem to exist. Logic and mathematics are examples. Although it may be hard to theorize how we know that $102 + 102 = 204$, we can be pretty sure we did not come to that knowledge by combining two piles of 102 objects and counting the resulting pile. We manage to get there by a process of calculation rather than through experiment or observation. Mathematics and logic are generally regarded as a priori bodies of knowledge, even if some philosophers have denied that a priori knowledge can exist and have attempted to reduce mathematics and logic to experience.

Hypothetical and Categorical Imperatives

For Kant morality is not an empirical body of knowledge, for it is not based on facts about humans: Morality has to be valid for all rational creatures, whether human or not. Hence the ultimate principles of morality are, Kant says, more like principles of logic than like scientific theories. But what is left if we exclude facts about humans? Only what Kant regards as "formal" features of morality. *Formal* is used in the sense of "relating to form" or, perhaps, "relating to the idea," just as we speak of "formal logic." And so Kant concludes that morality must be based on the form, or the idea, of the moral law.

The key formal elements of the moral law are (a) because it is moral, it is normative, in the sense of setting standards of behavior; and (b) because it is a law, it is universal. Therefore the good will is demonstrated through action in accordance with the pure idea of the normative, universal, moral law, unmixed with anything empirical.

To understand the idea of moral law more fully, two critical notions must be understood at this point: the distinction between the **categorical imperative** and **hypothetical imperatives**; and the idea of a **maxim of an action**. Let's turn first to the discussion of imperatives.

An imperative is an instruction to behave in a particular way. To understand Kant's distinction between categorical and hypothetical imperatives, it is best to start with the concept of a hypothetical imperative. Consider the claim "If you want to gain weight, you should eat more food." Few, I think, would disagree. And some people do want to gain weight if, for example, they are recovering from illness or they play a sport where being heavy is an advantage. But these days, people rarely want to gain weight rather than lose it, and the rest of us generally think it makes little sense to eat more food than we currently do. Hence, we can say, the imperative "eat more food" is hypothetical. Or perhaps it would be clearer to say it is conditional—something you should do only to achieve something else, in this case gain weight. Hypothetical imperatives, in Kant's system, have no moral content, as he illustrates:

> The precepts for a physician to make his man healthy in a well-grounded way, and for a poisoner to be sure of killing his, are of equal worth insofar as each serves perfectly to bring about his purpose. (1785/1996, 4:415, p. 26)

Kant says that the imperatives of morality are categorical, by which he means that they are not hypothetical. *Categorical* in this sense means "absolute" or "unconditional." "Don't tell lies" is a categorical imperative of morality, whereas "If you don't want to get into trouble, don't tell lies" is a hypothetical imperative of **prudence**, and anyone who tells the truth primarily to keep out of trouble is not demonstrating a good will by acting for the sake of duty. Kant would say that their action has no moral worth, even though it is in accordance with the moral law.

What about the statement "If you want to act for the sake of duty, don't tell lies"? This has the grammatical form or appearance of a hypothetical imperative, but we can reasonably say that it is really a categorical imperative in disguise. The conditional "If you want to act for the sake of duty" should just fall away because all humans ought to act for the sake of duty. This condition is unconditional. Indeed, as we have already noted, it falls not only on human beings, but on all rational creatures. If there are angels, Kant thinks, they will be just as bound by the moral law.

It is easy to understand how hypothetical imperatives can exist; in effect, they are instructions about how to achieve a particular goal. The idea of a categorical imperative is more puzzling because it gives instructions that are somehow justified in themselves rather than in pursuit of an external goal. But any particular categorical imperative, such as "Don't tell lies," will be justified insofar as it is in accordance with the supreme moral principle. Kant calls this the categorical imperative (expressed in the singular): "I ought never to act except in such a way that I could also will that my maxim should become a universal law" (1785/1997, 4:402, p. 15).

The Maxim of an Action

The statement of the categorical imperative that we have just seen includes reference to the idea of the "maxim" of your action. This is a critical part of Kant's theory, for he claims that an action has moral worth not in its purpose but in the maxim used in deciding on the action. Kant explains the idea of a maxim by calling it "the principle of the will," and he distinguishes the "will" from preferences or emotions.

Let's return to the butcher weighing and pricing his meat. The butcher who acts honestly but purely out of enlightened self-interest acts from a maxim or principle such as this: "Always treat your customers honestly if it will advance your business and reputation." The purely sympathetic butcher would follow something like the maxim, "Always treat your customers honestly if it makes them happy." But another butcher might act from the maxim, "Always treat your customers honestly." And only this butcher, Kant argues, acts with true moral worth. For only this butcher, Kant seems to suggest, would be able to will that the maxim of his action should become a universal law. Is Kant right that only the honest butcher has a maxim that could be willed as a universal law?

Kant does not, in fact, go through the particular details of this example. But let us pause for a moment to ask a question: Is the test that Kant sets out a plausible approach to morality? The essence of Kant's view is that an act is wrong if it would be impossible to will its universalization, as we saw in the case of the lying promise. This is an elegant and interesting moral view. And by *impossible* Kant, at least on a first reading, seems to mean "strictly, logically impossible" rather than "very difficult, undesirable, or troublesome." The first test for this theory, though, is whether it works. Can we explain all immorality as action based on a maxim that is impossible to universalize? And is everything based on a maxim that is impossible to universalize immoral?

To get a sense of the challenges, let's consider an example offered by the philosopher Marcus Singer (1926–2016). Suppose I want to become a carpenter. Is that morally acceptable? In normal circumstances it is hard to see anything wrong with it. But then suppose everyone wanted to be a carpenter. How could we live? There would be no farmers or tailors, and thus no food or clothes. Eventually we might all die. So it is impossible to universalize being a carpenter.

Now, a Kantian will not be impressed with this objection. First, it makes the confusion we have already identified between the impossible consequences of adopting a universal law with the (logical) impossibility of willing its adoption. There is nothing logically impossible about willing the adoption of the law, even though if we obey it strictly, human life would become very difficult. Second, even putting the first objection aside, there is a question of how to identify the maxim of my action. Is it "be a carpenter"? Or is it "follow a valuable profession you will enjoy"? Even if universalizing the first maxim creates difficulties, the second one seems unproblematic, assuming natural human variation in ambition.

However, this reply brings out a question that has been raised many times for Kant. How do we know what the "true" maxim of any action is? Any particular action could fall under a number of different maxims: "be a carpenter"; "follow a valuable profession you will enjoy"' "find a way of making money"; "exercise your talents"; and so on. With sufficient ingenuity we could multiply these maxims without limit. Is it even clear that there is always a single underlying maxim? Much of the time we don't have a single clear reason for doing something.

Why, for example, are you studying moral philosophy? Can you pinpoint the maxim of your action? Sometimes it is suggested that the maxim of your action is the aspect that "makes the difference." Imagine a situation in which the action did not have a particular characteristic; would you still do it? If not, then it seems plausible that the characteristic needs to feature in your maxim. Perhaps you are studying moral philosophy simply because you have distribution requirements to fulfill. In that case you would not have taken the course if it did not fit your plan of study. Or it might be that for a long time, you have been intrigued with the idea of philosophy and are also interested in morality; you thought it would be valuable to put the two together, and this is why you are studying moral philosophy. Still, the issue remains complicated. Even if you are studying for the intrinsic interest of the topic, you probably would not have taken the course if you did not get credit for it. But to say you are doing it for the credit makes your choice seem much more cynical and calculating than it may well be.

Identifying the maxim of any action is far from straightforward, although Kant does not seem particularly worried about that problem. Perhaps he thinks that an honest moral agent would never try to slip through the moral law by playing around with the formulation of the maxim of his or her action.

KANT'S EXAMPLES

To help understand Kant's position, let's look at some other examples that he helpfully provides to illustrate his approach. Kant runs through a series of four examples: suicide, false promises, neglecting your talents, and refusing aid to others. He says that all of these are morally wrong because in each case, the maxim of the action cannot be willed to be a universal law.

Kant does not pick his four examples at random. Rather he makes two distinctions, which crosscut so that four examples are needed. First, and easier to understand, is a distinction between duties to yourself and duties to others. The examples of false promising and failing to help naturally fall under the category of duties to others. Suicide and neglect of talents concern duties to yourself. Are there such duties? Kant certainly thought so; although in his later work *The Metaphysics of Morals*, he recognizes that the notion of a duty to yourself seems contradictory (1797/1991, p. 214). For if you had a duty to yourself, it seems you could release yourself from it. Hence there would be no duty if you didn't want it, which is no duty at all. Duties would therefore become optional, which defeats their purpose.

Kant resolves this problem by relying on the idea that human beings can be considered under two aspects: One is the natural being—the empirical being of experience—who, like other animals, has desires and seeks happiness; the other is the being with inner freedom, who acts in accordance with reason and, indeed, is capable of following the moral law (Kant 1797/1991, pp. 214–215). Kant seems to suggest that a duty to yourself is a duty to subjugate your desires to your rational freedom, much as an addict might try to suppress a craving for drugs or alcohol to achieve a type of "higher freedom." You might try to release yourself from this duty, but it is plausible that in doing so you are in some sense cheating yourself. Duties to yourself, then, are duties to overcome inclination, or desire, in order to follow reason and the moral law. Here we can see a powerful connection with self-respect: If you follow your cravings or inclinations at the expense of your rational freedom, you are likely to suffer from deep regret or even self-hatred.

The other distinction that Kant draws on is between **perfect and imperfect duties**. In the *Groundwork*, Kant goes over the distinction quickly, not really explaining it. One way of understanding this distinction is that a perfect duty applies in all circumstances, universally. If broken it undermines the condition of its own possibility, as Kant puts it. As we saw, he uses the example of lying to illustrate his meaning: You could not lie if everyone lied whenever they wanted. The breach of an imperfect duty, by contrast, logically could become a universal law; but, Kant says, it would be against our nature as rational creatures. This distinction may be hard to understand, and scholars still debate Kant's exact meaning.

Still, one natural way of understanding the point can be illustrated with examples. By this interpretation, imperfect duties should be acted on from time to time, but not necessarily always. Consider your duty to give to charity. In ordinary morality, most people would accept that moderately wealthy people have a duty to give to charity. But this surely cannot mean that we have a duty to give to every charitable cause that requests money. Bankruptcy may well follow; but even if not, giving more money to a small number of charities may be better than spreading it thinly among all of them. In effect, we have a duty to give to charity from time to time, perhaps to the limits of what we can reasonably afford. But we do not have a duty to give to all charities, or to any charity all the time, or to give away all our money. This, then, is what is meant by an imperfect duty: something we have to do from time to time. Doing it is not optional—it is a duty, after all—but we do have options regarding how and when.

So given his two distinctions, Kant needs four examples. The duty not to commit suicide is, on Kant's reading, a perfect duty to yourself. The duty not to make lying promises is a perfect duty to others. The duties not to neglect your talents and to help others are both imperfect duties—the former to yourself, the latter to others. Because they are imperfect duties, they tell us that we should not neglect all of our talents, and we should help others when we reasonably can.

Suicide

Let's consider Kant's first example: an individual contemplating suicide. This situation, Kant believes, involves a perfect duty: A person must never commit suicide. Here Kant imagines that the person contemplating suicide has the following the maxim of action: "From self-love I make it my principle to shorten my life when its longer duration threatens more troubles than it promises agreeableness" (1785/1997, 4:422, p. 32). This is a rather bland account of the mental life of someone contemplating suicide. Kant, in fact, discusses suicide several times in the *Groundwork*, and his first example does more to capture the highly anguished state of mind of someone contemplating suicide, supposing that "hopeless misery" has "taken away the taste for life" and therefore a person longs for death.

Kant argues that it is not possible to universalize the maxim to shorten your life under the circumstances described. For, he says,

a nature whose law it would be to destroy life itself by means of the same feeling whose destination is to impel toward the furtherance of life would contradict itself and would therefore not subsist as nature; thus that maxim could not possibly be a law of nature and, accordingly, altogether opposes the supreme principle of all duty. (1785/1997, 4:422, p. 32)

It is not easy to follow Kant's argument here. He seems to suggest that we have been given a natural instinct to further our lives, and so the resolution to take our lives contradicts that impulse. Yet it is not clear why we cannot will the universalization of this maxim: "End my life if the future balance of torment and agony over pleasure is likely to be negative." The example is puzzling.

There are two questions we can raise for Kant. First, is he right that suicide is morally wrong? Second, if suicide is wrong, can Kant's theory explain why? In Chapter 2 I used the example of suicide as an example of cultural difference about morality. In some societies suicide has been regarded as a sin—a mortal sin, consigning those who do it to eternal punishment. It has sometimes been a crime; horrifically, those who tried and failed to kill themselves were arrested and charged with attempted suicide, sometimes in their hospital beds as they recovered. In other societies suicide has been seen as an appropriate response to some sort of failure or humiliation. A military leader responsible for the loss of a key battle might be expected to take his own life, and the failure to do so could be criticized. Someone responsible for the death of others may feel he or she "does not deserve to live" and will commit suicide as a result. And still other societies have considered suicide tragic but morally neutral, at least in some circumstances; for example, when a person faces poverty, severely failing health, and the loss of many close friends and relatives.

Kant would consider such variation interesting anthropology but utterly irrelevant to morality. The supreme principle of morality rises above such merely empirical considerations, and it is true for all rational creatures, at all times and places. The test of whether a rule falls under the supreme moral principle depends on whether a person can will it to be universalized. And so, for Kant, customary morality and intuition tell us nothing important. The vital question is whether we can will the universalization of this maxim: "Take my own life when my future life's longer duration threatens more troubles than it promises agreeableness." Kant confidently says that willing the universalizing of this maxim contains a contradiction. Yet as we have already noted, his reason is not so clear. It does seem that a society could live according to this maxim; perhaps some of them do. But some philosophers, such as Schopenhauer and Nietzsche, suspect that Kant is too greatly influenced by his religious beliefs, and in this case is bending his theory to make it fit his religious prohibitions on suicide

There is support for Kant's case, though. Alongside suicide he also discusses what he calls mutilation, which we might now call self-harming. When we hear that a friend or family member is engaging in self-harming, usually by repeatedly and intentionally cutting the skin, we do not celebrate their freedom of choice. Instead we find ourselves greatly concerned. Even if they seem not to care, we feel that they *ought* to care. Is it a moral failure to harm yourself, in the sense of failing in your duty to yourself? The case is at least arguable, and this opens the door to thinking that Kant may well be on to something: that we do have moral duties to ourselves.

Another aspect of ordinary law and morality may well provide further support for Kant. In many aspects of life, we follow the doctrine of *volenti non fit injuria*: Where there is consent, there is no injury. For example, if you ask me to cut down your maple tree, normally you have no complaint if I do it; on the other hand, you would be outraged if I just came over and cut it down. But suppose you sincerely ask me to kill you, which I then do. Most legal systems still regard my action as a serious criminal offense: You cannot consent to your own murder. It is regarded as a "crime against society" rather than merely against the individual, even if that person sincerely wishes to die. And this is Kant's moral criticism of suicide. You may not consent to your own murder, even at your own hands, for the harm is done to society and not just yourself. And, so he claims (whether or not we agree), there will be a contradiction in your will if you do will to commit suicide.

False Promising, Neglecting Your Talents, and Failing to Help

Let's continue with Kant's four examples. We have just dealt with his discussion of suicide. Next is false promising. The failure to universalize maxims permitting false promises is highly plausible, although in Chapter 11 we will explore some perplexing issues Kant raised on the topic of lying. Because we have already discussed false promising, at this point we only need to consider the remaining two examples—neglecting your talents and failing to help others.

How convincing is Kant's claim that his approach rules out the cases of neglecting your talents and failing to help others? Kant acknowledges in both cases that it is logically possible to universalize the maxims. Is this an admission that his argument does not work? Not quite. We need to take another look at the formula of universal law: "Act in such a way that I can also will that my maxim should become a universal law." There is a subtle point here that I need to bring out explicitly. Sometimes it is impossible to will the universalization of a maxim because there would be some sort of contradiction in doing so, as in the case of telling a false promise—and, Kant thinks, in committing suicide. He suggests that where there is a perfect duty (one that must be adhered to in every case), there will be a logical contradiction in willing the universalization of the maxim. This would be an elegant theory if it worked. In the case of imperfect duties, the problem is not so much that there is a contradiction in universalizing the maxim, but rather that there is a *contradiction in willing* its universalization. And this, Kant argues, is the problem in the case of the two remaining examples: neglecting your talents and refusing to help people in need.

In the case of neglecting your talents and preferring to live in idleness, Kant supposes that what he called the "South Sea Islanders" live this way. In the 18th century many people believed that the islands of the south seas had such a bountiful supply of natural foods, such as coconuts and pineapples, that people living there would "let ... talents rust, and ... devote life to idleness, indulgence, procreation and, in a word, enjoyment" (1785/1997, 4:423, p. 33). From Kant's language it seems clear that he regards such a life as not fit for human beings rather than as the paradise it might seem to be for those with a different temperament. (In Chapter 11, we will look more closely at Kant's troubling attitudes about people of non-European descent.) Kant accepts that there is no contradiction in a universal law that would allow everyone to neglect their talents, but he says that willing this mode of life to become a universal law is contrary to the nature of a rational being that necessarily wills the development of its powers. In some ways this argument resembles the one he developed in relation to suicide: Kant must be presupposing a "higher" self of reason and a lower self of pleasure to support the argument that in neglecting your talents, you are failing in a duty to yourself and undermining your own self-respect. And again we can ask whether an implicit religious view is being smuggled in here; is the duty to your higher self easier to understand if it is a duty to your creator? (In Chapter 11 we will return to this question too.)

The final example of failing to help others does not concern neglecting or destroying yourself, but neglecting others. Thus it is a failure of a duty to other people, according to Kant's classification. Kant imagines a man seeing another person in distress and thinking:

> What does it matter to me? Let everyone be as happy as Heaven wills or as he can make himself; I won't deprive him of anything; I won't even envy him; only I have no wish to contribute anything to his well-being or to his support in distress! (1785/1997, 4:423, p. 33)

This is perhaps a version of ethical egoism (see Chapter 6). Again Kant accepts that a maxim of this sort can be universalized—it contains no logical contradiction—but the problem is that its universalization cannot be willed. For I might find myself needing the help of others, and would naturally will my own preservation; but a universal law of non-contribution would allow others to ignore me if they chose to. Therefore, Kant argues, my will would be in conflict with itself.

One critic who found fault with this argument was the German philosopher Arthur Schopenhauer (1788–1860). In in his work *On the Basis of Morality* (1840), Schopenhauer quotes a poem by William Wordsworth (1770–1850)—"Memorials of a Tour in Scotland, 1803, XI: Rob Roy's Grave"—to make the point:

> I can perfectly well will injustice and unkindness as a universal maxim, and regulate the world accordingly,
>> upon the simple plan,
>> That they should take, who have the power
>> And they should keep, who can. (Schopenhauer, 2009, p. 158)

Furthermore we should recall that the maxim is one that gives permission to ignore the plight of others, rather than forbids us to help. If others have the permission to pass me by if they see me in trouble, it doesn't follow that they will. Perhaps out of sympathy, rather than duty, they might help. If so, the conflict is not as clear as Kant supposes. Here his argument seems to be much closer to the "golden rule" of many religious traditions: "Do as you would be done by," or act in such a way as you would have others act toward you. Thus, in this example Kant has not shown any real difficulty in our ability to will a universal law of mutual indifference.

Indeed, in looking at Kant's argument, it is possible to have some sympathy with this criticism of Kant in Mill's *Utilitarianism*:

> This remarkable man, whose system of thought will long remain one of the landmarks in the history of philosophical speculation, ..., lay[s] down a universal first principle as the origin and ground of moral obligation; it is this: "So act, that the rule on which thou actest would admit of being adopted as a law by all rational beings." But when he begins to deduce from this precept any of the actual duties of morality, he fails, almost grotesquely, to show that there would be any contradiction, any logical (not to say physical) impossibility, in the adoption by all rational beings of the most outrageously immoral rules of conduct. All he shows is that the consequences of their universal adoption would be such as no one would choose to incur. (1861/2001, p. 4)

Mill uses this point to suggest that Kant is a tacit utilitarian after all—a suggestion Kant would have thought a monstrous distortion. Schopenhauer makes the related criticism that in many cases, and contrary to his own claims, Kant bases his arguments on what people would and would not desire—they would not desire to be ignored—rather than on what is and is not possible to will. If Mill or Schopenhauer is right, Kant has not eliminated the "merely empirical" from morality after all. In Chapter 11, we will see whether Kant has ways of responding to his critics.

CHAPTER REVIEW
Summary

In this chapter we looked at the basics of Kant's ethical position: its grounding in the idea of good will, the distinction between acting *in accordance with* duty and *for the sake* of duty, the distinction between categorical and hypothetical imperatives, and the idea of a maxim of an action. We also examined Kant's slightly problematic examples to illustrate his theory. These examples—of suicide, false promises, neglecting your talents, and ignoring the plight of others—also illustrate two distinctions. One is the distinction between duties to yourself and duties to others; the other is the distinction between perfect and imperfect duties. It should be clear that Kant is a rigorous, highly principled thinker and moralist, laying down what he believes to be the correct moral approach for all rational creatures. In the next chapter we will pursue some of these themes in more detail.

Discussion Questions

1. Why does Kant regard the good will as the only unqualified good?
2. Explain the difference between categorical and hypothetical imperatives.
3. What difficulties are there in identifying the maxim of an action?
4. How well do Kant's examples illustrate his theory?

Key Terms

consequentialism, p. 164	a priori, p. 169
metaphysics, p. 164	categorical imperative, p. 170
intrinsic value, p. 167	hypothetical imperative, p. 170
instrumental value, p. 167	maxim of action, p. 170
empirical, p. 169	prudence, p. 171
a posteriori, p. 169	perfect and imperfect duties, p. 174

Key Thinkers

Immanuel Kant (1724–1804), pp. 163–179
Roy Harrod (1900–78), p. 163
Jeremy Bentham (1748–1832), pp. 164, 169
John Stuart Mill (1806–73), pp. 164, 179
Karl Marx (1818–83), p. 167
Adam Smith (1723–90), p. 167
Friedrich Schiller (1759–1805), p. 168
Marcus Singer (1926–2016), p. 172
Arthur Schopenhauer (1788–1860), pp. 178–179
William Wordsworth (1770–1850), p. 178

Further Reading

▪ Immanuel Kant's *Groundwork of the Metaphysics of Morals* (1785) is available in many editions. Here I have quoted from the edition by Cambridge University Press (1997). Selections from this work are reprinted in Jonathan Wolff (ed.), *Readings in Moral Philosophy* (W. W. Norton, 2018), which also contains selections from Jeremy Bentham's *Introduction to the Principles of Morals and Legislation* (1789).

▪ The edition I have used of Kant's *Critique of Practical Reason* is from Bobbs-Merrill (1956). (Original work published 1788)

▪ Schiller's brief criticism of Kant is quoted and discussed in H. J. Paton's *The Categorical Imperative* (Hutchinson & Co., 1947).

▪ I have used the Hackett (2001) edition of John Stuart Mill's *Utilitarianism.* (Original work published 1861)

▪ Selections from Karl Marx and Friedrich Engels' *The German Ideology,* where they accuse Kant of resting his theory on "mere willing," can be found in *The Marx Engels Reader,* 2nd ed. (W. W. Norton, 1978), edited by Robert Tucker.

▪ I have used the Cambridge University Press (1991) edition of Kant's *The Metaphysics of Morals.* (Original work published 1797)

▪ Arthur Schopenhauer's "On the Basis of Morality" is printed in his *The Two Fundamental Problems of Ethics* (Cambridge University Press, 2009), edited by David E. Cartwright and Edward E. Erdmann. (Original work published 1841)

CHAPTER 11

Challenges for Kantian Ethics

So act that you use humanity, whether in your own person or in the person of any other, always at the same time as an end, never merely as a means.

IMMANUEL KANT, GROUNDWORK OF THE METAPHYSICS OF MORALS

FORMULATIONS OF THE SUPREME PRINCIPLE OF MORALITY

In Chapter 10, we discussed the most fundamental elements of Kant's theory. Still we were left with a puzzle. Immanuel Kant (1724–1804) illustrates his theory with a series of four examples: suicide, false promises, neglecting your talents, and not helping others. Yet it is not always clear that these examples work as well as we might expect, given that Kant himself introduces them to illustrate his theory. To overcome these difficulties and more fully understand how the theory and the examples are best understood, let's look into some further aspects of Kant's moral philosophy.

We should recall that Kant is looking for the "supreme principle of morality," valid for all times and places and for all rational creatures. This is a noble and highly ambitious project. In *Groundwork of the Metaphysics of Morals* he suggests, as we have seen, that the demands of morality must be "categorical." He also proposes that the supreme principle of morality is the **categorical imperative**, which is so far formulated as "act only on that maxim through which you can at the same time will that it should become a universal law" (Kant, 1785/1997, 4:421, p. 31). Naturally enough, this is known as the "formula of the universal law," and other moral rules (which should also be categorical in form) are to be tested against it. We have seen so far that very plausibly, Kant's theory will rule out telling a lying promise; but more problematic are Kant's claims that his theory also rules out suicide, neglecting your talents, or ignoring the needs of others. However, Kant offers two other main formulations of the categorical imperative (his text also includes many minor variations): the "formula of humanity" and the "formula of the kingdom of ends." Understanding these alternative formulations is important not only in comprehending Kant's theory but also in helping us with his examples.

The formula of humanity, also cited at the start of this chapter, is this:

> So act that you use humanity, whether in your own person or in the person of any other, always at the same time as an end, never merely as a means. (4:429, p. 38)

And the formula of the kingdom of ends is this:

> Act in accordance with the maxims of a member giving universal laws for a merely possible kingdom of ends. (4:439, p. 46)

The logic of Kant's position is confusing because these three formulations of the categorical imperative are supposed to be equivalent in some sense. But they seem to use different concepts, so their similarities are not obvious. However, they may well all have the same outcomes. Scholars continue to debate the question. Perhaps it will be easier to see that an act is wrong by measuring it against one, rather than another, formulation of the categorical imperative. In any case, we should take a closer look at the two new formulations.

The Formula of the Kingdom of Ends

The final formulation, that of the kingdom of ends, does seem close to the formulation of universal law. Both use the concept of universal law. The concept of the kingdom of ends may seem obscure; but Kant's purpose is to emphasize that each of us is one person among others and that as far as morality is concerned, each of us is both ruler and ruled. Kant wants us to understand morality as a system of laws that each one of us, as a rational creature, makes; but it is also a system that binds us. We make the laws through our own reason, but these laws must be universal—binding everyone, including ourselves.

This is an intriguing idea. Kant is asking you to consider what moral laws you could will if they were to be absolutely binding not just on other people but also on you as a lawmaker. The formula of the kingdom of ends helps us focus on this question. Nevertheless, because it is reasonably close to the first formulation, it probably needs no further comment—other than to point out that this aspect of Kant's view was one of the inspirations for the version of social contract theory due to John Rawls (see Chapter 7). Rawls wanted us to consider how we would want to order society if we did not know our place in it, which requires us to take up some kind of universal perspective.

The Formula of Humanity

The second formulation, the formula of humanity, does introduce something new. Probably the most famous element of Kant's moral philosophy, it contrasts the idea of treating other people as a means to your ends with the idea of treating them as an "end in themselves." On first glance this is another obscure idea—what is an "end it itself"?—but at least at some level, the point is obvious. The notion of using someone (merely) as a means to your own ends is well understood, and such behavior is considered highly questionable. It is close to the idea of exploiting or manipulating another person, ignoring their interests as long as you get what you want, which is common in bad or abusive friendships or relationships. Whether or not you wish to follow other aspects of Kant's moral philosophy, this idea stands out as a potentially essential part of anyone's moral code: It is wrong for you to use someone merely as a means to your own ends.

What, though, is it to treat someone as an end in themselves? It is easier to understand the idea of someone *having* ends of their own, rather than *being* an end. But the two ideas actually come together, for Kant. To treat someone as an end is to treat them as having their own interests, goals, and ambitions—and most importantly, their own will—rather than using them simply as a way to get what you want yourself. Treating another person as a mere means is an attempt to subjugate their will to your own.

In ordinary life, however, we constantly seem to use people as means to our ends. When I buy a ticket at a station counter, I'm treating the person who sells me the ticket just as I would a ticket machine: as an object or device that can give me what I want, and I am apparently indifferent to that person's own will. Of course I should treat the person with courtesy and respect, and I should avoid being rude or dismissive; but if I am simply businesslike in the transaction, have I really done anything wrong? The obvious reply is that although I do use ticket sellers as means to my ends, I don't use them as *merely* a means to my ends, without regard to their own concerns. But suppose I found that the ticket seller was chained to the desk, or doing the job as a slave, trafficked by the railway company. Then I ought to feel obliged to do something in my power to help. Essentially, then, under normal circumstances, when the ticket seller has freely consented to the job under good conditions of knowledge, I am treating him or her as more than a means, although there may be no way of expressing my concern through my actions. If, on the other hand, I felt that the conditions of the ticket seller's work were absolutely no concern of mine, then arguably I am treating him or her as a mere means; and so I can rightly be criticized. And this is not merely an academic example. Think of imported clothes and other goods sometimes made under the most brutal and exploitative labor conditions. Campaigners commonly protest the use of workers as "mere means," and we are often even more concerned about those—often

undocumented immigrants—who are deceived into taking jobs as sex workers and find themselves trapped because they lack the legal standing to
make a complaint.

If we look again at Kant's formula of humanity, however, we will see an
element that I have not commented on so far. It says: "So act that you use
humanity, whether in your own person or in the person of any other, always
at the same time as an end, never merely as a means" (4:429, p. 38). Notice
it mentions "your own person" as well as "the person of any other." Kant
argues, therefore, that it is wrong to treat yourself merely as a means, besides
being wrong to treat others as a means. This is another perplexing idea. If
you are treating yourself as a means, then it must be a means to an end. If
it is a means to your own ends, then you are treating yourself as a means
and an end at the same time, so it seems. How can you subjugate your will
to your own will? Perhaps you could treat yourself as a means to someone
else's ends; but that sounds, potentially at least, like self-sacrificing, altruistic action rather than an immoral action. How, then, can you treat yourself
as a means? Clearly this is an important idea for Kant because it will connect
with the idea explored above that you have duties to yourself.

In ordinary moral thought, people do have some similar ideas. For example, we use the concept of degrading behavior. Some forms of work are
regarded as problematic from the viewpoint of human dignity, such as sex
work (mentioned above) or abusive forms of domestic service; but some
people take on these roles for the money. Arguably they are treating themselves as means, but the puzzle reoccurs. A means to what? A means to
make money, presumably. In the *Groundwork* Kant, inspiringly, says that
humanity has a dignity, not a price (4:435, p. 42). But even if we agree, why is
it degrading to take on some jobs for pay, but not others? What is the difference between a lap dancer and a railway ticket seller, or come to that, a moral
philosopher? All of the people in these roles use their talents to make money.

Kant does not directly address these questions, but we can illustrate his
ideas by looking at how he uses the formula of humanity to explain again
what is wrong with suicide. Kant says of the suicidal person:

> If he destroys himself in order to escape from a trying condition he makes
> use of a person merely as a means to maintain a tolerable condition up to the
> end of life. (4:429, p. 38)

This phrasing is odd, because suicide doesn't provide a tolerable condition until the end of one's life. Rather, it brings one's life to a close to stop
the continuation of what is likely to be an intolerable condition. In addition
the language of ends and means is awkward here; the person who commits

suicide is not using a person as a means. Yet there is clearly something to Kant's thinking. Possibly the person who takes his or her life could be accused of failing to treat their life as an end in itself, or as something that has value in and of itself, or failing in self-respect.

Once we recognize that for Kant, life has this sort of intrinsic value, perhaps we can begin to understand his position better. Kant's position contrasts with an alternative view that life is essentially little more than a container for pains and pleasures. In such a view, a valuable life is one that contains a positive balance of pleasures over pains. People who hold this more utilitarian view have every reason to consider committing suicide if all they see ahead is torment or pain. But for Kant that would be to degrade life from intrinsic value to instrumental value, for then life is regarded as an instrument for delivering positive experiences. And in this thought we finally see how it is possible to treat life as a means—a means to pleasure—rather than as an end of intrinsic value. In short, a person contemplating suicide is already regarding life in the wrong way, as a means rather than an end in itself. This analysis may not be what Kant intended, but it is at least one way of making sense of his position.

Autonomy and Heteronomy

At this point it will be helpful to introduce another of Kant's key distinctions, between what he calls **autonomy** and **heteronomy**. *Autonomy* is a familiar term these days, normally taken to be synonymous with freedom in the sense that to be autonomous is to be free. Kant would have no complaint with this equivalence, but he would want to push the understanding of autonomy to a deeper level. From the Ancient Greek, *autonomy* means "self-law." And of course for Kant, the moral person is autonomous in this sense: He or she must act as if making law that would hold for all rational creatures. Thus for Kant, morality, reason, and freedom coincide.

The heteronomous person, in contrast, is essentially someone who acts non-autonomously, perhaps in self-interest or even out of sympathy for others. Suppose that you decide not to cheat your customers in order to preserve your reputation, or even because you like them. Then, although you are acting in accordance with the moral law, Kant would say your action is heteronomous, not autonomous, and therefore not of genuine moral worth.

Let's continue with Kant's examples in the light of his principle of humanity, which tells us not to treat others as a means only, but also at the same time as ends in themselves. We can deal quickly with the second example, the lying promise. The person who is told a lie is treated merely as a means. Kant's way of bringing out this point is to say that the person I lie to *could not possibly* agree with my action. And there is a strict logical impossibility here. If the person does agree, then I am no longer successfully lying, for my lying depends on actual deception. Kant's commentators have found here a powerful argument against deception as well as coercion. Both deception and coercion, by their nature, depend on the other party not agreeing. Therefore, if "possible agreement" is a necessary condition of a person's action being morally acceptable, then both deception and coercion are easily ruled out.

Neglecting your talents was the third example. We can again regard this example as sharing some of the characteristics of suicide: In Kant's view, the person engaged in this action is putting self-indulgence ahead of taking life seriously. Kant's discussion of this case is brief: He says that although failing to develop your talents is compatible with treating the humanity in yourself as an end, everyone has a duty to promote the end, and neglecting your talents fails to promote the end. Not only, then, does Kant think that life has intrinsic value, he thinks that we have a duty to cultivate our talents, and failing to do so is failing to promote the value in life. This is not an unusual view: In ordinary life we are unhappy to see those with great potential waste their talents, even if in other respects their lives go reasonably well. Think of someone with great athletic and academic ability who spends too much time partying, doesn't make the team, and fails some courses. We might observe that the choice is theirs, but we are likely to say so with a little sadness. This ordinary attitude makes even more sense in view of some religious assumptions. For example, if you believe that your life is a gift from God and that in return you have a duty to develop your talents, then not doing so is a violation of your religious duties. But even atheists seem to share something of Kant's attitude that is it somehow wrong to let your talents go to waste.

The final example from Kant was indifference to the suffering of others. Again it is hard to see how by ignoring someone, I am treating him or her as a means. But I am clearly not treating that person as an end. Consider, for example, how a Kantian should respond to a famine. It does not seem right that a Kantian should say, "As long as I am not the cause of the problem, I have no moral duties." Rather, as contemporary philosopher Onora O'Neill (b. 1941) has argued, a Kantian should consider not just how to address hunger (as would be the main concern of a utilitarian) but also how to help those who are suffering take control of their own lives again (O'Neill, in Wolff, 2018). Only in this way do you respect their humanity. Kant argues that to treat another as an end, we must take seriously his or her own ends too. This view also helps us understand Kant's idea that we form a kingdom of ends through our morally worthy action.

USING KANT'S THEORY

Now that we have an understanding of Kant's position, we can consider whether it solves the question of how, morally, we should act. To his immense credit, Kant has provided us with a method of testing whether any proposed action is morally acceptable. This is a philosophical breakthrough. Before Kant, although many philosophers provided reasons for and against acting one way or another, along with elaborate arguments, they offered little or no formal methodology to be used in calculating an answer. Kant regarded this deficiency as a disgrace and was determined to do better. We can represent his solution as proceeding in several steps. To apply it to a particular moral problem, you need to answer the following questions:

1. What action do you propose?
2. What is the maxim of your action?
3. a. Can you will that the maxim of your action should become a universal law?
   b. Are you proposing to treat yourself or another person merely as a means and not as an end in himself or herself?
   c. Are you acting in accordance with the maxims of a member giving universal laws for a kingdom of ends?

Of these questions, perhaps only the first is straightforward: What action do you propose? Still, we could make trouble even here. Do we always know what we want to do? Often, perhaps even most of the time, we just find ourselves doing things rather than making a conscious decision. But let's leave that complication aside for now. When we are confronted with a moral problem or dilemma, we generally do become highly aware of the options that face us.

So let's move to the second question: What is the maxim of your action? In the *Groundwork*, Kant seems to assume this query is relatively unproblematic. For each example—suicide, lying promises, neglecting talents, and ignoring the needy—he seems to have no difficulty in going directly to its maxim and does not raise the question of how a maxim is to be identified. We noted in the last chapter that this is not always a straightforward matter, using the example of someone who wants to become a carpenter. What is their maxim? "Become a carpenter"? "Follow your vocation in life"? There are many maxims we can offer, and some of them could be universalized and others not. Which maxims are genuine, and which are not? Remember that Kant said even we ourselves do not always know the maxim of our action, because we are all prone to self-deception.

Once More: Kant on Lying

Kant himself discusses a case that illustrates the problem of identifying the maxim of your action. Remember that Kant's argument seems to work best in the example of making a false promise. A slightly different example is telling a lie. Again the maxim of "tell a lie when telling the truth would lead to difficulties" seems incapable of being made a universal law. We can argue that having moral permission to tell lies would result in nobody taking anyone's word for anything, and so telling a lie would no longer even be possible. But might it be possible to have a principle that allows us tell lies in some cases rather than others? Kant is at least willing to have the conversation.

One relatively lighthearted case that Kant discusses comes from his book called *The Doctrine of Virtue*:

> Can an untruth from mere politeness (e.g., the "your obedient servant" at the end of a letter) be considered a lie? No one is deceived by it. An author asks one of his readers, "How do you like my work?" One could merely seem to give an answer, by joking about the impropriety of the question. But who has his wit always ready? The author will take the slightest hesitation in answering as an insult. May one, then, say what is expected of one? (1797/1991, p. 227)

Kant doesn't answer his own question here, which is interesting. It suggests that, contrary to common belief, he is prepared to entertain the thought that sometimes lying can be acceptable. However, another example of lying has attracted much more attention. In a short essay entitled "On a Supposed Right to Lie Because of Philanthropic Concerns" (1797/1994), Kant discusses the case of someone who is confronted at his door by a murderer intending to kill a person who is hiding in the house. The murderer asks whether the potential victim is there. This fictional example became a tragic reality in Kant's Germany around 150 years later, when the Nazis sought out Jews sheltering in the houses of their friends and neighbors.

Kant's principles seem to entail that you have a duty not to lie even to save a life. And astonishingly to some readers, this is what Kant actually says in response to the criticism of the Swiss French philosopher Benjamin Constant (1767–1830), who had argued plausibly enough that in the case of the potential murderer, lying is justified. Kant cites Constant's argument that in acting immorally, the murderer forfeits the protection of morality and so has "no right to the truth." We can read this argument in Kantian terms as supposing that if a lie were told, the maxim of the action would be as follows: "Tell a lie if it would save a life and the person to whom you are telling the lie has no right to the truth." Because the circumstances of this case are so specific, it may be possible to universalize this maxim without abandoning the practice of truth-telling. When murderers are around asking awkward questions, and people are petrified with fear, conventions of true communication are fairly chaotic to begin with, and so there may be no established practice to break down. Would a murderer really expect people to tell the truth in these circumstances anyway?

Kant does not approve of the idea that the murderer has no right to the truth. Telling a lie harms humanity as a whole rather than only the murderer, by weakening the practice of truth-telling. So should you tell the murderer the truth? Some will think the correct response might be simply refusing to say anything if you suspect that the visitor harbors evil intent. Kant also argues that telling a lie could backfire: Suppose you tell the murderer that the person is not there; but unknown to you, he has slipped out of the house. If the murderer leaves and then finds the person in the street, then through your lie "you may be justly accused as having caused his death" (1797/1994, p. 164). This analysis does seem harsh, especially when Kant also argues that if you tell the truth and then the murderer goes into your house and kills the person, you are blameless—at least from the viewpoint of "public justice," which presumably means you should not be punished. That argument may be right as a point about punishment, but it is harder to agree that morally you have done no wrong by helping the murderer in this way. Perhaps Kant is on stronger ground when he suggests that we humans are very bad at calculating consequences, and we do better when following firm principles; this was the insight, as we saw in Chapter 10, that leads to rule utilitarianism. But it is debatable whether this is a good argument for Kant's position.

I introduced the example of lying to a murderer as a way of illustrating the problem that any action can fall under more than one maxim and that it could be universalized under one maxim but not under another. Kant, though, refuses to take this way out, and he ends up with a rigorous theory about the morality of lying. Is it too rigorous? We will return to this question shortly.

Kantian Ethics in Real Life

For now, let's return to the question of how to use Kant's theory. One of his tests was whether you can will the universalization of the maxim of your action, and we saw that Kant suggests two ways in which a proposed maxim can fail that test. For perfect duties it is impossible to *universalize* the maxim, as in the case of lying or, more controversially, suicide. For imperfect duties it is impossible to *will* the universalization, as in failing to develop your talents or declining to help those in need. But we also have the appealing formula of humanity: Never treat a person, whether yourself or another, as purely a means to your ends; but at the same time, treat that person as an end in himself or herself. Another the formula is the kingdom of ends. If, as Kant claims, these are equivalent, then any action that passes one formula should pass them all. And equally, any action that fails one formula should fail them all. Kant does not demonstrate this argument in detail; and if the formulas are equivalent, it is not clear that we need more than one of them, although Kant plausibly suggests that they bring out different aspects of the moral law. Bearing this point in mind, in some cases it may be easier to judge the immorality of an act under one formulation than it is under another.

The key question for us, though, is whether Kant is right. Certainly his formulations of the categorical imperatives are useful guides to moral behavior. It will be significant to know whether or not a person can will the universalization of the maxim of his or her action. For example, if I am contemplating taking something from a shop without paying, I might ask, "Could taking goods whenever you prefer not to pay for them be universalized?" The answer, presumably, is that if theft became very widespread, then we would lose the concept of individual property because we would have lost the guarantee of safe possession. But without the concept of property, there is no concept of theft. Hence this fits neatly with Kant's account: It is impossible to will the universalization of the maxim of permitting casual theft. The institution of owning property would break down, and there would be no such thing as theft. This shows me that theft is wrong.

Here is another example: Suppose you agree to go to a party with a friend; but the day before the event, you get a more exciting invitation from someone you find more interesting and attractive. However, accepting the second invitation means letting down your friend. What should you do? You could do a range of things: just not turning up at the party, telling your friend you are sick, explaining the situation and seeing if your friend knows someone else who would equally like to go to the party, and so on. In some of these ways of behaving, you are recognizing that your friend is equally a human being to you—having his or her own will and goals, able to agree to and disagree with courses of action. Or, put another way, treating your friend as an end in himself or herself. In the cases of bad behavior you are not so much using your friend as a means, but rather failing to recognize him or her as an end—to recognize the humanity in his or her person, as Kant might put it. You would be ignoring your friend's interests and goals because those interests and goals no longer fit with yours. Having some of Kant's moral philosophy in your head will probably help you make better moral decisions.

But has Kant solved the problem of how to act? In other words, is passing Kant's test necessary for an act to be morally acceptable? (It cannot be morally acceptable if it fails the test of the categorical imperative.) And is it sufficient? (Anything that passes is morally acceptable.) We need to consider at least three questions.

First, as we have seen, it is not always clear whether an action passes the test. One reason this may happen is that there can be room for disagreement about the maxim of your action; and it is possible that you can will the universalization of one maxim, but not another. But even when there is no doubt about the maxim, it is not always clear whether you can will its universalization, as we have seen with Kant's own examples. Not all of these cases are obvious. A different philosopher may have argued for different conclusions in some of the cases Kant uses, even while using Kant's own method. These cases, then, turn out to be difficult matters of interpretation. I am not claiming that Kant is wrong in his interpretation of his own examples; I am saying we don't really know how to tell. Hence, although Kant gives us a formula, seeing how it applies is far from straightforward—at least in some cases.

The first question was about the difficulty of applying the formula. Now we need to look at the question of whether all morally correct action will pass the test. Consider the example of telling a lie to the murderer at the door. What is the right thing to do here? Personally, I'm attracted to the idea that the right thing is to tell the murderer that it is none of his business. But realistically, that response is unlikely to settle the matter. The next thing the murderer might do would be to take out his gun and point it at my head. At that point, out of fear, many people may well tell the truth; but a courageous person may tell a lie and say that the person is not in the house. Is his or her action morally wrong? Kant thinks so, apparently.

What if we disagree with Kant and think it is right to lie to the murderer, but we agree with Kant that the maxim of the action of lying to a murderer cannot be willed to be a universal law? Then we disagree with Kant's moral theory. Using this combination of views, we do not need to pass the test in order to act in a morally correct way. Alternatively, we might say we need to find a more specialized maxim of the action; but then this throws us back to the first problem of identifying the maxim.

We see, then, some reason to doubt that passing the test is a necessary condition of performing a morally correct action. What, then, about the third question? Is passing the test enough to show that an action is morally correct? (Is passing the test sufficient for acting morally?) In fact the same example shows the difficulty here. Telling the truth to the murderer passes the test, Kant says. Yet if we think this action would be morally wrong, then some morally wrong actions pass the test. Of course Kant would think we have simply gone astray in our judgments of right and wrong. Some will agree with Kant, others not. But in conclusion, we have to concede that it is far from obvious that Kant has solved the problem of how to know whether we have acted morally even though he has made some extremely important contributions to the question of how to approach moral problems.

FREEDOM AND MORALITY

At the start of this chapter, I mentioned that one of the key motivating ideas for Kant—and an idea that his contemporary defenders often emphasize—is that of freedom. The distinction between freedom and some form of determinism has already come up in the distinction between heteronomy and autonomy. Heteronomy was, in essence, acting on the basis of your desires, whereas autonomy—or freedom—involves acting on the basis of your reason. For Kant the main difference between humans and other animals is that human beings are capable of autonomous action, which is to say action based on reason. And that trait comes down to being able to override your desires and act according to the moral law: the law you create through your own reason. Freedom, then, is acting in accordance with the moral law.

This view may seem surprising. To act freely, many will think, is to act without constraint. But the moral law is a form of constraint. Therefore, some will argue, acting in accordance with the moral law is to act unfreely rather than freely. How can I be free if I have to follow the moral law? But Kant would argue that this argument gets everything upside down. Kant would pose the opposite question: How can you be free if, like the animals, all you do is follow your own desires and inclinations? Freedom is the act of overcoming your desires to act in accordance with reason; and reason, in turn, requires you to act as if through your will, your maxim would become a universal law. Reason—the exercise of freedom—yields morality.

Of course, we don't have to agree with Kant on this point; but we must, I think, concede that his position has some merit. Consider someone offered a large bribe to do something they know to be wrong, perhaps to award a scarce and undeserved university place to an applicant with poor test scores. Who has more freedom: the person who accepts the bribe or the person who declines it? Certainly we would say that the person refusing the bribe has some strength of character that the other lacks. We admire people who overcome temptation to do the right thing. Do they act with greater freedom too? It seems that the case can be argued. In any event we see here the firm connection for Kant between freedom, reason, and the moral law.

KANT AND CHRISTIANITY

In the main elements of his writings on ethics, Kant made it clear that he would not argue from religious premises or introduce any religious elements into his theory. In an earlier chapter we read a quote from the *Groundwork* that reveals Kant's position on the problem of a religious foundation for morality:

> [T]he concept of [God's] will ... made up of the attributes of desire for glory and dominion combined with dreadful representations of power and vengefulness, would have to be the foundation for a system of morals that would be directly opposed to morality. (1785/1997, 4:443, p. 49)

Yet critics have alleged that Kant's theory makes sense only in light of the type of protestant Christian views that he held. And in some of his writings, Kant does make a clear connection between morality and aspects of religion. We will return to Kant's explicit statements shortly, but first let's look at the ways in which critics have alleged that Kant's views may have a religious aspect. For example, we noted in Chapter 10 that Kant's arguments against suicide and against neglecting your talents would fit well with a religious view that we have been put on earth by God and that we are here to serve God's purposes, not our own. Duties to yourself, in this interpretation, make much more sense as duties to God, your creator. And this may be why some atheists deny that we do have duties to ourselves.

In fact Arthur Schopenhauer (1788–1860) alleged that Kant smuggled in a religious conception of ethics right from the start by assuming that morality takes the form of "law" or "command." In *On the Basis of Morality*, Schopenhauer argues that the "Mosaic Decalogue," by which he means the Ten Commandments, is the model and source for Kant's "theological" morals (Schopenhauer, 1840/2009, pp. 30–31). Friedrich Nietzsche (1844–1900) makes a similar claim in *Beyond Good and Evil* (1886/1999), suggesting that ultimately the basis of Kant's system is something like religious faith in a new form, consistent with the Lutheran Protestant tradition into which Kant was born and raised.

Kant himself gives these criticisms a surprising degree of support in his later work *The Critique of Practical Reason* (1788/1965). Recall that at the start of this chapter, I mentioned Kant's suggestion that the point of morality is not to make us happy, but to make us worthy of happiness. The highest good, Kant argues, is to be both virtuous and happy, which are apparently quite different things. But he raises an awkward question regarding someone who achieves virtue, and hence is worthy of happiness, but does not actually manage to achieve happiness in life. Kant seems to find this an intolerable state of affairs, and he insists that the morally virtuous person must receive his or her reward somewhere, somehow. This, and other arguments about the perfectibility of human beings, leads him to posit the existence of "the author of Nature," who will arrange matters in a more satisfactory way. This idea leads him to argue for the immortality of the soul and the existence of God.

Because of his insistence that the virtuous person acts for the sake of duty, not for happiness, and his argument against a religious basis for morality, it may be something of a shock to see Kant so explicitly incorporate elements of religion. Nevertheless religion enters not as the explicit foundation of Kant's moral beliefs but as a result of his moral position. However, if Schopenhauer and Nietzsche are right, Kant's moral philosophy is shot through with religious belief. In any case, the non-believer still can find great value in Kant's main insights about the importance of universalization of action and of not treating people as means.

MORAL PRINCIPLES, RACE, AND GENDER

We noted in Chapter 8 that John Stuart Mill (1806–73) was able to illustrate the strengths of the utilitarian approach to morality by deducing that it supported the liberation of women from male subjection. More problematically, in Chapter 9 we saw that Mill seemed to think utilitarianism supported the colonial enterprise—at least until "barbarians" had been raised to a level of civilization that would make them fit to receive their freedom.

In reading Kant's moral philosophy, it is natural to think that it could be an inspiring foundation for gender and racial equality. The idea that we should never treat others as a means only to our own ends appears to rule out domineering forms of marriage, slavery, abusive contracts of employment, and many social ills. The proposal that you should imagine yourself as a legislator for the kingdom of ends suggests that, as with social contract theory, you must take everyone's viewpoint into account. Doing so would seem to rule out all forms of discrimination, for why would you agree to a set of rules that might discriminate against yourself? Contemporary theorists seeking gender and racial equality have found much of use in Kant's work.

However, as Kant would have been the first to remind us, appearances can be deceptive. In looking at Kant's own writings, we do not find him developing his ideas in these directions. In fact, we find the opposite. Kant appeared to believe that only white males were fully capable of the level of rationality that made them full moral subjects. For example, he explicitly denied that women should have the vote, on the grounds that they lack economic self-sufficiently. Of course, this argument invites the question of why women do lack economic self-sufficiency. Kant would have argued that it is a matter of natural capacity rather than, as Mill insisted, unjust and discriminatory social structures. But the fact remains that Kant refused to take the opportunity to extend full moral equality to women. (For discussion of Kant and gender, see Herman, 2002.)

Even worse, perhaps, is Kant's position on race. Besides working on philosophy, he wrote and lectured on geography and anthropology despite never leaving his hometown of Königsberg in Northern Germany (an international port with a steady stream of visitors). Kant believed in a natural hierarchy of races with white Europeans at the top and other races ordered below. We saw that Mill held a similar view, although he believed the situation was temporary and full racial equality would eventually be possible. Underlying Mill's view of differences in achievement, there seems to be a commitment to ultimate moral equality of everyone. Not so for Kant, who argued that certain inherent characteristics in the various races explain what he saw as the different levels of intelligence, talent, and capacity for hard work (recall his comment about the "South Sea Islanders" mentioned in Chapter 10). (For discussion of Kant and race, see Hill and Boxill, 2000).

These facts about Kant's personal views are a shock, especially when compared with the deep commitment to equality in his writings. At one level, though, they appear to be relatively superficial—simply departures from the logic of his view in order to make it consistent with the common, though by no means universal, prejudices of the 18th century. The underlying logic of his position opposes sexism and racism, despite his own views

Nevertheless, in recent decades Kant's moral theory has come under pressure. Objections arise especially from feminist philosophers, although these objections could be applied equally to utilitarian theory. Kant's view, we have noted, emphasizes the importance of impartial reason as the foundation of moral thinking. This is where the criticism starts. The American social psychologist Carol Gilligan (b. 1936) developed the main argument, which is obvious even in the title of her book: *In a Different Voice* (1982/1993). As Gilligan argued, there is evidence that men and women reason about moral questions in different ways. Men, she argued, look for clear moral principles or formulas that they can apply to give answers to moral questions by using rational thought. Gilligan claims that women, however, pay much more attention to the particularities of situations. They emphasize the importance of relations between people, especially the "caring" emotions of love, sympathy, and empathy.

This argument is an extremely important development in moral philosophy. If Gilligan is correct, we should consider whether moral philosophy has, throughout its history, been "gendered": Does it ignore the ways that women think about moral problems? If so, then perhaps we need to rethink moral philosophy in very radical ways. But at the same time, while sympathetic to the criticisms of Kant, many feminists worry that Gilligan's approach allows back in the sexist assumption that men and women have essentially different natures that fit them for different roles in society. Many women will resent the apparent implication that abstract thought does not come as naturally to women as it does to men, and many men will resent the idea that they are less capable of caring than women. Given the importance of this issue, we will return to it in detail in Chapter 14.

CHAPTER REVIEW

Summary

In this chapter we saw that Kant offers three main formulations of the categorical imperative: the formula of universal law; the formula of humanity; and the formula of the kingdom of ends. Although they are supposedly equivalent, having the three formulations can help us apply Kant's theory. The formula of humanity, which tells us never to use others merely as a means to our ends, has been found especially inspiring. Kant's distinction between autonomy and heteronomy was also explained, and we looked again at Kant's key examples. We noted, though, that Kant's approach may seem overly strict because he believes it shows that we are required to tell the truth even to a potential murderer.

Kant's theory is strongly linked to notions of freedom. A significant link also exists between Kant's ethics and his religious belief, although the precise nature of that link remains controversial. We looked briefly at Kant's surprising views on race. I also pointed out that Kant's reliance on abstract principles of ethics at the heart of his theory has made him vulnerable to criticism from feminist writers, who point out the absence of attention to the "ethics of care" in his writing.

Discussion Questions

1. Explain the three different formulations of the categorical imperative.
2. Discuss Kant's views on the ethics of lying to a potential murderer.
3. How can you use Kant's theory to decide how to act in the face of a moral dilemma?
4. Is it fair to accuse Kant of smuggling religious doctrine into his moral philosophy?

Key Terms

categorical imperative, p. 182   heteronomy, p. 186
autonomy, p. 186

Key Thinkers

Immanuel Kant (1724–1804), pp. 182–197
John Rawls (1921–2002), p. 183
Onora O'Neill (b. 1941), p. 187
Benjamin Constant (1767–1830), pp. 189–190
Arthur Schopenhauer (1788–1860), pp. 194–195
Friedrich Nietzsche (1844–1900), pp. 194–195
Carol Gilligan (b. 1936), pp. 196–197

Further Reading

▪ John Rawls's *A Theory of Justice* was first published in 1971. I have used the revised edition published by Harvard University Press (1999).

▪ The edition of Kant's *Groundwork of the Metaphysics of Morals* (1785) used here is from Cambridge University Press (1997). Selections from this work are included in Jonathan Wolff (ed.) *Readings in Moral Philosophy* (W. W. Norton, 2018), which also includes selections from Rawls and from Onora O'Neill's paper "Ending World Hunger."

▪ Kant's *Doctrine of Virtue* is included in his *The Metaphysics of Morals*, and is quoted here from the edition by Cambridge University Press (1991). (Original work published 1797)

▪ "On a Supposed Right to Lie Because of Philanthropic Concerns" is available in Kant's *Ethical Philosophy* (Hackett, 1994), translated by James W. Ellington. (Original work published 1797)

- Arthur Schopenhauer's "On the Basis of Morality" is printed in his *The Two Fundamental Problems of Ethics* (Cambridge University Press, 2009), edited by David E. Cortwright and Edward E. Erdmann. (Original work published 1841)

- Friedrich Nietzsche's *Beyond Good and Evil* is available in an edition from Vintage (1989) edited by Walter Kaufmann. Selections from this work appear in Wolff, *Readings in Moral Philosophy*.

- The edition I have used of Kant's *Critique of Practical Reason* is from Bobbs-Merrill (1956). (Original work published 1788)

- Carol Gilligan's *In a Different Voice* is published in a revised edition by Harvard University Press (1993). (Original work published 1982)

- Barbara Herman's excellent discussion of Kant on women "Could It Be Worth Thinking about Kant on Sex and Marriage?" can be found in L. Antony and C. Witt (eds.), *A Mind of One's Own* (Westview Press, 2002), 53–72.

- Thomas Hill and Bernard Boxill's examination of Kant's views on race is "Kant and Race," printed in Bernard Boxill (ed.), *Race and Racism* (Oxford University Press, 2000), 448–469.

CHAPTER 12

Virtue Ethics: Aristotle

Our discussion will be adequate if it has as much clearness as the subject-matter admits of, for precision is not to be sought alike in all discussions, any more than in all the products of the crafts. ... We must be content, then, in speaking of such subjects and with such premisses to indicate the truth roughly and in outline, and in speaking about things which are only for the most part true, and with premisses of the same kind, to reach conclusions that are no better. In the same spirit, therefore, should each type of statement be received; for it is the mark of an educated man to look for precision in each class of things just so far as the nature of the subject admits.

ARISTOTLE, NICOMACHEAN ETHICS

ARISTOTLE'S MORAL METHODOLOGY

As we have just seen, Immanuel Kant and Jeremy Bentham (and by extension, utilitarians generally) sought a rigorous methodology to ground their moral philosophies. This search led them to propose abstract formulas to address moral problems. But almost 2,500 years earlier, the Greek philosopher Aristotle suggested that we cannot always expect to find precise answers to ethical questions because they are often messy, complicated, and ambiguous. Instead, as in this chapter's opening quotation, Aristotle proposed that sometimes we should expect the answers that we do settle on to be tentative or imprecise.

Aristotle, then, is trying to manage our expectations. He is not going to offer a formula to solve ethical dilemmas, although as we shall see later, this has not stopped some readers from trying to find one in his work. If you try this, you will come away frustrated. Therefore, in one sense, Aristotle's approach is an obvious disappointment. Life presents us with moral problems. What is moral philosophy for if not to show us how to solve those problems?

This has long been the hope of those who have turned to moral philosophy. Bentham thought he could show how all moral questions could be answered through the application of the theory of utilitarianism. Kant doesn't provide a formula as simple as that of the utilitarians; but he does provide a test, a systematic way to approach our moral problems, suggesting that any action has to match up to the **categorical imperative**. Aristotle, however, proposes that while moral philosophy can help us to think about moral questions and can help to guide our actions, morality cannot be reduced to a formula, or a simple set of rules, or even a test against which to judge actions. Acting morally requires what the Greeks called **phronesis**, or "practical wisdom," requiring judgment and experience. Unfortunately for those who crave clear solutions, morality, in this view, does not have a user's manual.

It may seem strange to discuss one of the earliest known moral philosophers so close to the end of this book. Aristotle lived from 384 to 322 BCE. He was a pupil of Plato (429?–347 BCE), and a member of Plato's Academy in Athens for 20 years, before going on to found his own school, the Lyceum. What can a thinker from the Ancient Greek world tell us about the world we live in now? Aristotle's world was very different from ours: In it, slavery was taken for granted, and women were not permitted to take part in politics nor in many areas of public life. Contemporary readers will be surprised by Aristotle's attempts to defend these then conventional, but now indefensible, elements of Greek life in his work *The Politics* (we will return to these issues in Chapter 13). Yet Aristotle's general approach to thinking about morality provides a fresh perspective for people today. We can best appreciate the appeal of a non-formulaic moral philosophy such as Aristotle's by seeing the difficulties of some more modern alternatives, as we have done by looking at utilitarian and Kantian theories.

But understanding Aristotle's theory is not a straightforward matter. His ideas date from a world of 2,500 years ago, and what he actually wrote down himself has been lost. The substantial body of his work that we have— almost 3,000 pages in standard editions—most likely consists of notes taken by his students. Sometimes they seem unfinished, obscure, or even contradictory. Reading Aristotle is always a matter of construction and interpretation, and Aristotle's *Nicomachean Ethics* (ed. Brown, 2009), the text we will focus on here, is an odd book by the standards of contemporary philosophy. It has many familiar elements, which include fascinating and insightful analysis of perennially important ethical questions such as defining when an individual should be held morally responsible for his or her actions. But much of the book reads almost like a self-help manual or one giving advice on personal relations.

Indeed, *Nicomachean Ethics* is often taken as an account of how to lead a good life, which after all is what many people hope for in a work of moral philosophy. For instance, we are told that although a father can disown his son in exceptional circumstances, a son should never disown his father (ed. Brown, 2009, 1163b20, p. 162). There are many pages on the nature of friendship and what friends can expect from each other. The advice is generally wise, but it is not always obvious that a philosophical problem is being addressed. Furthermore, it is hard to know what to make of some fairly disconnected observations, such as "in the theatre the people who eat sweets do so most when the acting is poor" (1175, p. 190).

Perhaps Aristotle would say that in the modern world, philosophers have made too much of a distinction between the subject of moral philosophy as a theoretical topic that may interest only scholars and the questions of how people should live their lives as a practical challenge that we all face. Much of the moral philosophy we have looked at so far in this book tells us how we should *think* about morality. Popular books on moral topics, such as business or medical ethics, might tell us how to *act*. Aristotle is concerned with both thinking and acting: the theoretical and the practical. But when we turn to the practical, Aristotle is mostly concerned about what sorts of *people we should be*: what *characters* we should try to develop. Of course character entails thought and action, but it also involves emotions and responsiveness to others. Morality requires us not only to think and act but to *feel* in certain ways: sympathy, guilt, pleasure, resentment, and so on. In this way Aristotle is presenting a much more holistic theory than many other philosophers did later.

Aristotle, then, is interested in the broad question of "How should I live?" not just "What is the morally correct way for me to act?" In answering his question, we will need to think about caring for others as well as ourselves. This point is worth emphasizing. Many people believe that morality often conflicts with self-interest; therefore, the principles of altruism and egoism often clash. Acting morally, in such a view, requires extensive self-denial. But for Aristotle, this idea of an intrinsic conflict between acting for yourself and acting for others is a mistake. Essentially, Aristotle's ambition is to show how these two sides of life can be brought into harmony (and in this respect, there are connections between Aristotle's thinking and the theory of ethical egoism we looked at in Chapter 6). With the right training and upbringing, concern for yourself will also be concern for others, and vice versa. As we will see, this view means that moral education will be a central topic for Aristotle.

THE GOOD LIFE

In *Nicomachean Ethics*, Aristotle begins by discussing what human beings want to achieve. His initial answer is no surprise: All agree—the multitude and the refined alike—that living the good life or doing well is the same as being happy. But what is it to be happy? Not, says Aristotle, a life of pleasure: "The mass of mankind are evidently quite slavish in their tastes, preferring the life suitable to beasts" (ed. Brown, 2009, 1095b, p. 6). Aristotle's view seemingly was echoed by John Stuart Mill, who claimed that it is better to be Socrates dissatisfied than a pig satisfied (see Chapter 9). This view contrasts with that of Bentham; he would have dismissed this claim as elitist prejudice, arguing that happiness is to be understood in terms of pleasure and that pleasures will vary in intensity and duration but not in quality.

Aristotle would reject Bentham's position as too simplistic. For Aristotle, happiness is a richer notion than pleasure. Indeed the Greek term he uses, **eudaimonia,** still does not have a single agreed-upon translation into English. Sometimes it is translated as "happiness," and sometimes as "human flourishing" or "fulfillment." It is also often left untranslated. The notion of human flourishing is perhaps the most helpful, and it is also similar to the term *thriving* and the associated problem, sometimes noted in children or older people, of "failing to thrive." A flourishing, or thriving, individual is someone who is physically and mentally healthy, enjoying life, and accomplishing a number of goals. He or she typically has friends, family, and a supportive social circle. Some of these ideas can extend to nonhuman animals and beyond: We know what it is for a dog or a horse to flourish, or even a house plant. A good human life is, for Aristotle, a life of human flourishing.

What, though, does happiness, or human flourishing, or fulfillment, involve? Not honor, says Aristotle, because that is too subjective, depending on what people choose to value for the time being. And not virtue either (a term we will come back to). As Aristotle says, perhaps rather oddly, "Even [virtue] appears somewhat incomplete; for possession of virtue seems actually compatible with being asleep, or with lifelong inactivity" (ed. Brown, 2009, 1096a, p. 7). To answer the question of the nature of human flourishing, Aristotle suggests, we need to understand the "function" of a human being. And this makes some sense. A flourishing plant is one that does what we expect a plant to do—grow taller, greener, and (in some cases) to produce fruit or flowers. A flourishing human being, then, would be one who does what we expect a human being to do:

> For just as for a flute player, a sculptor, or any artist, and in general, for all things that have a function or activity, the good and the "well" is thought to reside in the function; so would it seem to be for man, if he has a function. (1098a, p. 11)

Is it right, though, to think that human beings have a function? Is sensible to ask what human beings are for? We raised this question in relation to the theory of **natural law** in Chapter 5, and now we can see why Aristotle is regarded as one of the founders of natural law theory. In a religious worldview this question of whether man has a function may well make sense, for it is reasonable to ask why God has decided to create human beings. Indeed theologians have asked this question throughout history, especially in the context of Christian belief that God is perfect and self-sufficient. If so, then why create anything else? Human beings must have been created for a purpose, in some religious views at least. Aristotle, obviously, is writing in the pre-Christian era; and the Greek gods were a colorful and diverse group, far from perfect and with self-serving aims. Aristotle does not relate this question to a theological concern. Rather he seems to feel it will help make sense of the question about what happiness means for human beings if we consider their function. And this is what he does:

> Human good turns out to be activity of soul exhibiting virtue, and if there are more than one virtue, in accordance with the best and most complete. But we must add "in a complete life." (ed. Brown, 2009, 1098a, p. 12)

It is important to consider that Aristotle emphasizes the "activity of soul" exhibiting virtue; presumably, this is to get around his earlier observation that a person can be virtuous even when asleep. What's more, he emphasizes the importance of sustaining virtue over a complete lifetime. He also gives a critical role to the "intellectual virtues," going as far as arguing that reflection or contemplation leads to the highest degree of happiness because it is more godlike than anything else we do. Unlike the lower animals, Aristotle says, we humans are rational animals. He regards all animals as having a "locomotive soul" that allows them to move and a "nutritive soul" for growth and reproduction, but only human beings have a rational soul too. Here we have arrived at Aristotle's conception of happiness: to live a life in conformity with human excellence or virtue. But as we saw above, for Aristotle this is not a life of self-sacrifice, for the life of active virtue is pleasant. Indeed Aristotle argues:

> The man who does not rejoice in noble actions is not even good: since no one would call a man just if he did not enjoy acting justly, nor any man liberal who did not enjoy liberal actions; and similarly in all other cases. If this is so, virtuous actions must be in themselves pleasant. (ed. Brown, 2009, 1099a, p. 14)

In one way this statement contrasts with Kant's view, in which the moral motive was strictly detached from the motive of pleasure. Even though Kant too thought that acting morally would often be associated with a feeling of pleasure, he would not agree with Aristotle that you could not be a good person unless you enjoyed acting morally. Still, even for Aristotle it would be too much to ask for every morally required action to be pleasurable in itself. Morality will require self-sacrifice on particular occasions. Yet for the virtuous person, this is part of a broader pattern of life in which morality and self-interest can be brought into harmony over life as a whole.

ACQUIRING VIRTUE

We now need to look in a little more detail at Aristotle's important concept of **virtue**. This term is probably not used much in ordinary language: How often have you described someone as virtuous, and if you have, what did you mean? Aristotelian moral philosophy is a version of what is known as **virtue ethics** or, sometimes, virtue theory. Essentially, a morally admirable person is someone who "possesses the virtues," understood as a set of valuable, firmly held character traits. For example, courage is generally regarded as a virtue; and Aristotle listed others, such as truthfulness, modesty, and "temperance," by which he meant restraining your appetites. Other virtues might include kindness, thoughtfulness, or generosity. Acting morally is not simply a matter of doing the right things or following the rules, but being the right sort of person. A virtuous person is someone who deliberates and sees things in particular ways, and has the right sort of emotional response to situations. A virtuous person also acts on his or her perceptions of what ought to be done. This idea is called phronesis, or practical wisdom, as we saw above.

We can understand more about Aristotle's concept of virtue by asking a question that preoccupied Greek philosophy: How is virtue to be acquired? Interestingly, many modern moral philosophers discuss only fully formed moral agents, saying very little about children and adolescents. This makes sense if you think of morality as essentially a body of knowledge. The truth is one thing, and how it gets taught is quite another. But if we regard morality as a practical topic, then an important question concerns how it comes to be acquired.

What might the answer be? Aristotle's teacher Plato set out the most obvious likely answers in his dialogue *Meno*. Meno, a wealthy visitor from the city of Thessaly, asks:

> Can you tell me, Socrates, can virtue be taught? Or is it not teachable but the results of practice, or is it neither of these, but men possess it by nature or in some other way? (trans. Grube, 1980, 70a, p. 3)

If we ignore the open-ended phrase "some other way," three alternatives are expressed here. One possibility is that it can be taught as a form of theoretical knowledge, like geometry. Or it could be "a result of practice," like learning a language as an infant. You learn through immersion, which involves observation, repetition, advice, and correction. Finally, it could be a natural instinct, like breathing, and does not need to be taught at all. Are any of these answers a suitable model for how virtue, or moral knowledge, is to be achieved?

Is Virtue Natural?

Let's take the last suggestion first. Aristotle thinks it is clear that acting morally is not a natural instinct, arguing that

> none of the moral virtues arises in us by nature, for nothing that exists by nature can form a habit contrary to its nature. For instance the stone which by nature moves downwards cannot be habituated to move upwards, not even if one tries to train it to by throwing it up ten thousand times. (ed. Brown, 2009, 1103a, p. 23)

Aristotle is certainly right that you cannot train a stone to move upward by throwing it in the air, however hard you try. His argument seems to be that if a trait is natural, then it cannot be changed in any way. But of course we can train people to develop or even change their moral virtues. Therefore moral virtue cannot be natural to us, so Aristotle concludes.

It is not so clear, though, that this is a good argument. Earlier, breathing was used as an example of something that is natural to us. However, many yoga teachers and practitioners believe that we don't naturally breathe in the way that is best for us. They spend a lot of time in working on how to do it better, and in teaching and writing books on the subject. Of course, however hard we practice, we can't stop breathing and survive; but the way we breathe is something that can be trained. Could the same be true of the moral virtues? Aristotle meets the argument halfway by saying that nature gives us the capacity to receive the virtues, but only by practice can we fully realize them. And this is what a yoga teacher might say about breathing. After enough practice correct breathing becomes "second nature," a type of instinctive habit, though at first it is not instinctive at all, of course.

Can Virtue Be Learned from a Book?

The possibility remains that we could learn morality purely as a branch of theoretical knowledge, from either a good teacher or a book. To appreciate Aristotle's position here, it is helpful to understand a distinction now common in contemporary philosophy between **knowledge that** and **knowledge how**.

When I learn the capitals of the countries of the world, I acquire knowledge *that*: knowledge, for example, that the capital of Indonesia is Jakarta. This is often known as propositional knowledge: knowledge of a proposition that I can express by saying, "I know *that* Jakarta is the capital of Indonesia," or "I know *that* chocolate is bad for dogs." But there is another type of knowledge too: knowledge *how*. It is perfectly good English to say, "I know *how* to swim" or "I know *how* to ride a bicycle." In knowing these things, I know how to perform a range of actions. An interesting question is whether all of this knowledge could be written down as a set of instructions, such as "to turn to your left when swimming, twist your upper body slightly to the left while pulling harder with your arm on that side." There are, of course, manuals to teach you to swim or ride a bike. But it would be astonishing if anyone ever learned to do either of these things purely by reading the manual. However many books you read before you get into the water, and however hard you studied, it would be a miracle if you found yourself able to swim right away. This example supports the idea that the type of knowledge relevant to swimming is knowing how rather than knowing that, and such knowledge needs to be acquired by practice in both senses of the word: in practical terms and by practicing through repetition.

Aristotle suggests that knowledge of morality combines propositional knowledge, knowing that—such as the propositions contained in his own writings—with a large dose of knowing how. He illustrates this view by supposing that being a virtuous person is in many respects like being a skilled artist or craftsperson. In *Nicomachean Ethics* he remarks:

> For the things we have to learn before we can do them, we learn by doing them, e.g., men become builders by building, lyre-players by playing the lyre; so too we become just by doing just acts, temperate by doing temperate acts, brave by doing brave acts. (ed. Brown, 2009, 1103a, p. 23)

The importance of practice, what Aristotle calls habituation, shows that becoming virtuous, like becoming a swimmer, is something that cannot be learned simply by reading a book or listening to your elders, although these will help. A person becomes virtuous by practicing being virtuous. In Aristotle's view, this principle ought to be better known than it is:

> But most people ... take refuge in theory and think they are being philosophers and will become good in this way, behaving somewhat like patients who listen attentively to their doctors, but do none of the things they are ordered to do. (1105b, p. 28)

Habituation

We can, in fact, distinguish several aspects of full habituation. First, there is what Aristotle calls the knowledge of the *that* of morality, which seems to be a matter of understanding the general rules. This is like listening to the doctor and thus it is inadequate on its own. Second is another form of intellectual knowledge, which Aristotle calls the *because*—understanding why the requirements of morality are as they are. It is not enough just to know the rules; we also need to know the ultimate point of each rule. It is also a form of propositional knowledge, so in that sense it counts as knowledge *that*. But we could introduce a new concept: knowledge *why*. Knowing the *that* and the *because* (or the *why*) yield fuller moral wisdom. Yet Aristotle clearly thinks that you will not achieve an understanding of the *because* of virtue without having practiced it. Only practice will give you knowledge *how*, allowing you to develop and fine-tune the right moral sensibility: and the more you practice, the better you will become. But equally important is that the morally virtuous person finds a source of enjoyment in "noble and just" action. If virtue is a sacrifice, then—as we saw—in Aristotle's view it is not properly virtue.

Thus we have to be habituated into virtue, combining four elements: the *that*; the *because* (the *why*); the practice (the *how*); and the enjoyment (the *pleasure*, perhaps). And all of this habituation, according to Aristotle, requires the right upbringing. A young person naturally wishes to pursue pleasure. But when brought up well, he or she will also want to act well. The trick of a good upbringing is to link the two together, so that the mature person increasingly takes pleasure in acting well. This goal will not be achieved in a single step. To begin with, it will be a matter of learning the rules of morality—in the form of following orders from parents and teachers—perhaps not understanding entirely what should be done, and often suffering criticism or even punishment if it goes wrong. With experience, which inevitably will have meant making shameful mistakes, the virtuous person comes to see why the rules of morality exist. At this stage, he or she will have understood the *because* as well as the *that*, by knowing the point of the rules.

Importantly, this means that the virtuous person will be able to judge when the rules are an oversimplification and it is right to do something that, strictly speaking, appears to be prohibited. Kant's example of lying to a murderer is worth thinking about here. A virtuous person might reason that the point of truth-telling is to create a world of reliable expectations for mutual benefit. However, when someone proposes an action that so clearly goes against the public good, the normal reasons in favor of telling the truth are outweighed by other considerations. Slavishly following the rules may be better than never following them, but moral wisdom requires significant exercise of judgment, acquired through experience.

Interestingly, those who have acquired virtue typically will not use the idea of that particular virtue in their reasoning. For example, a courageous person does not ask, "What does courage require in this situation?" That question normally would be asked only by someone who is trying to acquire the virtue of courage and still needs to deliberate carefully. The truly courageous person, once habituated into virtue, simply sees what needs to be done; and he or she may well deny that the act was courageous when praised. It becomes second nature. Similarly, those who act out for friendship will not frame their deliberations in terms of "This is what a friend would do." Anyone who thinks that way may be pretending to be a friend, or perhaps training themselves to become a friend, rather than being a true friend. It seems generally true for the virtues that appropriate deliberation does not include reference to the virtue, although not without exception: In difficult cases, perhaps it will be essential for the just person to ask, "What does justice require?" This is what we would expect of a judge in court, however experienced. And, when facing a dilemma, anyone may well ask, "What would a true friend do?"

Given that moral maturity is a developmental process that needs the right sort of upbringing, we should ask what those who received the wrong sort of upbringing can do now to get back on the right track. Sadly, Aristotle's thoughts on this question do not seem to have been recorded: All those in his audience presumably were well brought up. But perhaps he thinks it would be almost impossible to achieve a life of virtue if you come to it late in life, just like those who come to learn a new language in adulthood rarely completely master it. With the wrong upbringing, you may struggle for the rest of your life.

VIRTUE, VICE, AND THE GOLDEN MEAN

We have, by now, a general idea of Aristotle's account of morality. But still, we are left with the central question. What does Aristotle think we should do? Perhaps the best-known aspect of Aristotle's position is the golden mean. The right way to act is the mean (i.e., in the middle) between excess and deficiency, which are two forms of vice—the opposite of virtue.

I mentioned earlier that the term *virtue* is not used much in contemporary life. We are more familiar with the word *vice*, although not exactly as Aristotle intended, even though the terms are related. Today as part of the police force, we have the "vice squad" that deals with prostitution, illegal gambling, pornography, and so on. We also have the term *vicious*, derived from *vice*, yet it now has a very different scope: nothing especially to do with drugs or pornography. *Vicious* is most commonly used when describing violence of extreme ferocity or in referring to malicious or spiteful gossip or criticism. For Aristotle, or at least in the way his work is conventionally translated, the terms *vice* and *vicious* are broader and used as the opposite of *virtue* and *virtuous*. If courage is a virtue, cowardice is a vice. Oddly, a coward is a vicious person with negative character traits. Although the language may be unfamiliar, surely the ideas are not too difficult to grasp.

Aristotle discusses a wide range of virtues and corresponding vices. The central thought framing his entire discussion is that virtues can be destroyed by both excess and deficiency, and so we can (almost) always go wrong morally in either of two ways. He illustrates the point with some interesting examples of how exercise and diet can affect bodily strength and health. To become physically fit, you need to exercise; but if you exercise too much, you will injure yourself and become weak. Therefore, too much exercise could be as bad for you, or worse, than not exercising at all. To be healthy you need to eat and drink; but eat and drink too much, and you will destroy your health as surely as malnutrition does, although in a different way. The idea is that healthy physical behavior entails finding a mean between overextending yourself and not doing enough. These examples seem sound, but are they a good analogy for what we might call healthy moral behavior? Aristotle is confident that this model is appropriate: Virtue is a mean between two extremes, which are both vices.

The Virtues

In *Nicomachean Ethics*, Aristotle's first example of virtue is courage. The person who runs away from everything is a coward, while the person who fears nothing "becomes rash" (ed. Brown, 2009, 1104a, p. 25). His second example is this:

> The man who indulges in every pleasure and abstains from none becomes self-indulgent, and the man who shuns all pleasure, as boors do, becomes in a way insensible. Temperance ... [is] destroyed by excess and defect and preserved by the mean. (1104a, p. 25)

Aristotle admits that he has had to make up the term *insensible*, for he says, "Persons deficient with regard to the pleasures are not often found" and hence there is no name for this vice (1107b, p. 32). Here Aristotle fails to anticipate one important strand in Christian morality, that of advocating voluntary poverty and self-sacrifice. This view was influenced by the Ancient Greek philosophy of **Stoicism**, which rose in Greece a few decades after Aristotle's death. On a first reading of Aristotle, it might even seem that he is advocating something very similar by using the term *temperance* for the virtue in question. But what he means by temperance is rather different from the modern idea of the temperance movement, which campaigns to reduce or eliminate the use of alcohol and is often depicted as rather joyless. Aristotle, as we have seen in several cases, thinks that the good life is one of enjoyment, though not of excess.

The difference between Aristotle's approach to life and a philosophy of self-sacrifice is well illustrated in his discussion of the importance of money and external goods for virtue:

> The liberal man will need money for the doing of his liberal deeds, and the just man too will need it for the returning of services (for wishes are hard to discern, and even people who are not just *pretend* to wish to act justly). (1178a, p. 196)

Indeed, Aristotle says the external goods needed for happiness go well beyond wealth:

> And there are some things, the lack of which takes the lustre from happiness— good birth, goodly children, and beauty; for the man who is very ugly in appearance or ill-born, or solitary and childless is not very likely to be happy, and perhaps a man would be still less likely if he had thoroughly bad children or friends, or had lost good children or friends by death. (1099a, p. 14)

This passage is fascinating, though troubling. As a psychological account of what makes people happy and unhappy, it is surely plausible. The question, though, is whether such misfortune in appearance, children, or friends should affect your ability to act virtuously. Arguably, Aristotle's discussion implies that it will be harder to act virtuously in these difficult circumstances. Such a position contrasts with the later Stoic view, mentioned earlier as influencing Christianity, in which virtue and happiness depend almost entirely on each person's inner state. The Stoics view what people own and how they look as having no bearing on whether they are good people. They say happiness can be achieved—even a higher grade of happiness—without external goods and regardless of how a person appears.

The view Aristotle described above (which he regards as the common opinion and so may not be his own) does seem to be widely held. In many cultures, for example, it is important to show hospitality and present gifts to others, and this practice is almost impossible without a reasonable level of wealth. And without children or friends to help you, it can be harder to help others. For Aristotle this aspect of ordinary life captures something important about morality, whereas for the Stoics and some Christians, it is a prejudice that we can and must rise above. Recall the biblical passage: "It is easier for a camel to go through the eye of a needle, than for a rich man to enter into the kingdom of God" (Matthew 19:24).

Aristotle's view, though, may be more moderate than it appears. His position probably is not that external goods, such as wealth and good looks, are morally good in themselves or essential to the good life. Indeed he argues that the pursuit of money for its own sake is morally problematic. Rather he presumes that it will be easier to live a life of virtue if you have the right resources behind you. And the morally good person will know how to use wealth well. With all respect to the passage from Matthew, Aristotle would probably disagree. It is easier for the rich man to live a life of virtue, but that does not at all mean that he will; nor is it impossible for the poor man or woman to do so. Nevertheless this view may be regarded as unfair, for it is a matter of pure luck whether we are born rich or poor, and those born poor will, on Aristotle's view, struggle to live a morally good life. Avoiding the influence of luck in this way was a motivation of the Stoic view, which concentrated on inner states rather than outward success.

Another way of looking at Aristotle's view is to remind ourselves that his concept of eudaimonia is not quite the same as happiness. It is closer to human flourishing, fulfillment, or thriving. Someone who has little money, and is friendless and alone in the world, may be perfectly happy and living a life of pleasure. But we would presume, at first sight, that their life is not going as well as it might. We would want to know more before we said that they are flourishing. Equally, someone who doggedly seeks money and external goods may fail to flourish due to neglect of family, friends, and the humble pleasures of ordinary existence. The pursuit of money, for Aristotle, is not the proper function of human beings, even if money can help us pursue forms of excellence.

The Golden Mean

Aristotle develops his view in a fairly systematic fashion. The idea that virtue lies between deficiency and excess has some plausibility, at least in the examples discussed so far. To be more precise, we might think of virtue as literally a *mean* in the sense of an average between two extremes, as Aristotle puts it. In another example, he compares achieving the mean to hitting the exact center of a circle—something much easier to fail at than succeed in. But can we really understand virtue this way? Calling something a mean seems to suggest it can be quantified or measured. Comparing virtuous action to the center of a circle infers that a precise standard can be identified. Yet these attempts at specification cut against Aristotle's warning that we should not expect high standards of precision in moral philosophy.

The notion of the mean needs to be taken metaphorically rather than literally. Furthermore, Aristotle himself points out that not all moral considerations can be represented as a mean:

> But not every action nor every passion admits of a mean; for some have names that already imply badness, e.g., spite, shamelessness, envy, and in the case of actions, adultery, theft, murder; for all of these and suchlike things imply by their names that they are themselves bad, and not the excesses or deficiencies of them. It is not possible, then, ever to be right with regard to them; one must always be wrong. Nor does goodness or badness with regard to such things depend on committing adultery with the right woman, at the right time, and in the right way, but simply to do any of them is to go wrong. (ed. Brown, 2009, 1107a, p. 31)

Justice provides another exception: It is, itself, the limit, and an excess of justice is not possible, says Aristotle. He could possibly have argued that always following the rules and never showing mercy is an excess of justice, although more likely he would regard mercy itself as part of justice. Interestingly, though, as we shall see later, in another text, Aristotle does represent justice as a mean existing between gain and loss.

Aristotle runs through a list of virtues and vices. He presents them as if they are examples rather than a complete account. Some of the examples may be surprising to a modern reader, even if they do fit in with Aristotle's overall picture that experiencing a moral life is more like being the host of a good party than being a monk. So in addition to the examples we have already seen of courage, temperance, and justice, Aristotle considers "pleasantness in the giving of amusement," saying:

> With regard to pleasantness in the giving of amusement the intermediate person is ready-witted and the disposition ready-wit, the excess is buffoonery and the person characterized by it a buffoon, while the man who falls short is a sort of boor and his state is boorishness. ... The man who is pleasant in the right way is friendly and the mean is friendliness, while the man who exceeds is an obsequious person if he has no end in view, a flatterer if he is aiming at his own advantage, and the man who falls short and is unpleasant in all circumstances is a quarrelsome and surly sort of person. (1108a, pp. 33–34)

These observations are amusing and insightful, and they show how little has changed in human manners in 2,500 years. Still, we might ask how much they have to do with morality. Certainly we enjoy the company of witty and friendly people and try to avoid buffoons, boors, the quarrelsome, and the surly. But is this a morally acceptable response, or should we try to tolerate everyone? Once again we see Aristotle employing a wider concept of morality than philosophers often do, though perhaps he is closer to ordinary understanding in not making a sharp distinction between a good life and a morally good life.

Nevertheless, from a slightly different perspective Aristotle is raising a familiar idea. Knowing when a situation calls for humor and when cracking a joke would be awful requires moral sensitivity. Joking about death at a funeral, for example, can sometimes be the right thing; but if done in poor judgment because of the content or timing, a joke can be terribly upsetting, verging on unforgivable. Being unfriendly can make life difficult for other people. If morality is largely a matter of our relations to others, then wit and friendliness are central to our moral lives.

Aristotle nowhere offers a complete list of virtues and vices. However, in the work *The Eudemian Ethics*—which partially overlaps with *Nicomachean Ethics* but includes extra material—Aristotle sets out the following table, which he says includes examples of vices and virtues (trans. Kenny, 2011, 1221a, p. 19). The oddity of some of terms shows the difficulty of translating aspects of the Ancient Greek world into our times.

Excess	Deficiency	Virtue
irascibility	impassivity	gentleness
foolhardiness	cowardice	courage
shamelessness	bashfulness	modesty
intemperance	insensibility	temperance
envy	[unnamed]	righteous indignation
gain	loss	justice
prodigality	illiberality	liberality
boastfulness	dissembling	candor
flattery	surliness	friendliness
servility	churlishness	dignity
softness	toughness	hardihood
vanity	diffidence	pride
extravagance	shabbiness	magnificence
cunning	naivety	wisdom

VIRTUE THEORY AND THE MEAN

Does Aristotle have a moral *theory*? I have preferred to use the term *virtue ethics* to *virtue theory*, for using the term *theory* can suggest that a type of formula or algorithm underlies morality and can be used to solve moral dilemmas. We have already seen that Aristotle warns his readers not to expect this sort of approach, given the complexities of what it is to live a good human life. However, for those who are used to the moral theories of Bentham, Mill, and Kant, it is tempting to want to read Aristotle as offering a theory—and various readers of Aristotle have tried to do just that. Consider, for example, the following excerpt from Kant. It is one of Kant's few discussions of Aristotle's moral theory—not in the *Groundwork*, which we discussed earlier (see Chapter 10), but in Kant's last work of moral philosophy, called *The Metaphysics of Morals*:

> The distinction between virtue and vice can never be sought in the *degree* to which one follows certain maxims; it must rather be sought only in the specific *quality* of the maxims (their relation to the law). In other words, the well-known principle (Aristotle's) that locates virtue in the *mean* between two vices is false. Let good management, for instance, consist in the *mean* between two vices, prodigality and avarice: as a virtue it cannot be represented as arising either from a gradual diminution of prodigality (by saving) or from an increase of spending on the miser's part—as if these two vices, moving in opposite directions, met in good management. Instead each of them has its distinctive maxim, which necessarily contradicts the maxim of each other. (Kant, 1797/1991, pp. 204–205)

This passage is intriguing. Kant correctly identifies Aristotle's view that (most) virtues are a mean between two corresponding vices. But he interprets *mean* as a mathematical average, which is one meaning of that term. Aristotle did not intend anything so precise. However, Kant's main idea is that we should read Aristotle as supposing that virtue is a type of compromise between two vices. You can get to "good management" by starting as a miser and gradually spending more and more; or you can start by spending too much and then gradually reducing your spending. But, Kant suggests, moral action is a matter of acting from the right law or principle rather than seeking a compromise between two vices. You need to start with a firm grasp of the moral law—in Kant's case, the categorical imperative—if your action is to have moral worth. Hence, Kant says, Aristotle's doctrine is "false."

How would Aristotle reply? To begin with, Kant has not shown that Aristotle is wrong to locate the virtues as a mean between two vices, in the sense that there are (generally) two ways of failing. And Aristotle did not say that virtue is a compromise between two vices. The most interesting point is that you cannot act virtuously by starting at one of the vices and then either increasing or decreasing the intensity of your action until you find yourself at the virtue. Or rather Kant's idea seems to be that if you did this, you might accidentally end up "acting in accordance with duty" but not "acting from duty."

Now, Aristotle does not use Kant's later idea of acting from duty, but I think he may well have replied that Kant has not completely understood his approach. The doctrine of the mean is not intended to be a decision procedure for a fully moral agent. There would be something odd about a person who said, "I want to manage my affairs well. I don't know how to do that but I do know how to be a miser, so I will start off in a miserly fashion and increase my spending until I get to just the right amount." Rather, the moral agent who has to exercise the virtue of good management is someone who has already received extensive training and habituation in the practice, and by now is experienced enough to know generally what to do without extensive reflection. Part of the earlier training may have involved reasoning in exactly the way Kant objects to. But if a person does reason by averaging or compromise, then although they may be on their way to moral maturity, they have not reached it yet. But in sum, Kant misreads Aristotle in thinking that the doctrine of the mean is a procedure for making moral decisions. It isn't. It is an example of philosophical reflection on the nature of virtue and vice, although one that can inform how students of morality may be habituated to virtue.

So we can see that an intelligent newcomer to morality, if there could be such a person, could not use Aristotle's ideas to solve moral problems without extensive training and experience. The general lesson is that if you try to construct a simple decision procedure from Aristotle, you will be disappointed. Either you won't find anything or, like Kant, you will have to push the text further than Aristotle intended. This effort could well yield a "virtue theory," but it likely will be one that is fairly easy to refute, as Kant thinks he has done. If Aristotle does have a theory of moral action, it is this: Act in the way a virtuous person would. Compare this idea to the way some Christians approach moral questions: "What would Jesus do?"

CHAPTER REVIEW
Summary

We began this chapter by exploring Aristotle's approach to morality, which contrasts with the more formulaic theories of Bentham and Kant. We looked at Aristotle's account of the good life, taking note of the concepts of *phronesis* (meaning "practical wisdom") and *eudaimonia* ("flourishing"). We explored Aristotle's account of "habituation" into morality, making use of the distinction between knowing *that* and knowing *how* to explain his account of possession of the virtues. We also noted the role of "external goods" in Aristotle's theory. We then went on to look at the idea of virtue as a "mean" between two vices of excess and deficiency, considering a number of examples and exceptions. We also considered Kant's critique of Aristotle, which appeared at least in part to be based on misunderstanding Aristotle's view. If someone of Kant's stature can misread Aristotle, then the rest of us need to be careful that we have understood Aristotle's thinking correctly.

Discussion Questions

1. How does Aristotle think that virtue can be acquired?
2. Is virtue a mean between two vices?
3. Does Aristotle's moral approach give too much weight to self-interest?
4. Assess Kant's objection to Aristotle.

Key Terms

categorial imperative, p. 201

phronesis, p. 201

eudaimonia, p. 203

natural law, p. 204

virtue, p. 205

virtue ethics, p. 205

knowledge that and knowledge how, p. 206

Stoicism, p. 210

Key Thinkers

Aristotle (384–322 BCE), pp. 200–217

Immanuel Kant (1724–1804), pp. 204, 208, 215–217

Jeremy Bentham (1748–1832), p. 203

Plato (429?–347 BCE), pp. 201, 205

Further Reading

▪ The edition of Aristotle's writings used in this chapter is *Nicomachean Ethics* (Oxford University Press, 2009), edited by Lesley Brown and translated by David Ross. Selections from this work are included in Jonathan Wolff, *Readings in Moral Philosophy* (W. W. Norton, 2018).

▪ *The Eudemian Ethics* is quoted from the edition by Oxford University Press (2011), translated by Anthony Kenny.

▪ Aristotle's *The Politics* is available from Oxford University Press (2009), edited by R. F. Stalley and translated by Ernest Barker.

▪ Plato's *Meno* is available in many editions. Here I have quoted from the second edition by Hackett (1980), translated by G. M. A. Grube.

▪ For an introduction to Stoic philosophy, see Tad Brennan, *The Stoic Life: Emotions, Duties, and Fate* (Oxford University Press, 2005).

▪ The Bible verse quoted in this chapter is from the New American Standard Bible.

▪ Quotations from Kant's *The Metaphysics of Morals* are from the edition by Cambridge University Press (1991). (Original work published 1797)

CHAPTER 13

Challenges for Virtue Ethics

In exercising a moral right I can do something cruel, or callous, or selfish, light-minded, self-righteous, stupid, inconsiderate, disloyal, dishonest—that is, act viciously.

ROSALIND HURSTHOUSE, *"VIRTUE THEORY AND ABORTION"*

CRITICISMS OF VIRTUE ETHICS

In Chapter 12 we looked at the outlines of Aristotle's account of morality. Has he captured morality correctly? We have seen some concerns that arose when we were trying to come to a clear understanding of his position. In this chapter we will look more systematically at some of the strongest challenges to virtue ethics, beginning with a reminder of some of the issues already raised.

We have already noted that Aristotle's conception of morality is very broad: he is unusually concerned with how much individuals enjoy their own lives and with external factors such as possession of wealth, good looks, and wit. One way of putting this comment is that it makes morality too much fun. Though that description sounds more like a strength than a weakness, it leads to the criticism that Aristotle has missed the target in his attempt to characterize morality. Some argue that he has included factors having nothing to do with morality. If, like many people, we understand morality as primarily the exercise of self-restraint in order to respect or advance the interests of others, then much of Aristotle's thinking is irrelevant.

Aristotle's response will be easy to predict. Who is to say that the "self-sacrificing" conception of morality is the correct one? Ultimately, then, the criticism presupposes a conception of morality that Aristotle would not share. Accordingly we see a disagreement here, not a clear objection, about the nature of morality. It is not easy to settle, and shows how difficult moral philosophy can be: There is not even a universally accepted definition of the nature and scope of morality. This line of criticism leads to something of a stalemate because it is unclear what moves are available to resolve it.

However, a more troubling follow-up leads us to a second objection. For Aristotle the good life, including the good moral life, partially depends on the possession of wealth, family, and other external factors. Therefore those with bad luck will find it very hard to achieve virtue in the highest degree. And this problem leads to the **Stoic** emphasis on internal states, which is developed in the Christian tradition and reaches fuller expression in Immanuel Kant's view that only "good will" has moral worth. Stoic, Christian, and Kantian philosophy contrasts starkly with Aristotle's view.

This second objection really comes down to a disagreement about whether the possibility of living a good moral life should be so dependent on external factors—or, put another way, on luck. Many moral philosophers would want to adjust what is required of you morally to what is possible for you. You might already have thought of this story from the Bible:

> And He looked up and saw the rich putting their gifts into the treasury. And He saw a poor widow putting in two small copper coins. And He said, "Truly I say to you, this poor widow put in more than all of them; for they all out of their surplus put into the offering; but she out of her poverty put in all that she had to live on." (Luke 21:4)

The widow's sacrifice, relative to her means, was much more significant than the lavish gifts of the rich, and many will feel it has greater moral merit. What are your intuitions? The view that the widow's gift is more praiseworthy than those of the rich is very appealing. But do you have any sympathy for the position that the rich, even if they inherited their wealth, are actually more praiseworthy because they gave a larger gift? If you are at all tempted by this view, then you side with Aristotle. If you disagree, then you side with the Stoics and Christians against Aristotle.

A third objection comes from another contrast between Kant and Aristotle. Kant, like Jeremy Bentham and John Stuart Mill, provides a test for what we should do. Often we face moral dilemmas: Should I give a false promise to get myself out of a difficult situation? Kant and Bentham have their own different ways of answering the question. In Kant's case it is the test of the **categorical imperative**, and for Bentham the greatest happiness principle (**utilitarianism**). Many people are frustrated when reading Aristotle because he offers no clear guide to help us solve our moral problems. Aristotle's official answer is that an action is right if it is what a virtuous person would do in the circumstances. But this is not much help if you don't yet match up to Aristotle's standards of virtue. In short, you can read Aristotle's writings on ethics and agree with them, but still be left not knowing what to do in difficult circumstances.

Aristotle could reply that moral philosophy aims not to tell people what to do but rather to give them insight into the nature of morality. But this suggestion is unsatisfactory, for of course he did regard moral philosophy as a practical subject; and it is disappointing when a philosophical approach gives no guidance. Understandably, readers might look elsewhere for inspiration. Thus it is worth looking at the question of how others have tried to apply an Aristotelian approach to moral issues, and we will do so in the next section. Before that, let's look briefly at a fourth and fifth problem for Aristotle so we have a list of them all now. Later in this chapter, we will explore these further objections in more detail.

The fourth issue arises from experimental work in social psychology. The virtue ethics approach concentrates, as we have seen, on an individual's character. Its aim is to habituate individuals into virtue so that they come naturally to do the right thing. This approach makes what looks like an innocent assumption: that human beings each have a character that exerts a great effect on how they act. But suppose this is not true, in the sense that how we act depends on external factors rather than our own characters. If so, as the results in social psychology might suggest, then Aristotle's view rests on a false assumption, for our individual character no longer determines how we act.

The fifth problem involves the important and sensitive areas of gender and race. Just as we have touched on these issues for Kant and Mill, we will also look at them in Aristotle's writings. In Chapter 14 we will move on to a fuller treatment of the ethics of gender and race.

VIRTUE THEORY AND ABORTION

The third objection mentioned above is that virtue ethics gives no real guide to action. Utilitarianism and Kantian ethics both offer practical guidance on how to make decisions in difficult moral situations, but Aristotle does not seem to do so. Hence the virtue ethics approach has been accused of being useless in real life. If this criticism is fair, it is a devastating blow for virtue ethics. Perhaps the best way of assessing the issue is to look at a detailed attempt made by a virtue ethicist to address a moral dilemma. Let's look at a paper called "Virtue Theory and Abortion" (1991). The author is Rosalind Hursthouse (b. 1943), a contemporary philosopher from New Zealand.

Hursthouse rightly points out that philosophical discussions about abortion tend to be framed in terms of two central concerns: first, whether a fetus has the status of a person; and second, whether a woman has the right to choose what happens to her body. Yet as Hursthouse points out, neither of these considerations really gets us to the heart of the agonized decision any woman in real life is likely to face. Suppose it is agreed that a woman does have a right to choose whether to have an abortion. As the author remarks, the right to choose should be enough to show that a law against abortion would be wrong. But for a woman in torment about whether to have an abortion, the question is not merely about her legal or moral rights. It is about what to do, or what to decide, about her situation. Of course if we were convinced that a woman had no moral right to have an abortion, then it would follow that having an abortion would be wrong. But the opposite does not follow. Remember that having the right to decide does not tell you what your decision should be; or that your decision, whatever it is, will therefore be beyond moral criticism. As Hursthouse puts it in the opening quote of this chapter:

> In exercising a moral right I can do something cruel, or callous, or selfish, light-minded, self-righteous, stupid, inconsiderate, disloyal, dishonest—that is, act viciously. (p. 235)

If the question of a woman's right to choose does not settle the issue, it might be thought that the second standard question of whether the fetus has the status of a person goes deeper to the heart of the issue. After all, if the fetus is a person, then abortion could be regarded as murder. But as Hursthouse points out, the status of the fetus is a hugely difficult metaphysical question on which philosophers throughout history have differed and continue to disagree. She argues that it is wrong to think we have to solve all relevant metaphysical questions before we can make moral decisions. Situations that call for decisions rush upon us. We cannot wait for a solution to long-standing philosophical questions, whether or not such a solution would be relevant—which Hursthouse doubts.

In discussing the factors that surround a woman's decision about having an abortion, Hursthouse emphasizes the importance of pregnancy, childhood, parenthood, and loving family relationships in human life. She also presents a whole host of emotional, factual, and practical issues that will affect different women in different circumstances. As we become aware of the complications in the individual circumstances of any woman, it becomes increasingly difficult to believe that a formula of the sort offered by Kantians or utilitarians could solve the question of what any woman ought to do in her particular, unique circumstances. In the end, Hursthouse suggests, all we can ask is that a woman has thought through all the relevant issues and has treated her decision seriously.

Someone who thought, for example, that an abortion was equivalent to getting a haircut or having an appendectomy—simply removing some unwanted human tissue—has not considered the issues seriously enough. To use Hursthouse's unusual phrase, that would be "light-minded." But suppose a woman has thought long and hard about all the relevant issues. She has considered the consequences for her and for others both of having and not having the abortion, including the emotional effect in both cases, and has discussed it with people who will be affected or are able to offer advice. Without doubt she has taken the decision seriously. And what more, morally, can we ask?

Two women, in seemingly parallel situations, could make different decisions based on very similar facts. But if both women have deliberated properly, it would be odd to say that one of them has made the morally right decision and the other the wrong one. Certainly the issue is not wholly subjective, for some considerations will be relevant and others not. For example, if a woman decides to have an abortion so she can fit into her party dress, we can surely call that a light-minded decision, or indeed much worse. But if she sincerely believes that she will be unable to care for or provide for a child, then her reasoning cannot be dismissed in the same way, even though many women in comparable situations will nevertheless have the child and manage perfectly well later. Based on this understanding, the virtue relevant to abortion is careful and serious deliberation, which is an objective position that makes room for subjective concerns.

Does this answer the question of how an Aristotelian theory can help us address moral problems? Once more, for those looking for a formula to use in approaching a question, it will continue to disappoint. But the Aristotelian approach suggests that expecting more is unrealistic, perhaps even immature. According to the virtue ethics approach, no textbook, computer program, or teacher can tell a woman whether having an abortion is the morally right or wrong thing for her to do in the circumstances she faces. Each person has her or his own moral thinking to do.

DO YOU HAVE A CHARACTER?

A very different, surprising, and powerful challenge to Aristotelian virtue ethics in recent decades is based on experimental findings in social psychology. Central to Aristotle's theory is that throughout a lifetime, human beings can be habituated into virtue through education, training, and practice. We thereby develop a stable and consistent character that leads us to act well in morally challenging circumstances. Some people develop courage, or generosity, or kindness, and so on; and the courageous, generous, and kind person is much more likely to perform courageous, generous, and kind actions than those who have not developed those character traits and virtues.

This view, that different people have different characters that partially explain their actions, seems almost too banal to be worth saying. Yet some fascinating experiments have put it to the test. Let's look at just two of several comparable examples.

First, in 1973 the American social psychologists John M. Darley and C. Daniel Batson published a paper reporting an experiment conducted at Princeton Theological Seminary (Darley & Batson, 1973). Seminary students who volunteered for the experiment were told they were taking part in a study about their future careers. As part of the procedure, they were instructed to give a short impromptu talk. Some were asked to speak on the biblical story of the Good Samaritan, who stopped to help a stranger who had been robbed and beaten. Others were assigned a quite different topic. They all were then informed that the talk was to be given in a room further down the corridor. Some students were told they had plenty of spare time before the lecture; others were told they were late and needed to hurry.

On making their way to give their talk, all the students passed a shabbily dressed actor slumped on the floor in the hallway. He was pretending to have suffered a collapse, and he groaned and coughed as the students went by. Thus, the actor gave each student the opportunity to put the tale of the Good Samaritan into practice. And because all of them were divinity students, you would expect them to be quite morally aware and highly motivated. The point of the experiment was to see which students would stop and help and which would ignore the apparently stricken man and carry on as normal. According to the experimenters, by far the most important factor in stopping to help was whether the student was in a hurry. Those who thought they were late were far less likely to help than those who had time on their hands. It did not matter whether they had prepared a talk on the Good Samaritan or the other topic, and no "personality" factor was found that correlated with the result.

This result is in some ways surprising and in others completely unsurprising. It is surprising that theology students who had just been reminded of the story of the Good Samaritan would not stop to help. But thinking of yourself in a comparable situation, isn't time often the most important factor in whether you will or will not stop to help someone? And this is true for many people, even if they are in a hurry to do something fairly trivial. Consequently, the experimenters' hypothesis is that what matters in "real-time" ethical dilemmas is the *situation* you are in, not the *type of person* you are. This view is sometimes known as **situational ethics**. If the experimenters are correct, then character seems to play little or no role in explaining actual behavior. And if that is so, then virtue ethics is in trouble because it is based on the false premise that character is all important in moral action.

A second, perhaps even more surprising experiment took place in shopping malls in San Francisco and Philadelphia and was reported in 1975 (Levin & Isen). The experimenters set up a telephone booth so that on some occasions, a person using the phone would unexpectedly get a dime on leaving. Just when the person using the phone left the booth, a woman would walk close by and "accidentally" drop a folder of papers. The purpose of the study was to see who would stop and help the woman pick up the papers. According to the study authors, there was almost a perfect correlation between receiving the unexpected dime and stopping to help. The hypothesis is that, in this case at least, mood rather than character is the key factor in explaining helping behavior. If you are cheerful or in a good mood, you are much more likely to help than you would be otherwise. Again this result will ring true for many of us.

These experiments, although small in scale, might suggest that human beings are embarrassingly shallow creatures. We act on the basis of minor considerations, such as whether we are in a hurry, or whether we are in a good or bad mood, rather than whether we have been "habituated into virtue." But do these examples really have such dramatic implications? On their own, probably not; but the literature contains more experiments of this kind, showing similar results.

Some philosophers have concluded that these studies show "lack of character" in human beings, and hence virtue ethics has to be abandoned. Others, rather suspicious of abandoning a philosophical tradition of 2,500 years on the basis of some eye-catching experiments, have argued that the experiments show only how difficult it is to be truly virtuous. After all, some people did stop to pick up the papers without receiving the dime, or offered help to the victim even when they were in a hurry. Still other philosophers point out that many experiments like this have now been attempted, and only a small number of them show such dramatic and surprising results. Hence the experiments could well be anomalous, and a statistical freak, rather than revealing something deep about human nature. Finally, even if the experiments do show something, some critics have dismissed them as too small in scale to show anything significant. They suggest that because they studies look at one-off situations rather than behavior over time, it is hard to say anything about the influence of character by observing only one action. Perhaps being virtuous makes only a small difference in each situation, but it adds up to a large difference over a person's lifetime.

Ideally we would do more experiments, but unfortunately it is now hard to conduct experiments of this type to test the issues further. The experiments critically depend on deceiving the study participants about the nature of the experiment, and modern protocols of research ethics make it difficult to conduct deceptive experiments (perhaps influenced by Kantian concerns about the immorality of deception). Nevertheless, the experimental results are striking and intriguing and do merit a response from the virtue theorist.

ARISTOTLE ON GENDER AND RACE

Earlier in this chapter, I described Rosalind Hursthouse's application of virtue ethics to the issue of abortion. Some readers might have noticed that it bears comparison with some aspects of the feminist **ethics of care** briefly described in Chapter 11. That is, it rejects abstract principles or formulas in favor of contextual and relational moral reasoning. Was Aristotle, then, a feminist? Sadly not. He says in *Politics*: "The relation of the male to the female is the superior to the inferior, the ruler to the ruled" (ed. Stalley, 2009, p. 16).

Now it was a great surprise to see Kant adopt sexist and racist views, given the premise of equality that was built into his moral theory, but it may be less surprising to see that Aristotle was prepared to advance a hierarchical view. After all, we have seen some potentially thorny problems in this area already. Notably, he argues that it is easier for a wealthier person to become virtuous than it is for someone who lacks wealth. So there is already a strong hint of an elitist element in Aristotle's view. Aristotle's idea that you cannot live the highest form of good life if you are a woman—or, we should add, a non-Greek—seems generally consistent with his elitism even though, of course, he could have stopped before making these additional claims.

It might be tempting to explain away Aristotle's prejudices by saying that in Ancient Greece 2,500 years ago, nobody knew any better. Thus it is wrong to blame Aristotle for holding what we now regard as deeply wrongheaded, discriminatory, and ultimately immoral views. But is it true that everyone in Ancient Greece held the same views as Aristotle? Importantly, one person held a different view about women: Aristotle's own teacher, Plato. Knowing that he is defending something outrageous at that time, Plato argues that men and women are both able to acquire the skills needed for positions of political power. Further, he says that some women will succeed. Physically men tend to be stronger than women, and Plato suggests that on average, men have a better chance of success than women. Nevertheless, he claims, there is no ultimate difference between the nature of a man and the nature of a woman that would make a man naturally the ruler of a woman. Plato, unlike Aristotle, turns out to be a type of early feminist. In the *Republic*, he says that women have the same potential to rule as men do:

> So, then, those men and women who display distinct aptitudes for any given kind of work will be assigned to do that work. If a critic can do no more than bring up the one distinction between man and woman—that the one begets and the other bears children—we shall see that for our purposes he has offered no proof of difference at all. We shall continue to affirm that our guardians and their wives should perform the same tasks. (Book 5, p. 145)

It is interesting to ask, though, why Plato seemed to believe that in a free competition a man would be more likely to win, even though occasionally a woman would shine through. In tests of physical strength this view may be fair enough, but what about other types of contests? What explains the statistical fact, true for most of human history and still true in many fields today, that men more often do better? One possibility would simply be that men are born on average more intelligent and more talented than women, and this would explain the statistical difference in achievement. However, the backward inference (an "argument to the best explanation" as this strategy is referred to in Chapter 1) from men's greater achievement to men's greater natural ability was known to be fallacious by all serious thinkers on women's emancipation.

These thinkers, even while applauding Plato for overcoming the prejudice of his day, would wish to dig deeper into the question of why women have been less likely to succeed in competition with men. If women have been raised in a sexist culture, they might be less successful for many reasons: (a) They may have been denied the education and training that men have received; (b) they may not be offered the opportunities for work or advancement that are open to men; (c) they may have been taught to underestimate their abilities and not strive to do well in competition; (d) others may underestimate their abilities too, and overlook them; and (e) they may face simple discrimination. Sexist social structures and sexist attitudes certainly impede women's achievement in many other ways too. Although women today continue to achieve power or high office less often than men do, this tells us nothing about men and women's relative talents.

We will return to the issue of gender in Chapter 14, but for now let's turn briefly to Aristotle's troubling statements about slavery and non-Greeks—or, as he calls them, "barbarians." In Aristotle's *Politics*, he says that while it is morally wrong to enslave Greeks, some other peoples are "slaves by nature." Now, once more we might try to excuse Aristotle by saying that as a person of his time, he took for granted what went unquestioned. But Aristotle himself acknowledges that "There are others, however, who regard the rule of slaves by a master as contrary to nature ... and so has no warrant in justice" (ed. Stalley, 2009, Book 1.3, p. 13). Having raised the issue, Aristotle must defend his view; he does so by claiming that non-Greeks have lower powers of deliberative rationality than Greeks, and they are more likely to be ruled by their bodily appetites. Non-Greeks are therefore not suited to the same level of freedom and should become slaves of Greeks.

It is worth trying to put Aristotle's argument into a more formal structure.

Premise 1: To be entitled to freedom, it is necessary to have a high degree of power of deliberative rationality.

Premise 2: Only Greek men have a high degree of power of deliberative rationality.

Therefore

Conclusion 1: Non-Greeks are not entitled to freedom.

Therefore

Conclusion 2: Non-Greeks should be slaves to Greeks.

We could question this argument in many ways. Let's start by comparing it with John Stuart Mill's argument (see Chapter 9) justifying the use of colonial rule over peoples who have not (yet) acquired the requisite level of civilization. Two differences are important. First, Mill thought that everyone was capable, eventually, of attaining the right level of rationality or civilization; Aristotle, like Kant, thought that intellectual and cultural potential is fixed by nature and there is no hope of development. But second, and more important, Mill argued that colonial peoples were to be ruled benevolently for their own good, just as parents take care of children. Of course the historical record shows that this did not happen, and colonial rule was often a matter of brutal exploitation. Mill's intellectual position was naïve, perhaps even self-deceiving. But unlike Aristotle, he did not argue that those who lack full rationality or civilization should be put in service to those of higher abilities. And it is hard to see how Aristotle thought his argument would justify the power of Greeks over non-Greeks for the benefit of Greeks. Aristotle's conclusion justifying slavery plainly does not follow from his premises. Therefore the argument is invalid, even if the premises are true. And indeed premise 2 is clearly false, and premise 1 highly controversial, to say the least. Because Aristotle presented no justification or evidence for premise 2, his position comes across as pure prejudice.

Arguably, however, Aristotle shows more honesty than many of his contemporaries who took slavery for granted and made no effort to justify it. We could also consider that he has done us the great service of showing just how weak the arguments in favor of slavery are.

Aristotle's is not the only attempt by a major philosopher to defend slavery. The English philosopher John Locke (1632–1704) presented another argument. If you are the victorious side in a just war, Locke suggested, you have the right to execute those who you capture. But if you enslave them instead, then both sides are better off. If the slaves disagree and prefer death, then they have that option and can take their own lives.

This is an interesting argument that could be challenged at several points. (Do you really have the right to execute those you capture, for example?) Locke was an influential figure in drafting early North American constitutions, especially the Fundamental Constitutions of Carolina (1669), which made provision for slavery in that state. Can Locke really have thought that Africans had been captured in a just war with America? It isn't plausible, and this account discredits Locke's integrity as a thinker, despite the immense value of the wide range of writings he produced.

Aristotle did no better than Locke in defending slavery. He barely attempted to do so, suggesting that some are already marked out at birth as fit to rule and others fit to be ruled. This failure to justify slavery is a lesson for us all: The implicit and unacknowledged protection of privilege can significantly distort our reasoning.

CHAPTER REVIEW

Summary

In this chapter we looked at some current questions related to virtue ethics. We began by reviewing some criticisms already raised in the previous chapter, that, first, Aristotle runs morality and self-interest together, and second, that he makes morality too dependent on external goods. Then we explored the objection that virtue ethics does not guide our actions, by looking at Rosalind Hursthouse's application of virtue ethics to the question of abortion. We also considered a surprising contemporary critique of virtue ethics: that social psychology experiments demonstrate that our actions are not explained by our characters, but by relatively trivial "situational" factors such as mood. Next we contrasted the views of Plato and Aristotle on women's equality with men, which led into a discussion of Aristotle's troubling views on women and slavery.

Discussion Questions

1. How can virtue ethics be used to address the question of the morality of abortion?
2. Explain the "situationalist" critique of virtue ethics.
3. Critically examine Aristotle's justification of slavery.

Key Terms

Stoic, p. 220

categorical imperative, p. 220

utilitarianism, p. 220

situational ethics, p. 224

ethics of care, p. 226

Key Thinkers

Aristotle (384–322 BCE), pp. 219–221, 226–229

Immanuel Kant (1724–1804), pp. 220–222, 226

Jeremy Bentham (1748–1832), p. 220

Rosalind Hursthouse (b. 1943), pp. 221–222

Plato (429?–347), pp. 226–227

John Stuart Mill (1806–73), p. 228

John Locke (1632–1704), p. 229

Further Reading

▪ Rosalind Hursthouse's "Virtue Theory and Abortion" was first published in *Philosophy & Public Affairs*, *20*, 1991: 223–246, and is reprinted in abridged form in Jonathan Wolff (ed.), *Readings in Moral Philosophy* (W. W. Norton, 2018).

▪ John M. Darley and C. Daniel Batson's study is "'From Jerusalem to Jericho': A Study of Situational and Dispositional Variables in Helping Behavior," *Journal of Personality and Social Psychology*, *27*, 1973: 100–108, and Paula F. Levin and Alice M. Isen's study is "Further Studies on the Effect of Feeling Good on Helping," *Sociometry*, *38*, 1975: 141–147. Both experiments are also explained in *The Person and the Situation: Perspectives of Social Psychology* (2nd ed.) by Lee Ross and Richard Nisbett (Pinter & Martin, 2011). An interesting philosophical assessment of this work appears in Kwame Anthony Appiah, *Experiments in Ethics* (Harvard University Press, 2009);

for more extended treatment, read John Doris, *Lack of Character* (Cambridge University Press, 2002).

▪ The edition of Aristotle's *Nicomachean Ethics* used here is edited by Lesley Brown and translated by David Ross (Oxford University Press, 2009); the edition of Plato's *Republic* is from W. W. Norton (1996). Excerpts from both appear in Jonathan Wolff, *Readings in Moral Philosophy*.

▪ Aristotle's *Politics* is quoted from the edition by Oxford University Press (2009), edited by R. F. Stalley and translated by Ernest Barker.

▪ John Locke's views on slavery can be found in his *Second Treatise of Government*, in many editions including one from Hackett (2011), edited by C. B. Macpherson. (Original work published in 1689)

CHAPTER 14

The Ethics of Gender and Race

As a woman, I feel I never understood that I was a person, that I could make decisions and I had a right to make decisions. I always felt that that belonged to my father or my husband in some way, or church, which was always represented by a male clergyman. They were the three men in my life: father, husband, and clergyman, and they had much more say about what I should or shouldn't do.

QUOTED IN CAROL GILLIGAN, IN A DIFFERENT VOICE

GENDER AND RACE: A REVIEW

We finished Chapter 13 by looking at Aristotle's views on slavery. Earlier in that chapter we discussed Aristotle and Plato's contrasting views on the potential for women to achieve the highest positions in society. In the context of exploring Plato's suggestion that only a small number of women are likely to hold elite positions—which is just starting to change in the 2,500 years since Plato wrote—we also examined how a sexist culture holds women back.

Those were not the first discussions of topics of gender and race in this book. Even in Chapter 2, when we explored cultural relativism, the question of different moral traditions associated with non-Western cultures arose. Cultural relativism has been criticized for providing no basis for objecting to the sexist practices of another culture. Later, in Chapter 8, we looked at John Stuart Mill's arguments against what he called "the subjection of women" in favor of equal freedom. While applauding Mill's conclusion that the inequality of women has no moral justification, we noted the rather shaky foundation of some of Mill's arguments. They relied in part on the idea that ending the subjection of women would benefit the general happiness, including the happiness of men. Although it would be a wonderful world if ending oppression really did benefit everyone, an alternative view is that women have a right to equality regardless of whether it affects total happiness. And in Chapter 9, we also noted that the utilitarian calculation led Mill astray in his discussion of colonial rule. Whether or not temporary despotism would improve the "civilization" of non-European peoples (a highly contestable claim in any case), many will argue that all people have the right to freedom and self-rule, even if it detracts from the general happiness.

We also looked at Immanuel Kant's writings regarding women and people of non-European descent (Chapter 11). Kant's moral theory is based on respect for all individuals. But it becomes apparent when taking his writings as a whole that for Kant, the scope of "all individuals" was implicitly "all adult white males"; women and those of non-European descent were treated as "lesser" beings. I suggested, though, that this perspective is really an aberration for Kant rather than something that follows from the logic of his view. Given its commitment to universal freedom and respect, Kantian moral philosophy can be used as a liberating theory for all human beings.

Nevertheless, we saw that even an expanded, truly universal Kantian view has come under attack from feminist writers. Provocatively, Sandra Harding (b. 1935), the contemporary feminist philosopher of science, has asked, "Should feminism set such a low goal as mere equality with men?" (1986, p. 21). In other words, Harding is asking if women should aspire to think, feel, and behave the way that men do.

One influential tradition has interpreted Kant, alongside utilitarianism, as offering an **ethics of justice** (or perhaps more accurately, an ethics of principle) in contrast to an **ethics of care**. In doing so, it is said, moral philosophy continues to exclude women's voices and concerns. Let's now look at this critique, and other feminist approaches, in more detail. We will then compare the new tradition of feminist moral philosophy with the emerging field of the ethics of race, as philosopher Naomi Zack (b. 1944) has called it. It is worth noting that in philosophy, race has been treated much more as a political and practical issue than one that generates its own distinctive approach to moral philosophy. It is fair to say, as Jamaican philosopher Charles Mills (b. 1951) has done, that throughout its history philosophy has tended to exclude or marginalize issues of race. The situation is beginning to change thanks to the work of Zack, Mills, and others. We will look at how the ethics of race is being developed later in this chapter.

THE ETHICS OF CARE

Earlier in this book we noted that utilitarian and Kantian moral philosophy both seek a formal, abstract principle that can be applied to address moral questions and settle moral dilemmas, such as the circumstances under which it can be right to lie. This approach to moral philosophy contrasts with Aristotelian ethics, which does not always expect precision, and for which the essential core of morality concerns developing the right type of character—one that exhibits virtues and avoids vices. For Aristotle, moral decision-making can be messy and contextual, often drawing on many different types of considerations, as we saw with Rosalind Hursthouse's discussion of abortion from the standpoint of virtue ethics.

The ethics of care (briefly introduced in Chapter 11)—a leading, but by no means the only, feminist approach to ethics—also takes contextual circumstances seriously. It attends to the details of each case rather than seeking a general formula. It also argues that emotional engagement and personal relations, especially the caring relations of love, sympathy, and empathy, are essential to moral thinking. This idea contrasts with the view that emotions and personal relations obscure the type of clear, impartial moral reasoning prized by some Kantians and utilitarians. Many leading feminist care theorists, such as Nel Noddings (b. 1929), point out the close connection between care ethics and virtue ethics.

Noddings perceptively adds that from the perspective of care ethics, "It is important to understand that we are not primarily interested in judging but, rather, in heightening moral perception and sensitivity" (1984/2013, p. 89). In other words, care ethics is not so much concerned with providing a list of moral instructions as with helping people develop the sensitivity to approach moral questions for themselves.

Abstract theories, especially Kant's, also tend to be complex and difficult to master. This issue leads feminist philosopher Alison Jaggar (b. 1942) to note, "A method of justification that ordinary people cannot use necessarily assigns final moral authority to those few philosophical experts who are able to use it. In western societies, such people are generally white, male and middle class" (ed. Fricker and Hornsby, 2000, p. 231). This type of elitism seems inconsistent with the spirit of a truly universal morality, which should be available to all. But in fairness to Kant, the principles of his theory are not all that difficult to master, and so this criticism is debatable. The feminist critique we are primarily considering in this section, however, is that abstract moral philosophy, despite its pretensions, fails to be universal in a slightly different way because it privileges male reasoning (of principle) over female reasoning (of care).

Jake and Amy

To understand the difference between the ethics of care and the ethics of justice or principle, let's look now at an example used by Carol Gilligan (b. 1936) in her book *In a Different Voice* (1993). One of her interviews with Jake and Amy, who were both 11 years old at the time, is especially helpful. The most famous discussion concerns the fictional moral dilemma of "Heinz," who is contemplating stealing a drug that he cannot afford in order to save his wife's life (this, of course, is another example of a thought experiment). When asked whether Heinz should steal the drug, Jake is clear that Heinz is morally permitted to do so, because "a life is worth more than money." Amy, on the other hand, says:

> Well, I don't think so. I think there might be other ways besides stealing it, like if he could borrow the money or make a loan or something, but he really shouldn't steal the drug—but his wife shouldn't die either. ...
> If he stole the drug, he might save his wife then, but if he did, he might have to go to jail, and then his wife might get sicker again, and he couldn't get more of the drug, and it might not be good. So, they should really just talk it out and find some other way to make the money. (Gilligan, 1993, p. 28)

The basic distinctions between the ethics of principle and the ethics of care are beautifully displayed here: finding a formula in contrast with engaging in contextual and sensitive reasoning. Jake finds a principle: "A life is worth more than money." For her part, Amy refuses to boil the problem down to simple terms. Gilligan considers the care perspective to be a more typically female approach to ethics, and it has some interesting and distinctive features. One is that it focuses on relations between people, including a proposed action's longer-term effects on these relations. Amy points out that if Heinz goes to jail, he won't be able to help his wife. She might also have said that if Heinz did steal the drug, how would he feel when he next saw the shopkeeper?

The concern with relations at the heart of the ethics of care is very important; as feminist philosopher Virginia Held (b. 1929) points out, it contrasts with Aristotelian virtue ethics, even though the two approaches have many similarities (Held, 2006). Aristotle says individuals cultivate the virtues in order to have a good life. Although, of course, how we relate to others is a key element in the virtuous life, the immediate concern for Aristotle is the individual agent rather than the relations between that agent and others. By contrast, caring starts from human relations. Here it is helpful to bear in mind Noddings's argument that the "ethics of caring" really grows out of **natural caring**, such as the care a mother has for her baby. Of course a mother normally wishes to be a good mother, but she wants to be a good mother for her baby's sake, rather than to satisfy a narcissistic concern to be admired for her mothering skills.

At the same time though, when caring goes well, it is not a sacrifice. As with virtue ethics, many of the demands of caring are not felt as demands. They are, says Noddings, the occasions that make life worth living. Ethical caring extends beyond the relations you have with your family, for caring relations can arise with strangers. This action often involves learned behavior rather than being instinctual or natural, but it bears many of the marks of natural caring. Here we need to be careful to distinguish *caring* from *caregiving*, which can be professionalized, as it is in homes for the elderly—and notoriously, can be done without caring. Of course, there is no denying that caregiving within the family can be hostile and grudging—or that professional caregiving is often very caring or even loving.

A further important feature of the ethics of care is that rather than considering emotion as an impediment to clear thought, as Kant did, it regards emotion as a key element in moral perception and thinking. In a fascinating observation, Noddings points out that when we are engaged in a moral dialogue with others, we want to look into their eyes and see their changing facial expressions (Noddings, 2013). Often people communicate more by tightening their facial muscles, or using uncomfortable body language, than by uttering any number of articulate verbal expressions. Anxiety, relief, pleasure, fear, and a host of other feelings are at the center of our moral experience. They enhance our moral understanding and can convey it to others rather than being an obstacle to experience and communication.

We have already seen yet another feature of care ethics: It attempts to understand moral situations in their complexity rather than reduce them to general principles. Earlier thinkers, especially the developmental psychologist Lawrence Kohlberg (1927–87), dismissed this type of unprincipled moral thinking as a form of "immature" moral reasoning. In response, Gilligan argues for its equal status with the ethics of principle (1993). Indeed, she often seems to hint at its superiority, or at least its function as an important corrective. In reading Jake and Amy's answers, we may well agree. And we should note that Gilligan's criticism generalizes to all forms of moral philosophy based on reason and abstraction, be it Kantian deontology or the utilitarianism of Jeremy Bentham and Mill. By supposing the only truly rational form of moral reasoning is that undertaken in a male style, these philosophers leave out what may be the most important aspect of our moral lives: caring relations and emotions.

It does seem that Gilligan has pointed out something vital. Moral philosophies based on the application of abstract rational principles seem to have little room for human relations, emotion, and moral complexity. Many feminist philosophers, including Virginia Held, have argued that we even conceive of our own identity in terms of our relations: you are a son, or a daughter, a brother or sister, a classmate, or roommate, a college member, a citizen of a country, and so on. Some of these relations you brought upon yourself, and some are temporary, but many are unchosen or permanent. All your relations and roles can affect your moral perceptions of what you might think important and less important, and also what you take to be your moral obligations. In trying to boil down dilemmas to their bare bones so that they can be solved by formula, approaches based on reason alone seem one-sided and leave out too much that is important. Even worse, perhaps, they imply that men are more likely than women to be "moral experts."

At the same time, for some feminists the ethics of care has set off alarm bells. There is a clear contrast between the ethics of principle and the ethics of care, but is it right to identify principle with masculine reasoning and care with feminine reasoning? This sounds like the dismissive attitude toward women all over again, except with the care element revalued as equal or superior. Such an approach is often called **essentialist**, assuming that male and female natures are essentially different, but also inescapable. Yet essentialism of this type is itself a common target of feminist critics who argue that social conditioning, not nature, may be behind different gender attitudes and roles. To push Gilligan's point too far is to play back into the hands of those who say that women are not capable of rational thought in the same way as men. As philosopher Annette Baier (1929–2012) writes:

> Some find it retrograde to hail as a special sort of moral wisdom an outlook that may be the product of the socially enforced restriction of women to domestic roles (and the reservation of such roles for them alone); that might seem to play into the hands of those who still favor such restriction. (1987, p. 44)

Political philosopher Jean Hampton (1954–96) pushes the point, observing that the ethics of care can set women up for exploitation by forcing them into caring roles inside and outside the home. Immersion in the care perspective, Hampton and others have argued, can lead women to ignore their own interests and sacrifice themselves to husbands, children, and elderly parents.

Gilligan would be horrified at the idea that the ethics of care could be detrimental to women's interests. She, and others on her behalf, have certainly wanted to avoid essentialism. To see how this can be done, it will be helpful to introduce a distinction now commonly made between **sex**, as a biological category, and **gender**, which is regarded as a social phenomenon. In the words of the French philosopher Simone de Beauvoir (1908–86), "One is not born, but rather becomes, a woman" (1949/2011, p. 293). Her meaning is that men and women receive extensive training in their social roles. These run from the extremely serious jobs that determine how individuals spend their time—such as who stays at home to cook, keep house, and look after the children—to the apparently trivial. For example, it seems that when drinking, women are more likely to tuck their elbows in while men stick their elbows out. It is not "ladylike" to drink with your elbow pointed out, and it is not "manly" to drink with it tucked in. Thus without ever realizing it, we are used to ideas of what is "masculine" and "feminine": it's just what we do. But, so the argument goes, we are socialized into gender roles rather than born into them. And indeed men can be feminine and women masculine; gender is increasingly being recognized as fluid and nonbinary.

Gilligan did not want to argue for the extreme essentialist position that men are by nature hardwired to adopt the ethics of principle and women the ethics of care. She noted that when prompted the right way, men and women do adopt both the ethics of principle and the ethics of care. However, many will accept the crude generalization that women are more attuned and sensitized to the ethics of care and men to the ethics of principle. Whether this notion is actually true is an interesting question. In a subtle critique, some have suggested that it is not even true that men and women reason differently; but it is true that men and women *think* that men and women reason differently. That is, we are partially blinded by stereotypes and do not see things as they are.

But even if the difference in reasoning is real, it could well stem from gendered training for social roles. In most cultures a mother, not a father, is the primary caregiver for children and elderly parents. Women are more likely to enter the "caring professions" such as nursing and elementary school teaching. And women may well be more likely to approach moral questions in the detailed contextual way exemplified by Amy, in which problems are solved by talking them out rather than applying a formula. Traditionally, men have been much more likely to take on managerial positions that involve directing large numbers of people or making decisions at a distance, in which case the only practical approach may be to use abstract principles. But according to the nonessentialist feminist, to the degree this difference exists, it is a matter of gender socialization rather than brute nature determined by our sex. This debate is helpful not only in making a feminist critique of abstract morality but also in helping us develop a more rounded approach to moral philosophy. It pushes us toward a principled approach to morality that needs to be supplemented with more attention to the details of the situation, the people involved in it, the relationships between them, and their emotions.

POWER, PRIVILEGE, DIVERSITY

Moral philosophy has certainly benefited from understanding the perspective of care in moral reasoning. But it is fair to ask whether the ethics of care has done very much to overcome the subjection of women, which—though not as marked as in the times of Aristotle, Kant, or Mill—still exists today. Indeed, as we have seen, the ethics of care presents some dangers. Many will argue that to achieve gender equality, women need to assert and insist on their rights; but their doing so seems to require support from the ethics of principle (recall that Gilligan called it the justice perspective). As Annette Baier points out (1987), for feminists there is absolutely no doubt that justice matters; the question is only how much other things matter too.

To make the issues clearer, a feminist moral philosopher could focus attention on at least three areas. The most concrete target is the organization of society, in which—to use Mill's word again—women still face subjection in the form of inequality and discrimination. In her book *A Vindication of the Rights of Woman* (1792/2009), the pioneering 18th-century feminist Mary Wollstonecraft (1759–97), for example, wrote a withering critique of the narrow, confined lives led by the women of her time.

Another target is not society directly, but the moral standards of the day: what we are brought up to think is right and wrong, and how we ordinarily approach moral problems. This is a form of commonsense morality, including rules such as "be kind to strangers" and "do not lie." But more perniciously, these rules often mirror social practices by providing apparent rationalization of injustice. So, for example, in the 19th century, women were not permitted to enter professions such as law and medicine. The practice was often justified by the claim that a woman's first duty is to her husband and children. "A woman's place is in the home" was part of the commonsense morality of the day, as it still is in many cultures today. Hence social practices, good or bad, can be supported by so-called common sense.

A third possible target for a feminist moral philosopher is philosophy itself. Gilligan, Noddings, and other care theorists focused on this area. They have argued that the philosophical tradition has privileged one form of moral philosophy and, by ignoring another form, has devalued it. The main thrust of their argument is aimed at reforming moral philosophy, but there will be connections with ordinary commonsense morality and with social practice. By accepting the reform of moral philosophy, we could strengthen and validate the ethics of care in ordinary life. And though this could lead to the dangers discussed earlier, it could also have the positive effect of giving women greater attention, respect, and influence in discussions about moral issues.

Our social practices certainly affect women's prospects for living the life they ideally would choose. A common thread throughout history has been an explicit set of laws that were detrimental to women, restricting their rights to vote, hold property or political office, or work in professional roles. In some countries these forms of **direct discrimination** still exist, but they have been overturned in most developed democratic countries. Nevertheless, many aspects of social organization effectively conspire against women in more subtle ways.

Just think of the different situation men and women face when they combine raising children with achieving advancement in a high-pressure workplace. For men, fatherhood rarely causes much of a problem, but motherhood often holds women back. Although the world was not designed to make having a career more difficult for women with children, such things as a late-night working culture and the need for short-term flexibility in scheduling appointments and meetings often turn out to be more difficult for women than men. Of course these problems arise because women still tend to take on a disproportionate amount of childcare and domestic work. When a set of practices is detrimental to one group, even if nobody designed it to be so, it involves **indirect discrimination**. And working and social practices work badly for women in other ways, ranging from social marginalization (being excluded from group activities) to sexual harassment to domestic violence. Even where a practice is illegal, the authorities do not always take violations seriously.

When reflecting about indirect discrimination and other practices of informal oppression, we can understand why many feminists have felt that although the ethics of care is an important step, it is still not enough to achieve equality. Even before the ethics of care was proposed, feminists argued for a radical rethinking of approaches to morality. For example, the African American poet and civil rights activist Audre Lorde (1934–92) famously remarked, "The master's tools will never dismantle the master's house" (2007, p. 110), meaning that the concepts used to support oppression are not appropriate to end oppression. As Lorde remarks, she is writing as a "forty-nine-year-old Black lesbian feminist socialist, mother of two" (2007, p. 114). It is thus easy to empathize with her feeling that the theories developed by heterosexual, financially secure white men (or indeed women) will not help her understand and overcome her own oppression.

Is it possible to contest Lorde's claim by suggesting that the master's tools, especially conceptions of equality and autonomy, can in fact dismantle the master's house if only they are used properly? We have seen this proposal from the beginnings of modern feminist theory, for example, in the approaches of John Stuart Mill and Mary Wollstonecraft. It can be summarized by saying that traditional moral theories contain everything required to argue for equal freedom and equality for women, but the problem in the past has been failure to use the theories to their full potential.

There are several ways of developing this argument. One is to say that sexist assumptions have meant that only men have been included in the scope of the theory. A second is that false assumptions have been made about women's interests and possible sources of happiness, which has led to diminished standing for women. And a third is that the theories contain resources that have not yet been applied, but some imaginative thinking can reap dividends. Some approaches probably combine all three criticisms.

Jean Hampton (1954–96) and Susan Moller Okin (1946–2004), for example, have each developed forms of the Rawlsian social contract that brings women into the social contract explicitly as equals to men. This may seem an obvious move; but even John Rawls considered the contracting parties as "heads of households." This view not only hinted that the men were the main contractors, but left relations within the family unexplored. Still, we can appreciate the power of the adaptation of Rawls's methodology by considering Susan Moller Okin's words:

> What Moslem man is likely to take the chance of spending his life in seclusion and dependency, sweltering in head-to-toe black clothing? What prerevolutionary Chinese man would cast his vote for the breaking of toes and hobbling through life, if he well might be the one with the toes and the crippled life? What man would endorse gross genital mutilation, not knowing *whose* genitals? (Okin, 1994)

More recently feminist philosopher Carol Hay has introduced a Kantian feminism that goes beyond simply adding women to the moral community. Hay also argues that women have a Kantian duty to themselves to resist their oppression out of self-respect. On this basis we can see that the master's tools have a lot of promise for achieving women's equality.

Nevertheless, Lorde's insight that new tools are needed remains important. Kantian and social contract theories are stated at a high level of abstraction; a great deal of work, in the sense of developing new concepts, is needed to connect those theories with the lived experience of many women. Oppression must be described before it can be confronted. We can understand

Lorde's point by reflecting on a comment from contemporary feminist philosopher Alison Jaggar:

> As a young woman … I was unable to articulate many vague and confused feelings and perceptions because the language necessary to do so had not yet been invented. The vocabulary I needed included such terms as: "gender,"… "sex role," "sexism," "sexual harassment," "the double day," "sexual objectification," "heterosexism," "the male gaze," "marital, acquaintance and date rape," "emotional work," "stalking," "hostile environment," "displaced homemaker," and "double standard of ageing." (2000, p. 238)

The example of **sexual harassment** is particularly interesting. By one account it was invented to help fight a court case for a woman named Carmita Wood, who felt compelled to leave her job because of the mental and emotional stress caused by extreme sexualized pressure in the workplace. She was unable to claim unemployment benefits because she had "voluntarily" left her job. To describe the intolerable situation she faced, Wood's advocates devised the term *sexual harassment*, which is now used so often that it is hard to believe it did not exist before the 1970s.

The Birdcage

To dismantle the master's house, then, perhaps we need to continue developing new tools, in the form of new concepts. But before dismantling anything, we would be wise to understand what it is and how it was built.

In this case we are looking specifically at social practices of female inequality and oppression in the sense of exclusion, discrimination, and even violence. Ultimately we want to know what resources are needed within moral philosophy to confront and end such inequality and oppression. First, though, we need to understand the structures that create and perpetuate our social worlds, controlling power, privilege, and disadvantage. In an influential early contribution to American academic feminist thought, feminist philosopher Marilyn Frye (b. 1941) insightfully used the metaphor of a **birdcage**. No single wire in the cage explains why the bird cannot escape, but the wires of the cage together create a trap. Frye suggests that for women and other disadvantaged groups, our world is like that. No single factor explains women's unequal experience of the world, but many factors working together.

> It is only when you step back, stop looking at the wires one by one, microscopically, and take a macroscopic view of the whole cage, that you can see why the bird does not go anywhere; and then you will see it in a moment. It will require no great subtlety of mental powers. It is perfectly *obvious* that the bird is surrounded by a network of systematically related barriers, no one of which

would be the least hindrance to its flight, but which, by their relations to each other, are as confining as the solid walls of a dungeon. (Frye, 1983, p. 5)

This description is immensely helpful. Inspired by Frye's observation, many feminist moral and political theorists, finding the ethics of care problematic, have instead attempted to identify and unravel the wires in the birdcage, one by one.

All we can do here is look at examples, so let's start with an issue that is often identified as one wire in the cage: pornography. The problem has been insightfully discussed by the radical feminist lawyer and philosopher Catharine MacKinnon (b. 1946), who developed her analysis in collaboration with feminist Andrea Dworkin (1946–2005). Traditional conservative opposition to pornography takes at least three main forms: (a) the argument that pornography is obscene; (b) the claim that those who use pornography are more likely to commit sexual assaults, including rape; and (c) the assertion that pornography harms the user, encouraging deviant sexuality and infidelity. These arguments have been used to draw the conclusion that pornography should be restricted or even banned.

MacKinnon has little sympathy for the first argument, that pornography offends common standards of decency, for those standards themselves can be questioned for suppressing and shaming women's sexuality. She does regard the second claim, that pornography can lead to sexual violence, as important; and she also accepts that pornography can damage relationships and expectations, typically to the detriment of women. We should note, though, that she distinguishes *pornography*, which she defines as graphic, sexually explicit subordination of women whether in pictures or words, from *eroticism*, which treats all participants as equals. Thus she is criticizing pornography in the sense defined, and not eroticism. However, MacKinnon's distinctive contribution is to draw our attention to two other arguments that seem much more forceful even though they have tended to be ignored in the debate.

One of these arguments is that, through interviews and memoirs, it has become clear that many women who take part in pornography—especially in violent pornographic films—say they do so out of coercion. Some of these women have become addicted to drugs (sometimes encouraged by the pornographers) and have no other way of feeding their addiction. These and other women are often bullied, threatened, and manipulated by powerful men. This is especially true for undocumented migrants. The harm to these women is significant and cannot be ignored; yet, before MacKinnon, their situation was rarely even mentioned in the debate.

Equally important is another argument: that the existence of violent forms of pornography helps reinforce a social environment in which women are treated as existing to serve men's purposes, to the great detriment of their own life experience and prospects. In a comment about having the right concepts and vocabulary (predating Jaggar's, quoted above), MacKinnon remarks:

> In pornography, there it is, in one place, all of the abuses that women had to struggle so long even to begin to articulate, all the *unspeakable* abuse: the rape, the battery, the sexual harassment, the prostitution, and the sexual abuse of children. Only in the pornography it is called something else: sex, sex, sex, sex, and sex, respectively. Pornography sexualizes rape, battery, sexual harassment, prostitution, and child sexual abuse; it thereby celebrates, promotes, authorizes, and legitimizes them. (1985, pp. 16–17)

One frequent response to this comment is that it is ridiculous to blame pornography for the subordination of women and the hostile and discriminatory environment that many women face. Advertising, the movies, TV, the workplace, and many other aspects of ordinary social life could well contribute just as much, so why single out pornography? But remember the birdcage analogy. No single wire explains why the bird is trapped, and removing just one wire probably will not allow an escape. But doing so—in this case, by challenging pornography—is one element in a broader program of countering structural injustices that work against women.

Feminism and Science

Pornography and other practices such as advertising are obvious targets for feminists. But many other less obvious practices can have similar effects and need careful examination. The birdcage that traps women is made of many different wires. Consider science, for example. Now, the whole idea of a feminist critique of science fills some people with scorn and even anger. Surely, it is said, science is an objective, rational inquiry; thus the idea of analyzing science from a gendered point of view is misguided, perhaps ideological. Sandra Harding remarks that "neither God nor tradition is privileged with the same credibility as scientific rationality in modern cultures" (1986, p. 16). But science can certainly be analyzed from a feminist point of view.

First, and most obviously, science has been male dominated. Historically, when women were attracted to practical activities, they were diverted to take up cooking or dressmaking rather than technical science. As Harding points out, many women have not seen science as a desirable occupation for themselves or other women (1986, p. 53). Many people know about the work of Marie Curie (1867–1934), who won two Nobel Prizes, developed the theory of radioactivity, and discovered the elements polonium and radium. But most people would find it difficult to name a second woman scientist, at least not without thinking hard. We could put this down to a generally sexist culture that would have its effects in science as in everywhere else. But even today, women are much less represented in scientific fields than they are in, say, law, politics, or the arts. Could there be something about how science is conducted that makes it less appealing to women or that makes it less likely for a woman than a man to succeed? We will return to this question.

A second issue centers on how science represents the nature of women, especially in relation to men. Of course biological science has to demonstrate the anatomical differences between men and women. But this effort can be pushed further than the evidence warrants. Consider, for example, "hysteria," once believed to be a medical condition. The behavior was thought to be related to the "wandering uterus," which broke free from its normal position, and hence was seen exclusively in females. Of course, no physical evidence was ever found for such a view. The uterus does not wander around. Later theories suggested that hysteria was a psychological condition, again predominantly female. Today hysteria is not believed to be a useful medical category.

This account of hysteria is often told as a type of historical curiosity about the charming and bizarre old days before modern science swept away a whole host of medical myths. But it has a much more sinister side. Many women with genuine and legitimate points to make were diagnosed as suffering from hysteria. Their impassioned arguments for justice, such as votes for women, were explained away by a roaming uterus or overflowing of hormones, and so they could—and should—be ignored. Pseudoscientific accounts describing the female nature served to justify women's domination and exclusion. Yet these claims hardly seem objective or rational, for they are pure speculations unsupported by what would normally count as scientific evidence.

The story of hysteria undermines the self-image of science: that scientists are always engaged in a curiosity-driven enterprise requiring obsessive, hyperintelligent, but rather eccentric and unworldly individuals to spend their lives in the lab engaged in going wherever the evidence and their experiments push them. In reality, though, much of science has other motivations: military success, political advantage (for example, the space race), and obviously, commercial gain—or, as in the case of the invention of hysteria, to maintain existing social order. Even when these goals are not directly discriminatory, given the ways that men and women are typically socialized, they are closer to "male" rather than "female" values. It must be said, of course, that many men do not accept these goals, and many women do.

In any case, the self-image of science as a realm of pure reason, logic, argument, evidence, and objectivity should be scrutinized. Many scientists have been known to hold on to their pet theory long after obtaining evidence that it is wrong. Often a theory will be popular not because of the evidence, but because of the charisma or domineering character of the person who holds it. Some scientific views are "fashionable" and others "unfashionable." Some lines of research are pursued because they are more likely to lead to fame and prizes; others are abandoned. This is hardly a pure realm of "objectivity" or "rationality."

Hence we have a twin attack here. First, the practice of science does not live up to its aspirational scientific values. Second, those aspirational values are biased toward the values that men have been socialized to prioritize: objectivity, rationality, competition, novelty, and technology. Along with these values we need to recognize many others such as empathy, in the form of a concern especially for the neglected; humility, in that human powers are limited; and democracy, allowing science to follow the values of society rather than suppose that it has its own entirely independent logic.

We can summarize the feminist critique of science as emphasizing that science is a *social practice* rather than a "special" realm of life shielded from ordinary concerns. As a social practice, it has internal values that can be debated and questioned. Most critically, however, social practices tend to distribute and reinforce power: Some people are insiders, others are outsiders; some people can set the agenda, others can only follow. And once a society acknowledges these points, it can see how women, and female values, have been excluded from science. For all its prestige, science as it has traditionally been practiced turns out to be a wire in the birdcage trapping women.

Morality and Power

With the model of science in mind, we can see that morality—in the sense of our ordinary commonsense moral beliefs and attitudes—can be viewed as a social practice too. Like science, morality has the potential to favor some groups over others and to reflect the values of the more dominant groups. In this book we have already seen such criticisms of morality. Friedrich Nietzsche supposed that morality is a conspiracy of the weak against the strong. Karl Marx and Jean-Jacques Rousseau supposed it is a conspiracy of the rich against the poor, who are kept in place by traditional morality.

The feminist critique of morality echoes the ideas of Marx and Rousseau, but it suggests that traditional morality is a device for enabling men to exercise power over women. The political theorist Carole Pateman (b. 1940), for example, has explicitly extended Rousseau's argument in this way, arguing that women are kept in their subservient place by a type of "sexual contract" (Pateman 1988). Mary Wollstonecraft objected to an idea of "feminine virtue," saying that women were taught to be soft, pleasing, and alluring, acquiring "gentleness of manners, forbearance, and long suffering" (1792/2009, p. 42) while men were brought up to be tough, knowledgeable, and independent.

These differences in what were considered morally appropriate virtues sealed the different fates of men and women for the rest of their lives. And they were cemented by a further element of traditional morality—the allocation of men to the role of moral experts or leaders.

As we noted, for most of human history religious leaders have been our moral experts, and they have been almost exclusively men. This seizure of power by men is self-reinforcing: Women were taught that their moral duty was to obey their husbands and fathers while men were taught that their duty was to be head of the household and command other family members.

We may feel that we have come a long way in recent decades, but we must recognize that the gender power structures of traditional morality are still with us in many ways. In many cultures, women are still trained to be emotional, submissive, and alluring while men are brought up to be rational, independent, and self-confident. And these traits will affect many aspects of later life, including career choice and advancement.

Critique of Moral Philosophy

The feminist critique of traditional morality that we are currently examining started from the idea that morality is a social practice. As such it is potentially a wire in the birdcage of female oppression. We can deepen the critique even further by exploring the claim that *moral philosophy* is also a social practice. This means that moral philosophy itself, even when used for liberating purposes, is "gendered" in a way that is unfair to women.

Consider, in parallel to our reflections on science, the place of women in moral philosophy. We have explored the ideas of Plato, Aristotle, Thomas Hobbes, John Locke, Rousseau, Nietzsche, Bentham, Mill, and others. All of them are men (and curiously, most of them never married). Even in a discussion of feminism in philosophy, the central early figure is Plato, and John Stuart Mill is a much-discussed more modern thinker. True, Mary Wollstonecraft is also a key figure. Many more women, some of them discussed in this book, have contributed to both moral philosophy and feminism in the past 100 years, and other earlier feminists are now being rediscovered. But the example of John Stuart Mill is particularly interesting in this context. As we noted, there is wide suspicion—even if no proof—that his central text on women (*The Subjection of Women*, 1869) was cowritten with his wife, Harriet Taylor (1807–58); but her name is left off. The standard explanation is that prejudices of the day meant that including her name would cause the book to be taken less seriously, even if Mill's name remained.

Why has moral philosophy been so inhospitable to women until relatively recently? One possible answer is that it is no worse in this respect than other fields of philosophy—or, indeed, than other fields of intellectual inquiry more generally. But nevertheless, it is surprising that, of all fields, moral philosophy has not been more open to women. It is hard to justify why women should have had less success in moral philosophy than in, for example, literature. But women arguably have been "bullied out" of moral philosophy by its emphasis on the importance of reason (in the Kantian tradition) and calculation (in the utilitarian tradition), combined with the sexist prejudice that only men are capable of calm, logical thought at the highest level. Hence moral philosophy became "colonized" by male values to the exclusion of women.

In the 20th century, with the revival of virtue ethics (partially led by female philosophers such as Elizabeth Anscombe, Philippa Foot, and Rosalind Hursthouse), women finally achieved a leading role in the discipline. This work has accelerated as attention became focused on topics in bioethics and applied ethics. Female moral philosophers are at the forefront, from feminist and nonfeminist perspectives, of issues such as abortion, reproductive rights, surrogate motherhood, and pornography. Perhaps the field was open because men had ignored moral issues that primarily affected women. Hence women took the lead on these topics; and now, equally with men, they are focused on many other topics too. Although good progress has been made, sadly, moral philosophy has until recently been yet another wire in the birdcage.

Beyond the Binary Divide

Carol Gilligan's work, we saw, has been used to argue that there are distinctively different female and male ways of approaching moral problems. We have seen this claim relaxed somewhat to avoid essentialism, but nevertheless it seems to be based on two related assumptions: (a) The distinction between "female" and "male" is clear (that it is exhaustive and exclusive); and (b) all members of the same sex have enough in common that it is reasonable to talk about a single female morality and a single male morality. Both assumptions are problematic.

First, we are increasingly realizing that the biological categories man/woman and the social categories male/female do not encompass the range of human life. This has been emphasized in the work of people such as the philosopher Judith Butler (b. 1956) in *Gender Trouble* (1990); the gender studies theorist Anne Fausto-Sterling (b. 1944) in *Sexing the Body* (2000); and writer Jeffrey Eugenides (b. 1960) in his novel *Middlesex* (2003). Some human beings have physical characteristics of both sexes, placing them in an intersex category, and others undergo surgery to change sex. Gender, arguably, is even more fluid. There are many examples of men taking on a female persona, and vice versa. Sometimes this is done secretly, sometimes overtly. In addition, a significant number of people are uncomfortable with being classified as either male or female. People who do not fall into conventional sex or gender classifications often face forms of discrimination, which creates a range of moral problems. Their existence causes difficulty for any theory that supposes all human beings can be assigned to a clear gender category regardless of whether it matches their biological sex.

An even greater challenge to the attempt to construct a single feminist ethic is the existence of human diversity. Just as the world has been constructed with a bias toward financially secure, white, heterosexual, Western, able-bodied men, some critics have argued that the feminist challenge has been biased toward financially secure, white, heterosexual, Western, able-bodied women. For example, a perennial concern of the feminist movement has been the exclusion of women from the workplace and their direction toward "refined" hobbies such as needlework and painting with watercolors.

But consider the words of Sojourner Truth (c. 1798–1883), an African American woman born into slavery before gaining her freedom, in a speech entitled "Ain't I a Woman?" (delivered in 1851):

> I have as much muscle as any man, and can do as much work as any man. I have plowed and reaped and husked and chopped and mowed, and can any man do more than that? I have heard much about the sexes being equal. I can carry as much as any man, and can eat as much too, if I can get it. I am as strong as any man that is now.

Sojourner Truth, in effect, points out that the problems of her social world are so far removed from the problems of the female white elite that what divides them may be more important than what they have in common.

And of course gender and race are not the only salient categories. Audrey Lorde lists sexual preference, class, and age as additional sources of different experience, and others have had added issues of health and disability. The term **intersectionality** was coined by the civil rights law academic and activist Kimberlé Crenshaw (b. 1959) to draw attention to those who belong to more than one disadvantaged category and to highlight the complex ways in which disadvantage interacts. To comprehend Sojourner Truth's oppression, it is not enough to understand female inequality and racial injustice. As a black woman, she suffers a fate that cannot be understood by combining the disadvantages suffered by white women and black men. The idea, then, that a single moral approach—whether the ethics of care or the ethics of justice—can address the situation of all women looks highly problematic.

THE ETHICS OF RACE

In earlier chapters, when examining the treatment of women in the major moral traditions, we also looked at the treatment of race. Writers of African descent, such as the pioneering African American philosopher W. E. B. Du Bois (1868–1963), have contributed significantly to bringing issues of racial injustice to the fore. Du Bois showed that the abolition of slavery was only one step toward racial equality, and to this day the journey remains far from complete. Discrimination and oppression continue to crush black aspirations.

Recently philosophers have rightly been appalled by racial discrimination. They have discussed the ethical acceptability and practical use of strategies such as affirmative action, especially in the workplace and education. They also express concern about media stereotyping directed at people of minority races, in addition to more general instances of unconscious bias and discrimination. The birdcage analogy is not restricted in scope to issues of gender; it also applies to all those who suffer from racial discrimination, because many diverse factors conspire to frustrate their goals and ambitions.

Nevertheless, nothing analogous to the ethics of care in moral philosophy has yet been developed as a way of attempting to capture the moral thinking of people of non-European descent. But of course as soon as the issue is formulated, the failings of a single theory are likely to become obvious. Although it was possible to suppose (even if it may not be true) that all women share something that underpins a common approach to morality, it would be absurd—and in itself deeply racist—to suppose that all people of non-European descent share something that could ground a moral theory in opposition to standard moral theories. It would be equally problematic to think that all black people, or all brown people, share some common approach to morality.

Recent philosophers who are turning their attention to race have, therefore, looked for more universal moral theories to capture what they believe an ethics of race should be. This effort parallels the move we saw in feminist ethics, turning away from the ethics of care to more universal Kantian or social contract theory. With regard to the ethics of race, Naomi Zack, for example, has taken elements from theories of natural law, utilitarianism, Kantian ethics, and virtue ethics (Zack, 2011). Charles Mills has argued for an extension of the theory of the social contract (Mills, 1990). Both philosophers point out that many moral theories have implicitly operated by distinguishing between the "fully human" and the "less than fully human," thereby treating anyone who is not a white male as a second class citizen, or even non-citizen. But of course the theories need to be fully universal to incorporate all people of all genders and races.

Zack sets out several principles that an ethics of race would need to incorporate, starting from this idea: "An ethics of race would have as its units human individuals and would assume the intrinsic value and freedom of every human individual" (2011, p. 167). This remark may seem so obvious as barely to need stating, but the tragedy is that although moral philosophers have often given lip service to this idea, in developing their theories they often failed to deliver what they promised. And this situation has a further problematic effect. A theory that is universal on the surface, but subtly racist or sexist at another level, can be harder to confront and oppose than one that is explicitly discriminatory.

However, race theorists know that once we try to appeal to a universal moral code, the risk of overlooking a specific problem or concern increases. We could hardly have a better example than the recent "Black Lives Matter" campaign to draw attention to the shocking number of people of African American descent—many of them unarmed—killed by the police in the United States. One common response to this campaign has been to reply that "All Lives Matter," and so it is unnecessary, deliberatively provocative, or even borderline racist to pick out one race in this way. Therefore, it has been said, the phrase "Black Lives Matter" should be dropped, and instead we should reinforce the universal message that all human beings matter. The problem with this approach, however, is that the campaign is needed precisely because the idea that all lives matter has not been enough to stop the disproportionate killing of black people. A universal morality provides a type of cover for ignoring, either willfully or by neglect, the cases of special concern. It is, says, Judith Butler in a 2015 blog interview with African American philosopher George Yancy (b. 1961), "important to name the lives that have not mattered."

Both Naomi Zack and Charles Mills, therefore, argue that a universal morality has to be supplemented with a project of repair that will involve considerable redistribution of material and social resources to put all people on an equal footing. There is much to discuss and argue about in detail. But if we remain content with a universal morality without taking history into account, although we will have made some theoretical progress, in practice we risk sliding back to where we started. Even if we adopted a fully universal morality tomorrow, the distribution of wealth, jobs, and power would still reflect the racist and sexist beliefs and practices of the previous decades.

TAKING ACTION

What, then, can be done? Critique is one thing; change is another. Although we have not gone into the details, it is not hard to see that from the stand-point of natural law theory, social contract theory, utilitarianism, Kantian theory, or virtue ethics, existing forms of structural injustice for women, people of color, and other disadvantaged groups cannot be morally justified. Stated another way, all moral theories discussed in this book can be used to object to the entrapment of people from disadvantaged groups in Frye's birdcage. This, in its way, is a powerful result. But recalling Audre Lorde's message that "The master's tools will never dismantle the master's house" we need to raise the question of whether existing moral philosophy is able to end the forms of discrimination that undoubtedly still exist.

To make some headway on this issue, for purposes of illustration, we will return to the example of science: What could be done to reform the unjust social practices of science so that it is no longer a wire in the birdcage that perpetuates inequality for women? The obvious point is that scientific prac-tice will have to change. But who is responsible for making that change? No one is in charge of science, even though it includes powerful organizations such as universities, learned societies, and the Nobel Prize committee. But although these groups can show leadership, their power is limited. Ulti-mately, each scientist will need to change his or her behavior.

Yet from the viewpoint of ordinary morality, it seems tough to blame any individual scientist for women's lack of inclusion in science. Any given sci-entist could personally be antisexist, even a political activist, but at the same time find that the best people to work with all just happen to be men. Do we want to blame this individual for perpetuating a sexist, scientific culture? It would seem unfair to single anyone out as being especially responsible, unless their actions are deliberate; but if we do not, then how are we to change anything? As we can see, a characteristic of structural injustice is that it makes responsibility very hard to locate because it is highly diffuse and shared.

The feminist philosopher Iris Marion Young (1949–2006) argued that ordinary morality implicitly relies on what can be called a "liability" theory of responsibility, in which an individual has to be particularly implicated in wrongdoing before it is legitimate to blame them (Young, 2003). In this respect, ordinary moral understanding is an obstacle to social progress because no change will be made in the type of case we have just discussed. Young suggests that in such circumstances, we need to move beyond the idea of blame to what she calls the **political responsibility model**, where we all bear responsibility for making whatever change is within our grasp. In this view, we should be less interested in the backward-looking question of who is to blame for injustice and concentrate instead on the forward-looking question of who is in a position to make beneficial changes. Without wishing to blame anyone, we can nevertheless call for everyone to review their practices and to take seriously the possibility that they are contributing to a set of practices that hold back women, people of color, or other disadvantaged groups. We cannot go into detail here about what this step would mean; but we can see that Young is proposing, at the level of moral theory, a change in our moral thinking that can push people into action that will improve social practices. Hence we can see the potential power of moral philosophy not just to analyze and critique, but to make the world a better place.

CHAPTER REVIEW
Summary

At the beginning of this chapter, we reviewed the discussion of gender and race in previous chapters. We then looked in more detail at the ethics of care. This view has been proposed as a moral philosophy that is more faithful to the way women approach moral philosophy than is the ethics of principle (or justice) found in utilitarian and Kantian moral theory. While recognizing the attractions of the ethics of care in terms of making room for relational, emotional, and contextual reasoning in contrast to abstraction, we considered the dangers of "essentializing" gender roles and values. The distinction between sex and gender was introduced to bring out the difference between biological and social characteristics of men and women.

Most feminist philosophers acknowledge that, while the ethics of care makes an important contribution, on its own this approach is not enough to combat sex inequality and discrimination. Some have revived forms of

Kantian or social contract reasoning. An important step toward developing a more comprehensive approach is to understand the social structures that sustain and reinforce injustice. We discussed the metaphor of a birdcage in explaining that many separate factors combine to entrap members of disadvantaged groups. We then looked at possible examples of "wires" in the birdcage, including pornography, science, ordinary morality, and even moral philosophy.

We also explored the less-developed field of the ethics of race. There is good reason to use universal moral principles in this field, provided that they are genuinely universal in the sense of encompassing all people and not just financially secure white males. At the same time, it is vital not to let the special concerns of disadvantaged groups become submerged and ignored.

Many different strategies will be needed to address problems of race and gender. These include developing a new language that will allow us to describe and oppose discriminatory and unjust practices, and generating new ideas of moral responsibility to motivate action. Moral philosophy can inspire and stimulate real social change.

Key Terms

ethics of justice, p. 233	direct discrimination, p. 240
ethics of care, p. 233	indirect discrimination, p. 240
natural caring, p. 235	sexual harassment, p. 242
essentialism, p. 237	birdcage, p. 242
sex, p. 237	intersectionality, p. 250
gender, p. 237	political responsibility model, p. 253

Key Thinkers

Carol Gilligan (b. 1936), pp. 234–239, 248

Aristotle (384–322 BCE), pp. 232–235

Plato (429?–347 BCE), p. 232

John Stuart Mill (1806–73), pp. 232, 247–248

Immanuel Kant (1724–1804), pp. 233–234

Sandra Harding (b. 1935), pp. 233, 244

Naomi Zack (b. 1944), pp. 233, 251–252

Further Reading

▪ Carol Gilligan's *In a Different Voice* is available in a revised edition by Harvard University Press (1993).

▪ A new edition of Simone de Beauvoir's *The Second Sex* was published by Vintage (2011), translated by Constance Borde and Sheila Malovany-Chevallier. (Original work published 1949)

▪ Sandra Harding's *The Science Question in Feminism* was published by Cornell University Press (1986).

▪ Naomi Zack's *The Ethics and Mores of Race: Equality After the History of Philosophy* was published by Rowman & Littlefield (2011).

▪ Charles Mills's *The Racial Contract* was published by Cornell University Press (1990).

▪ Nel Noddings's *Caring: A Feminine Approach to Ethics and Moral Education* (2nd ed.) is available from the University of California Press (2013).

▪ Alison Jaggar's paper "Feminism in Ethics: Moral Justification" was published in *The Cambridge Companion to Feminism in Philosophy* (pp. 225–244), edited by Miranda Fricker and Jennifer Hornsby (Cambridge University Press, 2000).

▪ Virginia Held's *The Ethics of Care* was published by Oxford University Press (2006).

▪ Annette Baier's paper "The Need for More Than Justice" was published in *Canadian Journal of Philosophy, 17*(suppl. 1), 1987: 41–56.

▪ Jean Hampton's "Feminist Contractarianism" is included in *A Mind of One's Own* (2nd ed.), edited by Louise Antony and Charlotte Witt (Westview Press, 2002).

▪ Mary Wollstonecraft is quoted from *A Vindication of the Rights of Woman* (W. W. Norton, 2009). (Original work published 1792)

▪ Audre Lorde's *Sister Outsider* (2nd ed.) is published by Random House (2007). (Original work published 1984)

▪ John Rawls's *A Theory of Justice* (rev. ed.) was published by Harvard University Press (1999). (Original work published 1971)

▪ Susan Moller Okin's paper "Gender Inequality and Cultural Differences" was published in *Political Theory, 22,* 1994: 5–24.

▪ Carol Hay's feminist reworking of Kant's moral philosophy is set out in her *Kantianism, Liberalism, and Feminism: Resisting Oppression* (Palgrave, 2013).

▪ Marilyn Frye's *The Politics of Reality: Essays in Feminist Theory* was published by Crossing Press (1983).

▪ Catharine MacKinnon is quoted from "Pornography, Civil Rights, and Speech," *Harvard Civil Rights–Civil Liberties Law Review, 20,* 1985: 10–68.

▪ Carole Pateman's *The Sexual Contract* was published by Stanford University Press (1988).

▪ Judith Butler's *Gender Trouble* (2nd ed.) was published by Routledge (2006). (Original work published 1990)

▪ Anne Fausto-Sterling's *Sexing the Body* was published by Basic Books (2000).

▪ Jeffrey Eugenides' novel *Middlesex* was published by Picador (2002).

▪ Sojourner Truth's speech "Ain't I a Woman?" was retrieved February 8, 2017, from http://voicesofdemocracy.umd.edu/truth-address-at-the-womans -rights-convention-speech-text/ (Original speech delivered 1851)

▪ W. E. B. Du Bois *The Souls of Black Folk* is available in an edition by W. W. Norton (1999).

▪ George Yancy's interview with Judith Butler "What's Wrong With 'All Lives Matter'?" was retrieved February 8, 2017, from http://opinionator .blogs.nytimes.com/2015/01/12/whats-wrong-with-all-lives-matter/?_r=0

▪ Iris Marion Young's views on political responsibility can be found in "Political Responsibility and Structural Injustice," the Lindley Lecture delivered at the University of Kansas (May 5, 2003). Young's paper is included in Jonathan Wolff (ed.), *Readings in Moral Philosophy* (W. W. Norton, 2018). This volume also contains many of the readings listed above, including those from De Beauvoir, Held, Baier, Rawls, Wollstonecraft, MacKinnon, Lorde, Du Bois, and Yancy and Butler.

CHAPTER 15

Developing a Moral Outlook

In the first chapters of this book, we looked at a number of philosophical challenges to moral philosophy: whether morality is culturally relative; whether we should be skeptics or subjectivists about morality; and whether we lack free will. The point of looking at these views was, initially, to see whether any of them stopped moral philosophy in its tracks. And on reflection we can now see that for two reasons, this was not so. Take, for example, the claim that morality is culturally relative. First of all, we saw that this view is not obviously true; in fact, it turns out to be remarkably difficult to formulate and defend. Consequently, even the attempt to short-circuit moral philosophy becomes a complex exercise in moral philosophy. Secondly, though, even if we think there is good reason to believe that morality is culturally relative, we will still experience times when we need to know what to do in difficult circumstances. Moral philosophy comes back in once more.

MORAL THEORIES

In thinking about how the moral person should act, we looked at religious and natural law morality, at ethical egoism, and at the theory of the social contract. We then looked in much more detail at the work of Jeremy Bentham, John Stuart Mill, Immanuel Kant, and Aristotle, four of the most significant figures in moral philosophy. We discussed these philosophers more or less in reverse chronological order because utilitarianism is probably the easiest of the theories to understand. It also has the greatest ambition: to provide a simple theory that can solve all our moral problems.

The difficulty that utilitarianism can apparently lead to injustice brought us to consider Kant's view. His theory also has the advantage of providing a systematic way of approaching moral questions while avoiding injustices of the sorts that utilitarianism, arguably, allows. But the Kantian approach, at least as Kant himself interpreted it, seemed in some cases overly rigorous and inflexible (for example, in not permitting lying to murderers).

Aristotle provided a much more flexible approach, concentrating on the nature of a virtuous person rather than providing rules of action. Aristotle helps us appreciate that the point of thinking about ethics is not simply to help us out in tricky moral cases. Perhaps even more importantly, it helps us understand how we should live our lives. But his failure to provide rules will make many readers think he has not achieved what people want in a moral philosophy. We also saw the rather problematic relationship between the views of all these thinkers and the demand for equality for those who fall outside the scope of the group of privileged white men.

Some readers nevertheless will think that one of the philosophers discussed here has come to the truth about ethics, perhaps because the objections are not important or because the objections can be answered. Those readers will want to delve much further into the thinking of those who interest them most. Others will come to the view that none of the views discussed here has arrived at the truth about morality; they will want to explore the work of other theorists, or perhaps even develop elements of their own original moral philosophy.

LEARNING FROM MORAL PHILOSOPHY

I will end this book with a few words about what I personally take from the discussion of the great moral philosophers. It is customary now in moral philosophy to present three "great traditions" of moral thinking: **utilitarianism**, Kantian **deontology**, and Aristotelian **virtue ethics**. It is also implied that a serious student of moral philosophy has to make a choice between them: Are you a utilitarian, deontologist, or virtue ethicist, in pure or perhaps modified form? Later chapters of this book may well have encouraged this approach, for seeing the theorists as competitors is probably the best way of comprehending their ideas. An alternative approach, however, tries to show that at the most fundamental level, different theories are compatible with each other. One example we discussed was Roy Harrod's development of **rule utilitarianism**, which attempted to incorporate Kantian deontology into utilitarianism. Arguably, John Stuart Mill attempted something similar; other writers continue to publish papers and books that attempt to show deep underlying connections between different theories.

My own approach is somewhat different. I find it hard to believe that any of the theories offered provides "the whole truth" about morality. At the same time, I cannot accept that any of the authors studied in this book are completely wrong. Their depth of thought and intelligence, and the attention—often over decades—they gave to the topics discussed makes it extremely unlikely that they have found nothing of importance. In my view the most common mistake in philosophy is to have found part of the truth, but think you have found it all. Yet this does not mean that it will be easy to put different insights together into a single theory. Rather, we might need to take parts of different theories to generate a general position.

So, what inspires my own moral outlook from the philosophers studied in later chapters of this book? From Bentham and Mill, I find it helpful to keep in mind the idea that if something cannot be shown to be bad for human beings or other sentient creatures, then it is very hard to understand why it should be thought wrong. Take, for example, the case of shops opening on Sundays. In my childhood in England, it was against the law for most shops to open on Sundays. Two different arguments were given for this policy. One was that Sunday is "the Lord's day" and should be observed. The second was that opening shops on Sundays disrupted the family lives of those who found themselves forced to work on Sundays as a condition of their employment. Based on the ideas of Bentham and Mill, the first argument has no general weight. Those who wish to observe Sundays can simply make that choice for themselves and have no business imposing their view on others. However, the second argument needs to be taken more seriously. Disruption to family life can have significant consequences if families do not have the opportunity to spend time together and, for example, children do not get the support they need. There are, of course, arguments on the other side, such as the boost to trade and tourism and general convenience that would follow from Sunday opening. Those arguments won the day; Sunday trading became permitted, although with some restrictions. But, as Bentham and Mill would insist, the argument has to be conducted in light of what harms and benefits people, rather than what is required to follow religious traditions.

Bentham and Mill, then, make us focus on the consequences of our actions and policies: What causes people harm, and what benefits them? The greatest difficulty for the utilitarian position, though, is that the max-imizing doctrine can lead to injustice. The Kantian moral position can be used as a corrective; and, as argued above, even those who reject the Kantian approach as the basis of their moral position can, as I do, take inspiration from at least two of Kant's insights.

First, the formula of the universal law asks whether you can will that the **maxim of your action** should become a universal law. Despite the problems in interpretation and application, the Kantian view makes you think about how you can justify your actions to others—and, in particular, renders problem-atic anything that will involve coercion or deceit. We might not want to push this all the way and say that coercion and deceit can never be allowed, but we would need a special argument to defend such practices in particular cases. The second of Kant's insights is the formula of humanity, which includes the idea of never treating others purely as a means to your ends. This formula rules out some of the injustices that utilitarianism seems forced to accept (those who are punished even though innocent are being treated as a means). It helps you consider what it would be like to have morally decent relations with those around you. It also requires you to be bound by your commitments, even if later you see advantages to breaking your word, for example. Yet at the same time, I accept much of the feminist "care" critique of Kantian (and utilitarian) ethics: We need to pay much more attention to the nature of relations between people, and to our emotional life, and to acknowledge the complexity of many of the moral situations we find ourselves in.

Finally, I take from Aristotle three main points. First, the distinction between a good life and a *morally* good life is more blurred than philosophers sometimes make it. A morally good life should also be a pleasurable life, as it will be for someone with the right upbringing. This leads to a second point: Ethics is about individual character as well as action. Therefore serious ethical questions are involved in the attitudes we have about ourselves and other people, and in the appropriate emotions to have on particular occasions in our dealings with others and with moral problems. Finally, the third point I take from Aristotle is that we cannot expect precision in morality, nor can we expect to find a moral code that provides all the answers we need. But once more, we must attend to the feminist insight that both morality and moral philosophy are social practices that can exclude women or even lead to their domination. We must always think about how anything we do can exclude or marginalize people who do not have access to the same privileges that we have.

I don't pretend that in taking different ideas from different moral philosophers, I have somehow reconciled their views. Furthermore, taking parts from different theories is bound to generate difficult questions about what to do on a particular occasion. What would the great moral philosophers make of what I have said? Bentham and Mill would probably argue that the picture I am painting is really only utilitarianism in disguise, taken in the long term. Kant, most likely, would have dismissed it as a "disgusting hodge-podge" of popular ideas. Aristotle would probably have been more forgiving, thinking that I was at least on my way to moral maturity, even if I had not achieved it yet. In particular he would have approved of using the writings of the great philosophers as a way of developing a moral outlook on life rather than studying them as a type of purely intellectual exercise. In this book I hope I have avoided giving the impression that moral philosophy is merely an academic pursuit.

key thinkers

Anscombe, Elizabeth (1919–2001). An important twentieth-century English philosopher who wrote on many topics but especially was noted for her work in philosophy of mind and action. Her works on moral philosophy were influenced by her devout Catholic faith.

Aquinas, St. Thomas (1225–74). Probably the most important theologian and philosopher in the Catholic tradition, notable especially for his *Summa Theologica* in which ethical and religious questions are treated together. A major natural law theorist.

Aristotle (384–322 BCE). One of the world's greatest and most influential philosophers. He was a pupil of *Plato* but disagreed sharply with many of Plato's doctrines. His works cover a huge variety of topics, from ethics, politics, and rhetoric to metaphysics and even biology.

Augustine, St. (354–430). An early Christian theologian and philosopher; most notable for his books *City of God* and *Confessions*.

Ayer, A. J. (1910–89). An English philosopher best known for his early work *Language, Truth and Logic* (1936), in which he introduced the philosophical writings of the Austrian "Vienna Circle" to an English-speaking audience.

Baier, Annette (1929–2012). A moral philosopher born in New Zealand. Baier spent her working life in the United States and produced influential works on feminism.

Beauvoir, Simone de (1908–1986). A French writer and philosopher whose book *The Second Sex* (1949) is a classic of feminist philosophy.

Benedict, Ruth (1887–1948). An influential American anthropologist; best known for her book *Patterns of Culture* (1934).

Bentham, Jeremy (1748–1832). An English philosopher and legal theorist who, in his copious writings, argued for substantial legal reform around the world based on "the greatest happiness principle," otherwise known as utilitarianism.

Butler, Bishop Joseph (1692–1752). A theologian and moral philosopher, Butler published much of his work in the form of sermons. He emphasized the importance of conscience in moral belief and action.

Butler, Judith (b. 1956). A feminist philosopher and theorist of gender; best known for her book *Gender Trouble: Feminism and the Subversion of Identity* (1990).

Camus, Albert (1913–60). A French philosopher and author, partially of Algerian descent. He was especially interested in questions of individual freedom.

Carritt, E. F. (1876–1964). A twentieth-century English philosopher; known for his critiques of utilitarianism.

Constant, Benjamin (1767–1830). A Swiss French political philosopher.

Copernicus, Nicolaus (1473–1543). A Polish astronomer and mathematician who developed a model of the universe with the sun, rather than the earth, at the center.

Crenshaw, Kimberlé (b. 1959). An African American civil rights law academic and activist, she is known for devising the concept of intersectionality.

Curie, Marie (1867–1934). A Polish French physicist and chemist who produced fundamental work on radioactivity. Curie was the first scientist to win two Nobel Prizes.

Darwin, Charles (1809–82). An English biologist and founder of the theory of evolution as explained in his most important book, *On the Origin of Species* (1859).

Dawkins, Richard (b. 1941). An English biologist who popularized the theory of the "selfish gene"; also well-known for his opposition to religion.

Dickens, Charles (1812–70). An English novelist; widely regarded as one of the greatest writers of the nineteenth century.

Dostoyevsky, Fyodor (1821–81). A Russian novelist, author of books that raise and address deep philosophical questions, including *Crime and Punishment* (1866), *The Brothers Karamazov* (1880), and *Notes from the Underground* (1864).

Du Bois, W. E. B. (1868–1963). A highly influential African American philosopher; Du Bois is the author of many important works including *The Souls of Black Folk* (1903).

Dworkin, Andrea (1946–2005). An American radical feminist; known especially for her work with *Catharine MacKinnon* on pornography.

Epicurus (341–270 BCE). An Ancient Greek philosopher, now associated with the term *epicurean*—cultivated pleasure seeking—but in fact a systematic thinker whose ideas about the search for happiness and freedom from fear were part of a broad vision about the nature of the world and the place of human beings within it.

Eugenides, Jeffrey (b. 1960). An American novelist and short story writer, author of the novel *Middlesex* (2002), which explores themes of intersexuality.

Fausto-Sterling, Anne (b. 1944). An American biologist and gender theorist known for extending the understanding of sex and gender beyond traditional categories.

Fénelon, Archbishop François (1651–1715). A French archbishop; best known for his novel *The Adventures of Telemachus*, which was said to have influenced the French Revolution.

Foot, Philippa (1920–2010). An English moral philosopher who helped bring about the revival of virtue ethics.

Frankfurt, Harry (b. 1929). An American philosopher known for his work in defending compatibilism as well as in political philosophy. Also known for his best-selling short book *On Bullshit* (2005).

Fricker, Miranda (b. 1966). A contemporary British philosopher; best known for her book *Epistemic Injustice* (2007), which draws together issues in moral philosophy and epistemology.

Frye, Marilyn (b. 1941). An American feminist philosopher who introduced the metaphor of the birdcage into feminist analysis.

Gandhi, Mahatma (1869–1948). The leader of the movement for Indian independence from British rule, Gandhi is especially noted for his advocacy of nonviolent civil disobedience.

Gilligan, Carol (b. 1936). An American social psychologist, Gilligan is especially noted for her book *In a Different Voice* (1982), which presents evidence that men and women approach moral questions in different ways.

Godwin, William (1756–1836). An English political philosopher known especially for his defense of anarchism.

Haidt, Jonathan (b. 1963). An American social psychologist specializing in moral psychology.

Haldane, J. B. S. (1892–1964). An English evolutionary biologist and mathematician.

Hampton, Jean (1954–96). An American political philosopher, especially noted for her work on *Thomas Hobbes* and the social contract. She made important contributions to feminist contractualist theory.

Harding, Sandra (b. 1935). An American philosopher of science and feminist theorist.

Hare, Richard (1919–2002). An English political philosopher; known for his work on the logic of moral concepts as well as his defense of utilitarianism.

Harrod, Roy (1900–78). An English economist; best known in philosophy for formulating the distinction between act and rule utilitarianism.

Hay, Carol. An American feminist political philosopher who has developed a Kantian form of feminism.

Held, Virginia (b. 1929). An American moral and political philosopher who has produced important works of feminist philosophy.

Herodotus (484–425 BCE). An Ancient Greek writer; said to be the first historian.

Hobbes, Thomas (1588–1679). A widely discussed English political philosopher; Hobbes argued that securing peace requires a social contract to submit to absolute government.

Hume, David (1711–76). A Scottish philosopher who produced extremely influential writings across a wide range of philosophical topics, even though in his own age he was better known as a historian.

Hursthouse, Rosalind (b. 1943). A New Zealand philosopher; an important figure in the revival of virtue ethics.

Jaggar, Alison (b. 1942). An English-born pioneering feminist philosopher who has spent her working life in the United States.

Kant, Immanuel (1724–1804). An exceptionally significant and influential philosopher who wrote on many topics. Born and lived in Königsberg, Germany. Kant is particularly noted for his fundamental but difficult writings on metaphysics, especially his *Critique of Pure Reason*, but equally renowned for his rigorous, principled approach to moral philosophy.

Kenyatta, Jomo (c. 1891–1978). The first president of Kenya. Trained as an anthropologist, he wrote a study of the Gikuyu people of Kenya called *Facing Mount Kenya* (1938).

Kepler, Johannes (1571–1630). A German mathematician and astronomer who formulated laws of planetary motion.

King, Martin Luther Jr. (1929–68). An African American civil rights campaigner, advocate of nonviolent resistance, and winner of a Nobel Peace Prize.

Kohlberg, Lawrence (1927–87). An American psychologist; he introduced a theory of stages of moral development that was criticized by *Carol Gilligan*.

Laplace, Pierre-Simon (1749–1827). A French astronomer and mathematician.

Libet, Benjamin (1916–2007). An American neuroscientist who developed experiments designed to test whether human beings have free will.

Locke, John (1632–1704). A major English philosopher; a key figure in empiricist tradition, Locke argued that all knowledge is gained by experience. Also a highly influential political philosopher who argued for the natural rights of the citizen against the power of the sovereign.

Lorde, Audre (1934–82). An African American poet, essayist, and activist.

Mackie, J. L. (1917–81). An Australian philosopher who wrote on a wide range of philosophical topics. He is best known for his book *Ethics: Inventing Right and Wrong* (1977).

MacKinnon, Catharine (b. 1946). An American lawyer, radical feminist, and activist. She is known especially for her work with *Andrea Dworkin* on pornography.

Mandeville, Bernard (1670–1733). An Anglo-Dutch philosopher and economist, author of the satirical economic text *The Fable of the Bees* (1714).

Maritain, Jacques (1882–1973). A French Catholic philosopher and contributor to natural law theory.

Marx, Karl (1818–83). A German political thinker, activist, and economist who inspired communist revolutions around the world.

McDowell, John (b. 1942). A contemporary philosopher, born in South Africa and now working in the United States. He is especially known for his writings on ethics, Greek philosophy, philosophy of language, and philosophy of mind.

Mill, John Stuart (1806–73). Born in England but of Scottish descent, Mill was initially a disciple of *Jeremy Bentham*; he later branched out to develop his own distinctive and highly influential moral views. He wrote on a wide range of moral, political, philosophical, and economic issues, including arguing for women's emancipation.

Mills, Charles (b. 1951). A Jamaican political philosopher and race theorist who has spent most of his working life in the United States. Mills has written several books on racial justice, including an analysis of the social contract from the viewpoint of race theory.

Moody-Adams, Michele. A contemporary African American moral philosopher who has produced a detailed critical assessment of cultural relativism.

Moore, G. E. (1873–1958). An English philosopher; in the early twentieth century, he was a key figure in the development of English-language philosophy.

Newton, Isaac (1643–1727). An English mathematician and physicist who formulated laws of motion and the law of universal gravitation. Newton made many other important discoveries.

Nietzsche, Friedrich (1844–1900). A German philosopher with a brilliant literary style, Nietzsche wrote primarily on moral philosophy, religion, and the philosophy of art. He was extremely influential, even though the real meaning of his writings remains highly debated. He had health problems for much of his life, and for his final ten years was incapacitated by mental illness.

Noddings, Nel (b. 1929). An American philosopher of education, especially noted for her book *Caring: A Feminine Approach to Ethics and Moral Education* (1984).

Nozick, Robert (1938–2002). An American political philosopher; especially noted for his defense of the political philosophy of libertarianism.

Ockham, William of (c. 1287–1347). A medieval English philosopher who is most famous for Ockham's razor: Do not multiply entities beyond necessity (i.e., we should prefer the simplest theory). He wrote on many theological, logical, and philosophical topics.

Okin, Susan Moller (1946–2004). Born in New Zealand, Okin was a feminist political philosopher who spent her working life in the United States.

O'Neill, Onora (b. 1941). Baroness O'Neill of Bengarve. Born in Northern Ireland, O'Neill is a moral philosopher especially known for her interpretation and development of *Immanuel Kant's* moral philosophy. She was appointed to the United Kingdom House of Lords in 1999.

Pateman, Carole (b. 1940). A British political philosopher and feminist who has spent most of her working life in the United States. Pateman is notable for her writings on democracy and her criticisms of the social contract from a feminist viewpoint.

Plato (429?–347 BCE). It has been said that all subsequent philosophy is "footnotes to Plato." Plato, an Ancient Greek philosopher, stands as perhaps the most significant of the founders of the Western philosophical tradition. He was a pupil of *Socrates* and teacher of *Aristotle*. He wrote in dialogue form, generally featuring Socrates as the lead figure in the debate.

Rand, Ayn (1905–82). A Russian American novelist and philosopher; Rand was highly influential in American public intellectual life as a defender of free market economics and, relatedly, a form of individualism.

Rawls, John (1921–2002). An American philosopher, regarded as the most important political philosopher writing in English in the twentieth century. Best known for his book *A Theory of Justice* (1971).

Rousseau, Jean-Jacques (1712–88). A highly influential Swiss French philosopher, known especially for his writings in political philosophy, such as *The Social Contract* (1762) and his treatise on education, *Emile* (1762).

Russell, Bertrand (1872–1970). An English philosopher and logician. He was famous for his academic works and for being a left-wing public intellectual.

Schiller, Friedrich (1759–1805). A German poet, playwright, and philosopher.

Schopenhauer, Arthur (1788–1860). A German philosopher known for his pessimism about the human condition. He engaged especially with the philosophy of *Immanuel Kant* and was also influenced by Indian philosophy.

Sidgwick, Henry (1838–1900). An English moral philosopher and economist; an important defender of utilitarianism.

Singer, Marcus (1926–2016). An American moral philosopher.

Singer, Peter (b. 1946). A contemporary Australian utilitarian philosopher; known for his uncompromising views on many issues of contemporary morality, such as animal liberation and the moral necessity to address global poverty.

Smith, Adam (1723–90). A Scottish economist and moral philosopher; particularly known for his book *The Wealth of Nations* (1776).

Socrates (470/69–399 BCE). An Ancient Greek philosopher, a key founder of Western philosophy, who left no written works. He is known primarily as a character in the dialogues of *Plato*, his student.

Stevenson, Charles Leslie (1908–79). An American moral philosopher and a leading exponent of emotivism.

Tangwa, Godfrey B. A contemporary Cameroonian philosopher who works particularly on ethics and bioethics.

Taylor, Harriet (1807–58). A feminist writer and philosopher; Taylor married *John Stuart Mill* after the death of her first husband and profoundly influenced Mill's later work.

Teresa, Mother (1910–97). An Albanian-Indian Catholic nun who devoted much of her life to helping the poor and sick in India. Although some have questioned the extent of her good works, she was made a saint in 2016.

Truth, Sojourner (c. 1798–1883). An African American civil rights activist. Born into slavery, from which she escaped. Noted for her speeches, especially "Ain't I a Woman?" (1851).

Turing, Alan (1912–54). An English logician and mathematician. One of the inventors of the modern computer, and a vitally important code-breaker in the Second World War. In 1952 he was tried for homosexual offenses and underwent hormone treatment. He died of cyanide poisoning in 1954, most likely suicide.

Turnbull, Colin (1924–94). A British American anthropologist; known for a highly controversial account of the Ik people in his book *The Mountain People* (1972).

Twain, Mark (pen name of Samuel Langhorne Clemens [1835–1910]). The American author of *The Adventures of Tom Sawyer* (1876) and *Adventures of Huckleberry Finn* (1885).

Wilde, Oscar (1854–1900). An Irish playwright. His works include *The Ballad of Reading Gaol* (1898), written after his release from two years in an English prison at hard labor for homosexual offenses.

Williams, Bernard (1929–2003). An English philosopher best known for his work in moral philosophy. In fact he produced influential writing on a diverse range of topics.

Wollstonecraft, Mary (1759–97). An English political philosopher; author of *A Vindication of the Rights of Men* (1790), soon followed by *A Vindication of the Rights of Woman* (1792), a highly influential early feminist work. Mother of Mary Shelley, author of *Frankenstein* (1818).

Wong, David (b. 1949). A Chinese American moral philosopher particularly noted for his work defending a form of cultural relativism.

Wordsworth, William (1770–1850). A major English poet, especially noted for his work *The Prelude*.

Yancy, George (b. 1961). An African American philosopher who is working on issues in the philosophy of race.

Young, Iris Marion (1949–2006). A feminist political philosopher who produced a wide range of influential works, including *Justice and the Politics of Difference* (1990).

Zack, Naomi (b. 1944). An American philosopher noted especially for her writings on the ethics of race.

glossary

abduction. Another term for *inference to the best explanation.*

act utilitarianism. A version of *utilitarianism* that defines right action in terms of whatever action maximizes happiness or *utility*. Compare to *rule utilitarianism.*

agent causation. The idea that if human agents have *free will*, then they, as agents, cause their own actions rather than having the ultimate cause of their actions lie beyond their own will or intentions in some sense.

analogy. Making a comparison between two areas of knowledge or investigation in the hope that what is known about one area will bring insight into another area.

a posteriori. Another term for *empirical.*

applied ethics. The exploration of a moral issue such as the permissibility of abortion by means of the application of philosophical reasoning.

a priori. Known by a method, such as logic or pure reason, independent of sensory evidence.

argument. The application of principles of reasoning to prove, or provide support for, one statement on the basis of other statements.

argument by elimination. Presenting an *exhaustive* set of options (i.e., a set including all possibilities) and providing compelling objections to all but one, thereby leaving one as the undefeated option.

argument from queerness. J. L. Mackie's *argument* that objective moral values would be such odd and unusual entities that they could not exist.

autonomy. Generally understood as self-rule. In Kant's philosophy, also related to the idea of acting for the sake of duty, following the *categorical imperative* of morality. Compare to *heteronomy.*

begging the question. Another name for a *circular argument.*

birdcage. A metaphor for oppression in which many different practices combine to create disadvantage, even if no specific practice is individually responsible.

categorical imperative. In Kant's system, the fundamental principle, or command, of morality. Compare to *hypothetical imperative.*

circular argument. An *argument* that uses what is intended to be the conclusion as a premise in the argument. Because it assumes what it is attempting to prove, it does not prove anything.

commonsense morality. Ordinary moral views, which are often used as a test for moral theories: Do they contradict commonsense morality?

compatibilism. The position that it is possible to reconcile *determinism* and *free will.*

conscience. An apparently intuitive belief in right and wrong that also affects emotion, motivations, and feelings of guilt.

consequentialism. Any theory that judges the morality of an action by its consequences. It normally defines the right (right action) in terms of the good. For example, *utilitarianism* is a consequentialist theory because it defines the right in terms of maximizing the good (happiness or *utility*). Compare to *deontology*.

contingency. A truth is contingent if, although true, we can imagine circumstances in which it would have been false.

contradiction. Two (or more) statements that, purely for reasons of logic, cannot all be true.

counterintuitive. A theory that supports actions that generate negative *moral intuitions*. For example, a theory that has the consequence that it can be right to kill innocent people is normally said to be counterintuitive.

cultural relativism. Also known as *moral relativism* or *ethical relativism*. The doctrine that morality is relative to each culture and that there is no overarching theory to assess or compare the moralities of all cultures.

deontology. Defines right action in terms of following duties, rather than in achieving desirable consequences. Deontological theories generally define the right independently of the good. Compare to *consequentialism*.

determinism. The denial of *free will*, arguing that our choices are ultimately determined by factors other than our will.

dilemma. An apparent forced choice between two (or more) *exhaustive* and *exclusive* options, each of which have compelling advantages (or disadvantages) but cannot both be selected.

diminishing marginal utility. The idea that a second unit of a good typically yields less pleasure or happiness

(*utility*) than the first, and so on. Typically used as part of an *argument* that maximizing utility favors equal distribution of goods.

direct discrimination. A policy intended to discriminate against members of a particular group. Compare to *indirect discrimination*.

divine command. In moral philosophy, the idea that moral requirements are the commands of God.

dogmatism. Adherence to a view without giving proper weight to evidence or *arguments* that might cast doubt on it.

emotivism. The idea that moral judgments are not strictly speaking capable of being true or false but in fact express our emotions.

empirical. Known through sensory evidence.

epistemology. The philosophical study of what we can know, and how we can know it.

equivocation. Using a word in more than one sense in an *argument*. Generally, to do so renders the argument invalid.

error theory. A view associated with J. L. Mackie. It argues that moral judgments express genuine beliefs, but since no objective moral values exist they are all false, for all moral judgments presuppose the existence of objective moral values.

essentialism. In the context of feminist theory, normally used as an accusation that typical attributes of men and women are treated as if they are essential, unchanging features. Opponents of this view claim that such traits are the result of socialization, not essence.

ethical egoism. The theory that each individual has a moral duty to pursue his or her own self-interest.

ethics of care. Commonly associated with feminist approaches to ethics, this term emphasizes the importance of relations between people and the complexities of particular situations, in opposition to the ethics of abstract principles that look to bring different situations under general rules. Compare to *ethics of justice.*

ethics of justice. A formal, abstract approach to moral reasoning, based on the application of general principles to particular cases. Compare to *ethics of care.*

eudaimonia. Aristotle's notion of human well-being. Sometimes translated as "happiness," although "flourishing" may be a more accurate rendering.

exclusive. Two or more beliefs or options, of which only one can be selected.

exhaustive. A range of options that cover all possibilities.

expressivism. Sometimes used as a synonym for *emotivism,* although sometimes used as a broader term, suggesting that moral judgments express something other than emotions, such as attitudes.

fact/value distinction. The claim that there is a sharp distinction between issues of fact and issues of values, accompanied by the claim that it is a logical fallacy to try to derive value conclusions purely from factual premises.

false dilemma. Two (or more) options presented as a *dilemma,* but in truth fail to be so, normally because the options are not *exhaustive* (other options are possible) or *exclusive* (more than one option can be chosen).

form of the good. Plato's version of *moral realism,* in which perfect values exist outside the empirical world, whereas what we encounter in the world are imperfect copies.

free riding. The case where an individual relies on the cooperation of others without themselves offering cooperation.

free will. The idea that human beings are able to make free choices about their decisions and to act on those choices.

game theory. An area of economics and psychology that attempts to reduce social situations to formal structures (or "games"). Doing this allows researchers to model the available strategies and to determine, by mathematics and probability theory, which is the optimum "move" in each case.

gender. The social roles typically associated with masculine and feminine behavior. Gender is generally regarded as far more socially contingent than biological *sex.*

government house utilitarianism. The theory that although *utilitarianism* is true, happiness will be maximized if ordinary people are taught it is false and the truth reserved for the moral elite.

group altruism. The theory that groups whose members display altruistic concern toward each other are more likely to survive and flourish than groups that do not display such concern.

heteronomy. In Kant's system, to act heteronomously is to act on the basis of your desires, rather than on the basis of the moral laws. Compare to *autonomy.*

hypothetical imperative. A conditional imperative, of the form "If you want to achieve *x,* then do *y.*" According to Kant, the imperatives of morality are *categorical imperatives* (unconditional), not hypothetical.

incompatibilism. The idea that if *determinism* is true, then human beings lack *free will.*

indirect discrimination. A policy that causes difficulty for members of a group although not designed to do so. Compare to *direct discrimination*.

individual subjectivism. The view that the truth about morality is to be determined by each person for himself or herself. There are no universal moral standards that limit or constrain what any individual may think on moral questions.

induction. Providing support for a general hypothesis by observing repeated instances of it. For example, the hypothesis that all swans are white can be supported through induction by finding many examples of white swans. However, induction is never proof.

inference to the best explanation. Arguing for a theory on the basis that it provides the best explanation of some observed phenomenon. For example, it is generally believed that the best explanation of the correlation between smoking and lung cancer is that smoking causes lung cancer, even though other possible explanations are also available.

infinite regress. Term used to describe cases where a proposed solution to a problem generates exactly the same problem it is intended to solve. Hence the problem will repeat itself to infinity if the same solution is applied each time.

instrumental value. Something has instrumental value if it is valued not purely in itself but because it is likely to help bring about something else of *intrinsic value*. It is possible for something to have both intrinsic and instrumental value.

interpersonal comparisons of utility. Measuring and comparing the happiness of one person with that of another.

intersectionality. The idea that the experience of a person who suffers from more than one form of oppression—for example, a black woman—cannot be reduced to the combination of the oppression of the two groups to which she belongs.

intrinsic value. Something has intrinsic value if it is valuable in itself. It is possible for something to have both intrinsic and *instrumental value*.

kin altruism. The theory that people who are closely related are likely to behave altruistically toward each other. It is highly compatible with the theory of the *selfish gene*.

knowledge that and knowledge how. "Knowing that" is a shorthand term for knowledge of a proposition: knowing that something is true. "Knowledge how," in contrast, is knowing how to do something in a practical sense. It is generally thought that knowledge how can be acquired without being able to articulate exactly what you know (e.g., knowing how to swim is a matter of acquiring a skill, not learning a set of propositions).

liberalism. A family of views that gives great weight to individual liberty and autonomy, accepting that different individuals and groups have different values. Liberalism opposes the idea that anyone has the right to impose their moral ideas on anyone else.

libertarianism. An ambiguous term in philosophy; it is sometimes used as a name for the theory that we have *free will* and sometimes as a name for a position in political philosophy that argues for minimal government intervention, especially in the economy.

logical form. An *argument* in ordinary speech can often be reconstructed as a step-by-step logical argument, thereby revealing its logical form.

logical validity. An *argument* in which, if the premises are true, the conclusion must also be true. In a logically valid argument, negation of the conclusion contradicts the premises, and this is how the logical validity of an argument can be tested.

maxim of action. In Kant's moral philosophy, every action has a "maxim" that might be thought of as the reason for taking the action. It is used to test whether an action is performed for the sake of duty. The test is whether the maxim of the action can be *universalized*.

meta-ethics. The study of the nature of moral value and our knowledge of it.

metaphysics. The philosophical study of what, ultimately, exists in the universe.

moral egoism. The theory that the right thing for a human being to do is always to follow his or her own interests.

moral intuition. A reaction to a situation, whether real or a *thought experiment*, that expresses the opinion that what has been described is morally acceptable or unacceptable.

moral motivation. In normal circumstances any action is motivated by an agent's belief and desires. According to some moral theories, such as Kant's, an action has moral worth only if it is done for the right moral reasons.

moral nihilism. The idea that there is nothing to morality at all. There are no moral truths or standards of right or wrong action.

moral realism. A form of *objectivism* claiming that values are in some sense real objects that exist in the world.

moral sense. The idea that human beings are able to perceive right and wrong through some sort of built-in capacity.

natural caring. Caring that takes place as part of normal life, such as a mother's care for her child, or family members for each other.

natural law. The idea that certain laws exist independent of human action. Such laws are often believed to be discoverable by *natural reason*.

natural reason. The idea that human beings naturally have particular powers of reasoning that can deliver substantive conclusions independently of experience or other sources of evidence.

noncognitivism. The view that moral judgments do not state genuine "cognitions" or beliefs, and therefore cannot be true or false. *Emotivism* and *expressivism* are examples of noncognitivist positions.

normative ethics. The study of what morality requires of human beings.

objectivism. In moral philosophy, the idea that statements about morality can have a validity that goes beyond subjective opinion, often involving the idea that moral ideas are somehow grounded in the nature of reality or are valid for all people at all times.

objectivity. See *objectivism*.

original position. The situation of people behind the *veil of ignorance*.

paternalism. Overriding an individual's own choices on the grounds that another course of action would be better for them, as a parent may do for a child.

perfect and imperfect duties. The distinction can be used in various ways, but it is most commonly understood in these terms: A perfect duty is one that applies in all circumstances, such as not to commit murder; an imperfect duty is one that is required from time to time, but not always in every case where it might apply. The duty to give to charity is a common example.

phronesis. In Aristotle, the idea of "practical wisdom" or knowledge of how to act.

political responsibility model. The claim that responsibility for ending injustice does not lie only with those people who can be blamed for causing it, but that the responsibility is more widely shared.

prisoner's dilemma. A two-person situation or game in which the pursuit of each person's self-interest leads to a worse outcome for both of them than they could have achieved through cooperation.

prudence. The pursuit or preservation of a person's own rational self-interest.

pseudo-relativism. The view that each society has the right to live according to its own values, and no other society has the right to interfere. It differs from *cultural relativism* in accepting the universal value of noninterference.

psychological egoism. The theory that human beings are, in some way, psychologically compelled to follow their own interests.

public goods problem. Public goods are goods that, if supplied at all, can be enjoyed by people who have not paid for them—for example, street lights on a public road. Such goods are regarded as a problem because the apparently rational strategy for any individual is to wait for someone else to pay for their supply; but if everyone does this, the goods will never be supplied, even if they are collectively beneficial. See *free riding.*

reciprocal altruism. The theory that altruism can or will emerge through mutual cooperation between individuals.

revaluation of all values. Nietzsche's proposal that it is necessary to reassess all traditional values to determine whether, in fact, they are actually valuable.

rule utilitarianism. A version of *utilitarianism* that defines right action in terms of acting in accordance with rules that together would maximize happiness of *utility.* Compare to *act utilitarianism.*

selfish gene. A biological theory proposing that genes have a built-in drive to preserve the identical gene either in the same individual or in other individuals.

sex. The biological and physiological characteristics used to define the categories male and female.

sexual harassment. Unwelcome behavior or speech of a sexual nature, especially in the workplace, aimed at a particular person.

situational ethics. The idea that the right thing to do varies with the details of each particular situation, rather than falling under general principles that can be applied to different cases.

slave morality. Nietzsche's assessment of the traditional—largely Christian—morality of his time: that it was fit only for slaves.

social contract. A family of views in moral and political philosophy in which the authority of morality, or of the state, is said to rest on the agreement, in some sense, of the people.

Sophist. Initially a member of a group of Ancient Greek philosophers who were paid by wealthy Athenians to help them develop their skills of reasoning. Now a term used to describe someone who willfully engages in fallacious reasoning to pursue his or her own interests.

soundness. A valid *argument* derived from true premises. If the premises are not true, an argument is unsound even if it is *logically valid.*

Stoicism. A major school of Ancient Greek philosophy. The Stoics had views on a range of topics, but in moral philosophy they emphasized the importance of moral reason and the rejection of the emotions as an influence in moral decision-making. They also emphasized the importance of our inner states rather than outward show or achievement.

teleological view. Directed toward, or justified in terms of, some goal or purpose.

theory of the good. An account of the good or desirable elements in the world. For example, the *utilitarian* theory proposes that happiness or pleasure is the sole good.

theory of the right. A theory of how human beings are to act if they are to do so in a morally correct way.

thin and thick ethical concepts. A distinction formulated by Bernard Williams. Thick ethical concepts, such as "courageous," have a particular descriptive content as part of their meaning. Thin concepts, such as "right," do not.

thought experiment. Creating a fictional scenario to illustrate a theory or to test it against our intuitions.

universalization. Considering the moral appropriateness of an action by imagining a world in which everyone did what you propose to do.

utilitarianism. The moral theory that the right thing to do in any circumstance is to bring about the greatest total balance of happiness over unhappiness.

utility. A measure of subjective well-being; closely related to happiness and pleasure.

veil of ignorance. An idea introduced by John Rawls to ensure that in applying *social contract* theory, we are not biased by our own interests. Accordingly, Rawls suggests that we should make our agreement assuming that we do not know personal facts about ourselves, such as our race, religion, sex, talents, family background, values, and so on.

vice. The opposite of a *virtue*. A disposition of character that leads a person to reason, feel, and act in a morally problematic fashion.

virtue. A disposition of character that leads a person to reason, feel, and act in a morally admirable fashion.

virtue ethics. An approach to ethics focusing on individual character, building on the concepts of *virtue* and *vice*.

index